THE LOGIC OF
RACISM

THE LOGIC OF RACISM

E. ELLIS CASHMORE

London
ALLEN & UNWIN
Boston   Sydney

**Allen & Unwin (Publishers) Ltd,
40 Museum Street, London WC1A 1LU, UK**

Allen & Unwin (Publishers) Ltd,
Park Lane, Hemel Hempstead, Herts HP2 4TE, UK

Allen & Unwin, Inc.,
8 Winchester Place, Winchester, Mass. 01890, USA

Allen & Unwin (Australia) Ltd,
8 Napier Street, North Sydney, NSW 2060, Australia

First published in 1987

British Library Cataloguing in Publication Data

Cashmore, Ernest
    The logic of racism.
1. Racism
I. Title
305.8   HT1521
ISBN 0–04–301255–8
ISBN 0–04–301256–6 Pbk

Library of Congress Cataloging-in-Publication Data

Cashmore, Ernest.
    The Logic of racism.
Bibliography: p.
Includes index.
1. West Midlands (England) – Race relations.
2. Racism – England – West Midlands.   3. Social classes –
England – West Midlands.   I. Title.
DA670.W495C37   1987   305.8'009424'9   86–14106
ISBN 0–04–301255–8 (alk. paper)
ISBN 0–04–301256–6 (pbk. : alk. paper)

Set in 11 on 12 point Garamond by Nene Phototypesetters Ltd
and printed in Great Britain
by Billings and Sons Ltd, London and Worcester

Contents

The Logic of Racism

PART TWO
Visions of Youth

PART THREE
Perspectives in Later Life

Contents

Acknowledgements

The author and publishers would like to thank the following organizations for their assistance in the production of this book: the Economic and Social Research Council, which supported the project on which the book is based; the Afro-Caribbean Community Development Association; the Commission for Racial Equality; the Community Relations Council; the Department of Health and Social Security; the Department of Environmental Planning; the Greater London Council; the Gingerbread organization; the Handsworth Action Scheme; the Housing Departments of Newtown, Chelmsley Wood, Kingshurst; Kingshurst Labour Club; Kingshurst Neighbourhood Centre; Newtown Community Centre; NACRO; the Neighbourhood Team of Birmingham Settlement; Newtown Residents' Association; the Probation Services; the Residents' Action Group of Kingshurst; St Andrew's Youth Club, Chelmsley Wood; St George's Centre, Newtown; St Paul's Community Workshop, Lozells; Wallace Lawler Centre, Newtown; the schools of Edgbaston, Chelmsley Wood, Newtown and Solihull, West Midlands; the Departments of Social Services of Birmingham and Solihull; the Education and Housing Departments of England and Wales, which responded to requests for information; and the independent schools which volunteered information. The many individuals who co-operated in the development of the project are too numerous to mention.

The names of all people in the text with the exceptions of Denis Howell, MP, Dame Jill Knight, MP, Iain Mills, MP and John Taylor, MP, have been changed in the interests of confidentiality, and any resemblance to actual people is coincidental.

Chapter One

Introduction: Social Vision

It's easy to be a liberal in Exeter

'We're not talking about something as absolute as a mathematical problem where I can say, "Two and two makes four; you're wrong to say two and two makes five",' argues John Taylor, MP for Solihull in the West Midlands. He continues:

Prejudice exists. It would be a fool who says it doesn't. But it would also be a fool who tried to make moral judgements about that prejudice and said, 'Prejudice is wicked.' You can't cut everything down in those kind of terms. People will think and feel what they think and feel. Some of the indigenous population rather resent the numbers, resent the incomers making no contribution to their own culture and feel, in a sense, that they are threatened. Not just in job terms: I think they feel their environment is threatened. Some people spent their childhoods in what were then mediumish white suburbs, which they now find inexorably changing character. People are unhappy about that.

Pursuing this line of thought, we arrive at the conclusion that most people are conservative for no reason more mysterious than that they want stability and order. They take for granted a stable environment that provides a secure enclosure in which they can work out their own problems.

Occasionally, events crop up which threaten to disrupt the stability; natural catastrophes, economic disasters and military coups are dramatic examples. The stable pattern is upset, and people, to use Mr Taylor's phrase, 'feel their environment is threatened'. People become more reflective; they construct theories and launch arguments in defence of the order under threat.

In the forty-odd years since the Second World War, people have seen their social environments change, in some cases very rapidly. They have seen others whom they previously identified only as characters in *Tarzan* films move in as their next-door neighbours. They have seen their streetcorner shops become Indian-run food stores. They have seen their workmates and colleagues replaced by newcomers, migrants from New Commonwealth countries with unfamiliar beliefs, languages and lifestyles. They have felt their self-assurance change to indignation, their complacency to aggression.

If we accept that people are ordinarily conservative, then we can grasp a certain logic in their response to change. For the most part, they have neither the time nor the inclination to probe their environments; when they feel threatened, they are given occasion to think more deeply about the nature of them and how they can be defended. Racism in modern society typically arises in defence of the established order of things against perceived challenges. And in this sense, it can be seen as a logical response. A logic of racism? A logic of one of the most intolerable of all evils in modern Western society? Yes, and the purpose of this book is to reveal that logic – through the words of the people for whom race relations are not an academic study but a pressing and urgent reality.

The people whose views are studied in this book *live* race relations. They are all resident in the West Midlands, an area which was the target for many migrating groups seeking employment in the 1950s and 1960s and which has in the 1970s and 1980s been the site of considerable disorders arising out of race-related issues. The residents have confronted the changes since the war directly. Some live at the 'nerve centre' of the inner city, with its large ethnic populations and seething competition over housing. Others live in the relative sublimity of almost exclusively white middleclass suburbs.

It will become apparent in the chapters that follow that the logic of racism has an intricate, twisting and irregular quality and is fused with relevance by different groups of people in quite dissimilar circumstances. Yet the reasoning of people is so coherent, consistent and, given their particular circumstances, plausible that it informs many of their day-to-day judgements and, in turn, actions. John Taylor's understanding of this logic has stemmed from talking to his constituents; he knows that it is not embodied in some universal system such as mathematics, but is contained within particular communities, especially those that feel under some kind of threat. He doesn't believe that absolute concepts like 'wicked' can be applied with any degree of precision or moral certitude. Wickedness derives from the particular circumstances in which it occurs. This doesn't imply that prejudice is not wicked; it simply means that, in the specific case of Solihull, assessments of the way people think and judge have to be set against a background of changing social conditions. The next exercise is to discover exactly how they interpret those changes and what effect this has on their overall impressions of and approaches towards race relations. This is exactly the task of this book.

The logic of racism is not the special preserve of any one social class, age group, or residential zone. Position in the class structure, age and place of residence all affect how one regards and feels about other groups. Yet there is a consistency to the reasoning; racism obtains in all groups regardless of class, age and place. To understand both the nature of this logic and the reasons for its resilience in the face of anti-discrimination laws, multicultural education and any number of social policies aimed at its elimination, it becomes necessary to probe the thoughts of those who hold the logic and of those who suffer because of its persistence. To this end, an investigation began at Aston University, Birmingham. Its foci were four housing areas in the West Midlands. Two were located near Birmingham's centre: one a workingclass council estate, the other a middleclass residential area. The other two were outside Birmingham, again one workingclass and one middleclass area.

The Newtown estate is a product of Birmingham's massive public housing rebuilding programme of the 1960s. Built on the site of a series of smaller, traditional workingclass areas adjacent to the city centre, it originally rehoused families that were reluctant to move far from their previous homes. Its location near industrial sectors made it attractive for Birmingham workers, particularly those employed at Lucas, whose factory is actually in the centre of the estate. Since the early 1970s, Newtown has received a steady influx of migrants, so that 13.4 per cent of its residents are now of New Commonwealth background or descent (mostly Caribbean). Unemployment is running at 23.7 per cent, which is a problem for an area with a relatively young population: 47.5 per cent under 30 (23.8 per cent under 16). More than 80 per cent of the estate's families are without cars.

Edgbaston never experiences the kind of 'trouble' that has in the past afflicted nearby districts like Ladywood and Handsworth. Although geographically part of Birmingham's inner city, it has all the characteristics of suburbia, including property valued in six figures, a smallish unemployment total of 4.2 per cent, only 21 per cent lacking cars, roughly the same age structure as Newtown and small (9 per cent) public housing stock. Edgbaston tends to be favoured by professionals and entrepreneurs who need ready access to the city centre. The area has a small (6.1 per cent) Asian population, which has grown over the past eight years.

Ten miles outside Birmingham is Chelmsley Wood. Here is another council estate, where the small ethnic presence (3.5 per cent) is less apparent than in Newtown. There are few concerns over race relations here, and many residents opted for a move from the city for precisely this reason. In the 1970s, the nearby Rover car factory was the magnet for many young Birmingham couples, and this is reflected in Chelmsley's age structure: 54.8 per cent under 30 (33.1 per cent under 16). Redundancies and lay-offs, however, have driven unemployment up to 16.3 per cent. Rehousing from Birmingham is slowing appreciably as a consequence. In less than fifteen years since its construction, Chelmsley, a monstrous sprawl of highrise blocks housing an overspilled population, has become what locals regard as a 'dump estate'. It is ironic, in a council estate virtually founded on the car industry, that 52 per cent of families lack cars. Chelmsley stands as a workingclass oasis in a suburban desert.

Silhillians, as residents of Solihull — one of the most palatial districts in the Midlands, lying ten miles west of Coventry — call themselves, feel they are superior, with their one per cent ethnic population. Solihull is the epitome of white affluence: a very limited stock (8.9 per cent) of council housing, just 4.2 per cent unemployment and only 14 per cent without cars. There are a half-dozen independent schools in the area, and 38 per cent of its population is under 30 (20 per cent under 16).

The fact that living in a particular area affects one's experiences and therefore perceptions of race relations is not lost on the residents themselves. As Joan Harrington, 40, of Edgbaston, remarks:

It's very easy to be a liberal in Exeter. But it's a lot more difficult when you live in Brampton Road, Sparkbrook, and you've seen lots of changes happening, and different racial groups have become part of your district. It's very difficult then, because your social vision has changed very dramatically and you're always going to blame what you see around you. It's very easy for a professional person to be liberal; the majority of professionals don't come into contact with West Indians or Asians. It's much harder to be liberal when they live next door.

The sentiment is endorsed by Mary Painter, of Newtown: 'It's all very well for politicians and the rest of them to say "love thy neighbour" and all that shit. They haven't got 'em [ethnics] living next door playing the jungle drums all day or stinking the street out with their cooking curries and whatnot.'

There is an alternative account of how experiences affect one's perspective. Those who share the view of Solihull resident John Prosser believe that, contrary to the previous argument, familiarity breeds not contempt but tolerance: 'Lower down the scale, where people live and grow up together, attitudes have changed through people mixing. Where we get to know more about our coloured neighbours, racism disappears. Living here in comfortable Solihull, we aren't really aware of the problems while we sit here, ignorant, pontificating.' In this view, racism tends to proliferate in areas where there is little or no opportunity to experience contacts with ethnic minority groups, and ignorance is sustained. The sense of threat is thus not a necessary condition for the growth of racism.

Ignorance is best conquered by detailed knowledge, so there would seem to be a relationship between age and racism. The young, having most opportunity to familiarize themselves with ethnic minorities at school, would seem less likely to hold racist beliefs than their elders, who in all probability were denied this chance when their ideas and attitudes were still fluid. To test the validity of this view, the populations of the areas in focus were divided into age brackets. The youth, or under-21-year-olds, are people who have grown up in what is a genuinely multiethnic society and have seen no particularly significant changes in their environment, having been born after the peak of migration from the New Commonwealth. The middle-band age group ranges from 21 to 50; this broad group of people have experienced changes in their environment, presumably making adjustments in attitudes and postures. Their perspectives open the book and establish a kind of 'base-line' against which to compare those of the more extreme age groups. The elderly, or over-50-year-olds, would all have been reasonably well established in their occupations and domestic arrangements by the onset of migration in the 1950s and 1960s. Most of the people in this group were in their thirties, at least, when they were made to recognize that dramatic changes were afoot. As a consequence they had to assimilate changes in mid-life, when routines, habits and ideas are less easily rearranged.

The book is divided according to these age groups. Part One reflects the views of the middle age range. Part Two focuses on the youth, and Part Three on the over-fifties. Within these parts, the perspectives of workingclass, middleclass and ethnic minority residents of the chosen areas are presented. Additionally, Part Four is devoted to the thoughts and opinions of people who are not necessarily residents but who are in practice involved with the communities' race relations: teachers, social workers and politicians.

What race relations mean to people is the central theme of this book. I have tried to make sense out of their perceptions of profound change, not by imposing any kind of structured theory, but by reaching reactions and emotions as people express them. I have allowed the residents to speak as frankly and freely as they wished, simply absorbing their views with the help of a tape recorder. In all, eight hundred unstructured interviews of varying lengths were completed by myself and my research assistant, Carl Bagley, over a three-year span.

One of the questions the book asks is why racism, despite offending some of the most important moral values by which society lives, burns on like an Olympic torch that cannot, it seems, be extinguished. It is a complex issue and one which lends itself to all sorts of theories, some of which reside in the minds of ordinary people. Granted we are creatures of habit, but we do not think and behave mechanically; rather we reflect on or speculate about ourselves, about our experiences and relations with others. Race relations enter into these reflections.

The propensity to see physically different groups as different in some fixed and inferior way is not just a product of competition over jobs or accommodation, although this always sharpens perceptions of allies and enemies. It is something much more enduring and repetitive and has its roots in a view of the world that originated in the era of colonial expansion when theories about the innate inequality of human beings abounded. Some would say that its origins predate this and argue that there is a near-universal, transhistorical quality to racism. The history, however, is less important than the present in this context. I have written before of a colonial mentality, a mode of thinking which follows the attempts of colonial Europeans to explain and justify their supposed superiority over groups falling under their domination. The central principle of this outlook is that whites are in some, probably many, senses naturally suited to dominate because of their inherent superiority. Any attempts to challenge that superiority should be repelled, and whites should try to keep their edge by whatever means available. Although its source is in bygone ages, this style of thinking has a persuasive presence in all areas of modern society – as the book will demonstrate.

Were this a purely philosophical puzzle, unravelling the

logic of racism and exposing the premisses on which it rests as fallacious would be a relatively straightforward exercise. After all, the validity of the very concept of race has been so totally discredited that anyone presented with the evidence would not, we must presume, fail to see the absurdity of believing in an essential inequality of so-called races. Humans simply do not divide neatly up into such categories. But the logic of racism has a self-validating property. Historically, those who have followed the logic, beginning with the exploring Europeans of the seventeenth century, have generally created the social conditions under which it has been possible to appear to confirm racism. It was relatively simple for slavers to hold fast to racist beliefs, pointing to blacks as pitiful, uneducated creatures more akin to animals than to themselves. They could then deny those slaves education and the other facilities necessary to prove that they were anything other than this image. In much the same way, blacks and Asians in the UK could be cited as examples of groups which have shown neither aptitude nor motivation in certain sectors of the occupational sphere, in business or the professions. This could then be used as evidence supporting the view that they are not capable – mistakenly (or conveniently) ignoring the fact that for decades they have not been permitted the opportunity to excel in those sectors. Racism works to deny opportunities, then justifies the denial.

This is one of the reasons why racism has become a great diabolic problem of our time: because it appears to receive continued validation from experience. Every black solicitor or conspicuously successful Asian business man or woman defies the logic in a small way, but their numbers are tiny compared to the overwhelming majority of blacks and Asians who exist at the margins of society and perform only to the level of whites' expectations of them. In the pages of this book, those expectations and the way ethnic minorities react to them will emerge. Such expectations and reactions deeply influence the pattern of relationships between whites and ethnic minorities. To take a crude, but not too unrealistic, example: if people believe that blacks belong to a group that is biologically and permanently different and possibly inferior, they will fashion their relationships with blacks on the basis of this belief about them. Blacks will be able to behave only within certain limits. During each encounter, the groups will add new detail to the information of each other and either confirm or invalidate the original suppositions. The soundness of the whites' original belief may or may not be called into question. But, in the process, both whites and blacks construct lines of reasoning, a logic, fitting together pieces of information into coherent and consistent perspectives.

In examining the contents of such perspectives, we will see modern Britain through the eyes of whites, blacks and Asians. It is not exactly a sight to be proud of. In reproducing faithfully the testimonies of the subjects interviewed, I have brought to light a vista which contrives to be both intellectually candid and, at times, politically repellent. This book is not intended to reassure, less still to comfort. As a social warning, it can do neither.

Part One

Views from the middle years

Chapter Two

The Scramble for Houses
– White Workingclass

They're ten times better off than we are

Dear Sir,

I am writing to complain about my problems in getting suitable housing. I feel that I am a victim of unfair discrimination. After seventeen years residence in Newtown, I have been trying for an exchange. The only places I have been offered up to now have been a flat, a maisonette but no house. I said 'no way'. I am going to get a place that suits me and until then I'll stay put. I don't think this is fair because people who have been born here and lived in this country all their lives whose parents lived here and fought for this country cannot get a house. Other people, who haven't been in the country so very long, they're given a choice and they always seem to get better places to live in than our people.

Dorothy Jameson added two more paragraphs of complaints about the alleged inequities of the housing allocation system and addressed the letter to the Director of the City of Birmingham's Housing Department. That was in May 1985; she is still awaiting a reply, but doesn't seriously expect to get one. 'What can they say?' she asks. 'It's the truth.' Mrs Jameson's letter was an attempt to bring perceived injustices to the notice of the relevant authority. She feels that her sentiments are shared by most of Newtown's white tenants. 'If you want to know what

Newtown is like, you go down to the housing office and see how many white people are sitting there compared to coloured people. It's all coloured going for accommodation; half the places around here, now, are empty and they're going to coloureds, not whites. With housing, we don't stand a chance of getting what we want.'

Of all the issues that work to divide innercity council estates like Newtown, housing is the most important. In the eyes of white residents, it is a continual reminder that their suspicions about blacks' and Asians' receiving preferential treatment from the state are based on fact rather than on fantasy. 'Don't you think that it's too easy for them to come to this country?' Mrs Jameson inquires. She goes on:

They're given money to live, aren't they? The state gives them money to keep them. There's a lot of them do want to work, but there's a lot who don't bother. And not only do they get places to live, but they get what they want – *new* houses. Look at the houses down Church Road; they're new houses and nearly every one has coloured people in them. It makes people bitter 'cause when we came here we had no choice; these were the only places; they hadn't finished building when we moved in. We've seen them building in this area, yet we're still in our old places. We don't stand a chance.

Mrs Jameson is 43. She and her family have secured one move in seventeen years, from one block of highrise flats to another. At the time of the move she considered it a marginal improvement, but developments about her made her resentful. The spacious new houses were exactly what she wanted, but her requests for a move came to nothing. She couldn't help but notice that the houses were increasingly occupied by ethnic minority families. The offers she received from the housing authority were for other flats or maisonettes. She refused the offers, not because they didn't constitute improvements on her current dwelling, but because she saw ethnics in better property and felt

14

unjustly treated. 'If they can have good houses, I don't see why I should put up with worse.'

The housing issue is part of a more general syndrome in innercity estates. It is summed up by 24-year-old Carole Mansfield, who says of ethnic minorities: 'They're better off than we are; they make out they aren't, but they are. They're ten times better off than we are. We suffer worse than them.' Such a perception is exaggerated in times like the present. Unemployment, housing scarcity and rising prices sustain a mood of depression, and people tend to compare their own problems with those of others. In times of relative affluence, the comparison might yield a zest for improvement, a little status-boosting competition to see who drives the better car or goes on the more extravagant holiday. But during a recession, comparisons lead only to mistrust and an aggravated sense of grief. Everybody else seems better off in some sense. Ethnic divisions become pertinent as tenants grow aware of possible inequities. Observations, rumours and newspaper reports lend credence to beliefs about preferential treatment. Blacks appear to be grabbing the best houses. Asians seem to be taking over all the local shops. They are, in the eyes of people like Mrs Mansfield, 'ten times better off' than struggling whites.

Ruth Johns, who is 48, endorses this view, asking:

Why should it be them that seem to get things, especially housing? Why should they get the places and yet we've lived with our parents? We were born in this country and yet we're still stuck in a place like this, whereas others, who're comparatively new to the country, are getting the houses. They're the ones getting the houses, and we don't seem as if we can get what we want. I suppose if you're going to blame anyone, it's not them; it's the ones who allocated accommodation. They should make it equal as regards giving out new housing. This might come across as sounding like prejudice, but it isn't; it's just that I feel hard done by.

The suspicion of preferential treatment is the primary

generator of cleavage in Newtown. The secondary factor is nuisance, which we will come to shortly. The two are in a way complementary, for many white tenants are convinced that blacks, in particular, are excused the consequences of their many misdemeanours – which, if committed by whites, would surely draw punishment. There is a sense in which white residents feel that, as Mrs Mansfield puts it:

Things have gone too far in the other direction. We know coloureds might have had it rough in the past, but now they've got it made. Nobody thought about whites when they brought in these Race Relations Acts. What happens if we think we're being discriminated against – which we do? Nothing. If you call 'em 'niggers' you get prosecuted. But they can call you a 'white bastard' and they won't touch 'em for it.

'With the Race Relations laws,' says Joan Humphreys, for fifteen years a resident of Newtown,

I think they cause more trouble than anything. If I say they're getting good houses while I'm stuck in my poxy maisonette, can I go and complain that I'm being discriminated against? No. They can; and they play up to it. When they made up the rules, they didn't consider whites enough. I don't think our lives will be worth living in about thirty years' time. Everybody's moving further and further out. The coloureds have got everything on a blooming plate for them. They won't have to move; they get the best houses in the most convenient places, while the whites are pushed out of the city. Eventually, they'll put us all on a boat and send us away.

This genuinely felt belief that state departments pander to the interests of ethnic minorities has a rupturing effect on the community. Whites believe they are being ground down to the status of underclass. The point is emphasized by Mrs Mansfield:

Some coloureds think they own us; they think they own the country now; they really think they're it. A lot of them come over here from Jamaica and they get a house just like *that*! [She snaps her fingers.] We can't. We're losing our jobs, losing our money; it's us white people that work and pay tax and give them their dole money. I don't think things like that are right. If I was the government, I'd give them one area and make them stay on their own. I'd say, 'No coloureds allowed in Newtown.' I think everybody around here would be pleased if no coloureds were allowed in; they're all turning against them around here.

Indians, Pakistanis and Jamaicans should accept that they've been let into this country and should do nothing wrong. If we went over to their country and we started playing up there, what would happen to us? We'd probably get a spear in our back. It's our country, and they're destroying it, and we're getting nowhere. They're getting everything they like. They only have to go to the Housing and say, 'We want a move.' I've been down many a time and they just say, 'You only get points if you have medicals, health, things like that.' I've been down the doctor's this morning complaining about my asthma and my eczema and a mild arthritis that's starting in my legs. But I can't get a move.

The supposed reversal has affected education, according to some parents like Mrs Johns, whose daughter goes to the local Aston Manor School:

The headmaster is all for the coloureds. Many a time, Barbara has said to me, 'If my face had been black, I would be all right at this school.' Whites get into trouble; blacks don't. I kept Barbara away from school for three days last week in protest 'cause a white lad got sent home when he went to school without his school uniform. An Indian lad doesn't wear his uniform and nothing's said. At Christmas I went to the school play and there wasn't a single white child in it. I nearly walked out in disgust.

Mrs Johns has successfully managed to negotiate a move out of Newtown after nine years' residence. 'It used to be lovely,' she reflects:

They were all whites over this side, a real friendly lot; all used to keep their balconies clean. Then they all started to move out, and coloureds began to move in. One lot were all right and the next family wasn't a bad lot. But next door, we got rastas playing records.

17

Boom! Boom! Boom! All my ornaments used to fall off my shelf with the vibrations of it. You got no peace whatsoever in here.

The tensions created by nuisance, especially noise, are likely to be as exaggerated as the concern over the perceived injustices or the reversal of discrimination. For, surely, no one can disregard every research finding that indicates that ethnic minorities have had and continue to get an unreasonably rough deal in securing quality accommodation or loans with which to start new businesses. It just appears that way when judgements are influenced by one's own materially disintegrating circumstances. It's like sitting in a reversing train and imagining the stationary train alongside is moving forward while you are still. Blacks and Asians haven't taken any mighty steps forward; if anything, workingclass whites of the inner cities have been thrust back. But nuisance? This is the subject of major debate in Newtown, a problem that exacerbates a condition of cut-throat competition over housing. Mrs Johns isolates the problem's starting date at 1981: 'It goes on all day – not just music but general noise, kids racing about and shouting. And when the parties go off, well, you might as well forget sleep for a couple of nights.'

Mrs Mansfield tells of what she calls 'the best block on the whole estate': 'No trouble, no nothing. Then they just put one rastafarian kid in on his own and he terrorized the bloody lot with his music, with his comings and goings, with his abuse when they told him to behave.' The youth was evicted eventually, though Mrs Mansfield still insists: 'They think we pick on them, but we don't. I have my stereo on, but not at full blast so it upsets everybody. If I did, I'd soon get slung out.'

It would be facile to dismiss the complaints about nuisance as symptomatic of a general intolerance to different cultural habits. Many white Newtown residents object to the smells associated with the Asian cuisine, but have learned to accept them, perhaps grudgingly, in a way which they haven't noise. The result is a virtual consensus over the unbearably high decibel level of many black households: not only this, but the round-the-clock aspect of the noise. Stories of three- and four-day parties abound in Newtown. The reggae beat pushed out through 200-plus watts per channel is truly deafening for anyone living within four floors of the sound system. What's more, blues parties are said to be the mainspring of all manner of immoral activity, according to offended white residents. Anyone who has spent some time in Newtown knows that the thin and often cracked walls between flats and the single-glazed windows facilitate the transmission of noise. The sound of allnighters rings out, but so does that of do-it-yourself home-improvers, families arguing and fighting and the traffic roaring along the main New John Street West, which bisects the estate. To live in Newtown, one must have a reasonably high threshold of resistance to noise. Yet the sound of reggae seems to reach above that threshold for many residents. It does so because it symbolizes the massive and, in their eyes, destructive changes that have taken place over the past ten years. It may be the beat of bass guitars and drums, but for many white residents it might as well be the sound of bulldozers, so certain is the demolition, social if not physical, of Newtown.

The widespread abhorrence of loud music is matched by the fear of street violence. This is, of course, regarded as much more than sheer nuisance. People recognize that poverty, unemployment and a general instability are contributory factors which affect all sections of the community but, at the same time, isolate black youths as the main culprits of street crime. As Mrs Humphreys phrases it: 'I wouldn't say 100 per cent of the mugging is done by coloured kids, but it's not far off.' Newtown's demographic mix, which ensures a young and, given employment prospects, footloose population, obviously strains the area's facilities. The play areas by each highrise block are pathetically small. The estate's community centre is barely adequate. Gangs of bored young people with little to do and no promise of meaningful employment roam the passages and culs-de-sac and the labyrinth of roads in search of something to do: in short, an ideal culture for youthful street crime. If the youths are not on the streets, they remain indoors, preferring to play music into the small hours rather than watch tv. They have no reason to set their alarms early in the morning, so they go to bed late. The resentment arising from the perception of inequities in the housing market gathers new detail as white residents prepare for Armageddon.

Colour's everything *to do with it, 'cause nothing else is*

Two couples in their mid-twenties: Bob and Jenny Hawkes have lived most of their lives in Newtown; Graham and Claire Curtis have been residents of Chelmsley Wood for six years. Before that, Graham, who was born in Liverpool, lived in Castle Bromwich, Birmingham, and Claire in Perry Barr, Birmingham, where she was born. Bob has a definite view of racism. 'Most of the people I know who've got bad opinions about the blacks haven't personally had any contact with them.' Both Jenny and Clair readily admit they have had no sustained relationships with members of ethnic minorities. Neither grew up in an area of high ethnic density, and, as they observe of Chelmsley: 'There aren't many coloured on the estate at all, just an odd couple of families here and there.' So Bob's argument might be tested against the Curtises:

Because they don't mix, or can't mix, they get to hear about any trouble, and if it's 'trouble with blacks' it's highlighted. How do you expect them to feel? If I see a pair of skinheads coming down the road, I'll cross over because I 'know' they're out for trouble. It's just like blacks; they don't know one black person's different from another, like one white person's different from another, troublemakers and decent people. They class them all the same, and that's how it goes on.

'Honest to God. I am not in the least bit racialist,' Graham Curtis prefaces his comments. 'I believe they are human beings; they just have a different skin colour.' However, there are certain aspects of the ethnic minorities that he finds disagreeable:

Blacks aren't too bad, but it's Indians and Pakistanis that I don't like, the main reason being that they don't take to our ways. At least blacks have; they talk our language and dress like whites; they try to adopt our ways. But Indians and Pakistanis don't. They'll talk one language and dress their own way. They're making themselves a separate community from everybody else, with their own special food in their own shops, and clothes. We don't have any coloured neighbours, but it would bother me if an Indian moved in next door. Not so much 'cause they're Indian, but because of their ways. I've been to some Indian and Pakistani houses in my work as a [health authority] counsellor and the smells nearly killed me – the smell of the oils and the way they talk and everything else.

I've lived in a few parts of Liverpool. There was one bloke there, he was absolutely fantastic. He was coloured himself and he used to go around 'paki-bashing'. He was a great bloke. It's the same in Chinatown up there; you can get on great with most of them 'cause of the way they have adapted to Liverpool ways. We should give them the opportunity – either to adapt to our ways or go back. They shouldn't be allowed to let their children go to schools in trousers; English girls can't, even when there's six foot of snow. And the religious sects: they have to have the great big swords and they're allowed to walk about the streets carrying them. But if you get a white boy with a chain around his neck, he's pulled in by the law. The law says you've got to wear a crash helmet, yet some Indians go around with just a turban. Keep their religion, yes; but not when it infringes the laws of our land. It's got to stop.

21

Neither Mr Curtis nor his wife has too much sympathy with victims of racialism either in covert or overt forms. 'A lot of the time they're just asking for trouble,' argues Claire Curtis.

They deliberately provoke people by walking round, looking different. OK, you see white blokes going round dressed as skinheads and everything else. But people like rastas go out looking for trouble. They walk down the street, and you've got to move out of their way. It may be their belief that they are almighty God, but this is still deliberately provoking for a lot of English. You see some of them with white women as well. As far as I'm concerned, there is enough white blokes to go with white girls and there is enough black blokes to go with black girls. It's not just that. Fair enough, you get married; but what if you have children? I mean, which religion do they follow, Catholic or rastafarian? Then you've got the colour of their skins. You would have one white child, and the next one could be black. It could bring a load of problems for the family, then. I don't believe in mixed marriages; it's something that makes me sick to see, a white girl with a black boy or a white boy with a black girl.

Mr Curtis goes further: 'I think I would actually make it illegal because it's so disgusting.'

Mr and Mrs Curtis have been in what they regard as an unsatisfactory maisonette since they moved to Chelmsley. They have applied for a move, but without success. Yet they're adamant that the decision to move out of the city was a correct one, if only for the sake of the children they intend to have in the future. 'I think the kids will have a much better chance out here,' Mr Curtis states. His wife agrees:

Yes, because I went to school with a few coloured and two Pakistani lads, and they could get by with their English reading, but they hadn't a chance with their writing. So I know from personal experience that the teachers had to spend half an hour each with them to explain how to write a sentence when there was four or five white kids who needed just a bit of help who couldn't get that attention. Now, life is hard enough for kids as it is, without putting them under that kind of pressure. It held the whole class up.

It would be misleading to describe Mr and Mrs Curtis as typical white Chelmsley dwellers, yet they do voice many of the concerns that pervade the estate. One issue in particular tends to dominate, and this is the alleged propensity of ethnic minorities to isolate themselves culturally. The retention of values, beliefs and behaviour patterns specific to an ethnic culture is regarded as somehow offensive, an affront to white culture. It is seen as part of a general reluctance to participate in society; ethnics are *in* society but not *of* it. Asians, for instance, are popularly seen as having an instrumental attitude to British society, which offers them opportunities for making money. Blacks, being less entrepreneurial, settle for less in the eyes of many white council residents. They are content to amble along in a parasitic way, sponging off the state and augmenting their unearned income with the spoils of robberies. Neither group shows any inclination to assimilate. Outercity residents are less aggravated by this, as the volume of ethnic residents in their areas is too small to constitute the kind of threat that unsettles Newtown. There is still an apprehension that the problem could escalate, as Mrs Curtis points out: 'Here we don't have to worry too much as there aren't enough to make a football team. If there were three times or even twice as many, we'd have to look over our shoulders, though.'

As we have seen, the Curtises are anxious that the children they plan will not have their educational progress impeded by slow learning black and Asian children. Were they familiar with the most recent research findings on the subject, they would have their fears allayed. Asian children especially are achieving admirably in terms of qualifications and entry to higher education. One might even argue that the presence of motivated high achievers at school could be inspirational to their peers.

The thoughts of parents in their middle years naturally turn to the future. Concerns about the welfare and development of their children prompt them to speculate on the years to come. Chelmsley parents believe assimilation should spread to all sectors of society and resent the exceptions made for different cultures. 'They should all go into dinner together and all get the same food, no matter what their beliefs,' argues Lilian Allibone, 24, a mother of three children, who has lived in Chelmsley for five years. 'I wouldn't let my kids go to a school where there was more than about a quarter coloureds.'

Newtown parents, although not without anxiety, do not feel their children's welfare and development are endangered by the perceived failure of ethnic minorities to assimilate and their accommodation by schools. If they have not learnt to accept cultural diversity, they have at least established a way of enduring it. The reality of having their children educated in a multicultural environment is not nearly so problematical as Chelmsley parents might imagine. The thought of their son or daughter bringing home a black or Asian friend, or even of having different-coloured grandchildren, isn't so appalling as some Chelmsley folk find it. Bob Hawkes, who believes that the holders of bad opinions about blacks are people who 'haven't personally had any contact with them', would find plenty of support for his contention amongst Chelmsley Wood's parents. But, as we have seen, he would also find 'bad opinions' amongst Newtown parents, whose anger is stoked by the preferential treatment they understand is meted out to blacks and Asians. Mr Hawkes and his wife are both aged 26, and have two children. As long-termers in Newtown, they have witnessed firsthand the changes in ethnic composition and are slightly depressed at the persistence of racism even amongst their peers.

'Negative attitudes are still there. There's no acceptance, no breaking down of old ideas,' observes Mrs Hawkes:

But I feel it will change if you have more whites and blacks in schools growing up together. I also believe the black kids today are going to rebel against their parents, who've told them, 'White men are no good; you don't want to go mixing with white people.' They will and they'll mix well.

I don't believe in anything that highlights the differences – things like being taught about the 'homeland'. They're living here; they're English. Colour's nothing to do with it; or, to put it another way, colour's *everything* to do with it, 'cause nothing else is. Race isn't. They're English, born here, and they're going to live here all their life, so the only thing left to hold against a person is their colour.

Having both grown up in the area, Mr and Mrs Hawkes feel well qualified to comment. Additionally, Mr Hawkes's late father was Italian and, as he puts it:

When I was a kid, they used to take the piss out of me. I suppose that's had an effect . . . There's a diffeerence between English and Europeans, let alone English and blacks or Asians. It's far reaching is racism; it's going to be hard to overcome. I think it helps to root it out in the schools, learning about other people's cultures. Because it's lack of understanding of the way people are that's a cause of tension.

Mrs Hawkes recounts how her youngest daughter, aged 7, arrived home one night and excitedly told her how she'd been to a mosque with her school party. 'She said, "Oh, I enjoyed it. There was only one thing – I had to take my shoes off." That was fair enough. Asians and blacks shouldn't have to change. We should learn about them, and they should learn about our ways.'

'The only thing is,' intercedes her husband, 'they've had to take stick before they get accepted. It takes time. The Poles and Italians went through it. They had to take stick for sitting on the step and playing loud music, which is what they used to do back home.' (Of course, young blacks have taken over their mantle nowadays.)

The Hawkeses' vision of the future for their children as seen from Newtown is very different from the Curtises' vision in which the numbers of ethnics are limited, and differences in values and beliefs are flattened out by a monocultural education system. The Hawkeses see diversity and challenge; the Curtises homogeneity and conformity. The differences are not attributable solely to the locations. On the other hand, the strength of experiences in a specific kind of environment should not be underestimated. In a way the Hawkeses *need* to think positively for the sake of their children. They are too aware of the important issues to want to take refuge in an outercity area. They know that the problems they see about them do not spring from sheer quantities of ethnics, but from a more basic breakdown in relations. Such relations need attention. The Hawkeses are not uneasy about the prospect of black or Asian neighbours, as are their contemporaries in Chelmsley. They have had ethnic neighbours for years. They don't have time, nor inclination, to indulge in the 'should've', 'might've', 'could've', 'would've' speculations of many Chelmsley residents: 'should've put the block on immigration in the 1950s'; 'might've had a less congested city then'; 'could've had a better standard of living as a result'; 'would've had a better future for our children'.

As Mr Hawkes puts it: 'The problem's *here*, it's mainly about ignorance and it's going to be hard to overcome. But it has to be accepted.'

For the Hawkeses, education is the key to the future. Both their daughters go to schools with high ethnic intakes, and as parents they are satisfied that both schools' efforts at instigating multicultural education programmes are effective reforms. If there is a resolution to the problems that beset race relations in the innercity, or indeed anywhere, it lies in education (and we will consider this proposal in Chapter 11).

A poison streak

The sense in Mr Hawkes' argument is plain to see. After all, he has spent a good portion of his life amidst social change and has been forced to adapt to the new order of Newtown. He was not taken aback by the changing face of his environment, as were some of his older and perhaps more staid neighbours, but changed himself. His experience of growing up in a district in transition structured his present outlook. He has been misled into thinking his peers' experiences yielded a similar result. His Italian connections and glimpses of prejudice rendered him more sympathetic to the problems of first- and second-generation migrants of whatever extraction. This may be the factor that he has overlooked; personal contact, even over a long period, may be a necessary condition in the breaking down of racist barriers, although it is not in itself a sufficient condition. But when it combines with some personal grasp of the practical problems that face ethnic minorities, then a certain sympathy can result.

An Irishman like Liam Flanagan serves as an example. 'I can't see any way out of this immigration problem because the government brought them into this country in the first place,' he admits:

Just after the war, they used to be calling people in for jobs; you could walk from one job to another, and they had so much work that they just couldn't get the workers. I'm Irish myself, but I've been over here for thirty-four years. My family was born over here, so I've no prejudice against anybody. But, as I say, the Englishman himself didn't want the jobs in those days; they wanted the top priority jobs. It was the Irish first that they picked on, but then when the coloureds came over they stopped on the Irish and they picked on the coloureds.

Mr Flanagan, who is 56 and has five children, believes that the present experience of blacks and Asians is by no means unique. Itinerant Irish, who have travelled to England and Scotland in search of work since the seventeenth century (particularly after the 1845–9 potato famines), have been subject to similar treatment. Irish migrants of the nineteenth century, both seasonal and permanent, became industrial and agricultural labourers, occupying lowly positions in the labour market in much the same way as West Indian and Asian migrants did in the 1950s and 1960s. In areas of large-scale Irish settlement, they formed a reserve labour pool and, on occasion, acted as strike-breakers. Once the Irish were seen as competitors in the job market, other differences, such as their devotion to Roman Catholicism, became salient, and a strong anticatholicism on the part of the native British lasted well into the twentieth century. Irish labourers were widely discriminated against and became the subject of political controversy. A study by Robert Miles highlights how, in the late seventeenth century, the Irish were conceived of as a physically separate 'race' and 'attributed with a range of negative social and cultural characteristics ... [including] violence, drunkenness and theft ... Irish immigrants were held responsible for overcrowding, inadequate sanitation and the spread of disease' (1982, p. 140).

In 1952, the year Mr Flanagan moved from Dublin to England, the migration from the New Commonwealth was on the upswing. Mr Flanagan remembers black and Asian workers:

They took all the bad jobs, cleaning toilets, scrubbing walls, labouring jobs in factories; and, if they did put them on machine jobs, they'd make them work for less money than whites. They were underpaid. It was the exact same thing as when the Irish first came here in the old days. The Irish have more or less had enough of it now, but there was no difference. The blacks were coming in by the busload; I'd hardly seen one back home, except during the war when I'd seen a few Americans stationed there. They were getting jobs, but they were all crap jobs, and that's after the war

28

when Britain was a prosperous country. 'Come one, come all,' they said. They couldn't get enough for work.

Exploitation is the factor common to the Irish and New Commonwealth migrant experiences. Skin colour is, in Mr Flanagan's view, an additional aggravating element in an already volatile situation. Just as hostility was vented against the Irish, and Catholicism was plucked out as a cause of conflict, so skin colour has also been wrongly identified as a cause. Closer examination reveals a more economic basis to the conflict. Mr Flanagan is also aware of the historical aspects to the present situation: 'It's the white men; they exploited all the Caribbean and the rest of the Common-wealth countries; they took the slaves to America to sell. This is where it all originated from, and it's going on today. White men have exploited nearly every country. This was the mother country. Lots of countries were very, very under-educated, and people were kept ignorant.'

Mr Flanagan's knowledge of his own ancestry and his familiarity with Birmingham's changes over the past thirty-odd years have given him an interesting, broad and comparative understanding of the present scene:

If you're a Catholic back home, you're brought up in a Catholic district and you're taught to hate Protestants. Protestants are the same. Same here with whites and blacks: brought up to hate. Some areas around here are ghettos, and any time a black family moves into a white area you'll find, nine times out of ten, someone saying, 'Oh, I don't want those black bastards living next to me.' The music starts, then there's trouble in the places where they go.

Mr Flanagan holds up a printed sheet addressing the residents of Newtown and imploring them to unite against black nuisances. 'Then you get things like this through your door telling you to join a residents' association.'

He appreciates that the elder black population may have felt resentful at their wanton exploitation and, as he puts it, 'put a bit of hate into their children'. He sees this as justified in a way. Equally, he can comprehend how the children of early migrants have found their parents' posture uncomfortable:

I'm not sure whether the children have learned it themselves, but the young ones are getting bad. I'll give you an example. At one time, you could walk up the street and see loads of them, but you even look at a black kid now and it's, 'What the fuck are you doing?' and all that. They stand round corner shops, round chip shops, round bookies, and you daren't look at them. This amazes me because, at one time, I used to get on great with coloured people. But now it's got to the point . . . well, it's changed. The old ones are forgotten about now, and the young ones have taken over and they don't want the jobs their parents did; they want good jobs.

The advantage of being part of a minority – albeit a few generations removed – and having been brought up in an atmosphere of cultural preservation, is that the attempts of others to resist the degradation of their forebears is not only comprehensible but also commendable. Even more so in the 1980s because, according to Mr Flanagan: 'Everybody is exploited now. There's no work for anybody.' Blacks, like the Irish before them, were exploited in work; now they're exploited by being kept out of work. 'The black kids today have got the same attitude as our own kids,' says Mr Flanagan, alluding to the fact that one of his own sons is unemployed and becoming feckless:

They think, 'What's the use of learning? We're going to end up with nothing anyway.' Black kids of 18, they've got a terrible chip on their shoulder, because they've been kept down for so long. And now they're standing up and they don't want to be educated. But they are getting enough education to know their rights and wrongs and they know – 'My old man's had his day; you're not going to do it on me, mate'.

His impression of many Asians is quite different:

I work with a lot of Pakistanis, and they turn round and say they won't have their children educated in this country. I've said, 'But why? You have the children here, you're getting a living here, you're working here, you've bought your own house.' They all buy their own houses, you know. I'll tell you how it used to work. They all stuck together, and one would buy a house and then about ten of them would live in that house and all work and pay that off. Then the next one would buy a house, and this is what they'd do for one another. Same with businesses. They're all family concerns; they don't have to pay high wages or expenses; they can keep their costs down and they can all live happily and make a profit. I admire people like that, for getting on, but I don't think the Jamaicans, West Indians, are inclined to be business-wise. They're more like the Irish. All they want is a day's work, a bit of money in their pockets, go out and have a drink or a smoke and they never think of the next day. I was like the coloured people. I never thought of the next day; I lived for one day and then, next day, I took what came. I was a master butcher back home, but I had to get out, because I couldn't stick any more about religion, because my missus was a Protestant and I was a Catholic, so we had to get out. We were hounded out and we came over here to make a living. I couldn't get enough money as a butcher, so I had to take any job. So I went where the big money was: the car factories. I was lucky, I got a job but, as I say, fifty per cent of the people that's got a job today, they don't want to know about the ones who haven't, because they're frightened. They've got to hold on to that job. The other fifty per cent who've got jobs, they're not getting enough money to live on, so they're going to start complaining. And then you've got your coloured problem, which is the worst. Everybody's going to start hating each other.

Patricia Beech has the advantage of seeing the world from a number of perspectives. Born in the Small Heath district of Birmingham, she moved to London as a young girl, moved back to South Birmingham with her parents when aged 14 and secured a council home in Newtown when she married. Her husband, Horace, is a Jamaican by birth but has lived in Birmingham since he was 12. They are both 27 and have a 3-year-old son, Marcus. Only the colour of Mrs Beech's skin is white; her hair is tightly plaited and in a decorative headwrap; she dresses in long, loose clothes and flat sandals; she cooks food Caribbean-style, switches speech patterns effortlessly from Brummie to West India patois and regularly attends blues parties as the only white. She numbers only one white girl – who also lives with a black man – among her friends. Culturally, Mrs Beech is black.

'A lot of people round here say, "Oh, Patricia, what's got into you?" But, to me, it's modern,' she notes about the difference between her and her neighbours. 'My old man hasn't got locks like rastas; he's just a plain, simple black guy. He's quiet, doesn't smoke the funny stuff, doesn't go to blues that often, doesn't drink, doesn't abuse women. But he won't go to a white person's party and he expects me to go to all-black parties. So I've been drawn away from whites, really. Jo is my only white friend and she's had it worse than me, really. Not from whites.'

Joanne Harbourne's head is also wrapped, but her hair is locked *à la* rasta. She is a year older than Mrs Beech and is perhaps culturally 'blacker' by virtue of her rastafarian beliefs, which have served to separate her from her white former associates and to deepen her involvement with the black community. She recalls an incident which captures her paradoxical position:

I was in town once – I'd just had my baby – and two rasta girls stopped me, and one of them said to me that I couldn't go back to Africa for one simple reason: I'm not black. They told me my baby could go as he was black and were going on about his rights and all that sort of thing. I didn't really want to know. And they asked how could I be rasta when I'm not black. I said that as long as you believe in love, peace and unity, that's what being rasta is, not colour. They didn't like that and they dragged my wrap off. It shocked them to see I had locks; they thought my hair was combed. I couldn't control my temper and I went to hit one of them. 'You call yourself true rasta?' I said. 'You're nothing to do with rasta.' That incident stuck with me. It put me off for a bit, and I started having my hair Afro'd for a while. Then you get it from whites; they think because one rasta's mugged an old lady, the rest of them are going to do it.

Mrs Beech concurs. 'Black girls give you trouble. You'll be at a friendly, sociable party, and they'll come over to you and say, "Girl, what are you looking at my man for?" That's happened a couple of times with me. I'll say, "I don't need to look at your man. I'm married." It's those that live with black men; the ones who live with white men are really friendly, very different.'

Joanne Harbourne can also appreciate this: 'Have you noticed how, if a white person calls a black man a "black bastard", he hits the roof, but if the black calls the white bloke a "white bastard" the white just laughs it off?' She sets out the problem before explaining the difference in experience.

It's because blacks have got an inferiority complex. Take this black girl who lives by me. I don't know her, but she kept giving me dirty looks. So I went over to her and said, 'If I've done anything wrong, I apologize, but why are you giving me dirty looks?' She says, 'Because I don't like you.' I says, 'Don't look at me, then, in that case.' And she called me 'a white whore'. I said, 'If anybody's a whore around here, it's you, you black bitch.' She went berserk. A lot of blacks call me 'a white bastard', and I just say I'm proud of it. I'm proud of my colour. But blacks don't think about their colour in those terms; they can't just laugh it off.

The reason why blacks are unable to 'laugh it off' is apparent to both women. They have become sensitized to the problems facing blacks, if only by association. 'Only the other night, Horace and I were drinking at a pub nearby,' said Mrs Beech:

And it was nearly closing time, when this bloke walks in and he looks round to us – there was about six of us, mostly black – and says, 'Am I in the wrong pub?' You'd think most of them would have got used to black people by now. But even our neighbours are a bit funny. My mum never believed in mixed marriages or mixed relationships; now she's had to get used to it. As she said to me, it's *my* life I'm living. When she was my age, there were hardly any blacks to be seen.

Horace, her husband, interjects:

What her parents don't realize is that, when my mum and dad came to this bloody country, my mum had to wash sheets and things for other people for pennies. Now my generation can't work even a forty-hour week. We had trouble with her [Patricia's] mum when we started going together, until one day when I said to her, 'Listen, either you accept me or you don't; there's no halfway point.' She was all right for about a year, then she went funny and started talking behind my back. One day, her parents came down to my mum's. My dad offered her dad a drink and he said, 'Yes.' But her mum never said anything. There was just silence. Now her mum won't go near the place. The only time is if her dad specifically wants to come over, and then her mum will sit in the car. She doesn't come near our place either.

'We call it poison,' Mrs Beech goes on.

When they're prejudiced, they've got a poison streak. There's a guy in the next block who's terrible. Only recently, I was out with Marcus, and one of his kids came over. Well, he dashed out of his house and shouted at his kid, 'Simone, don't you dare look at that child!' So the next time I saw her, Marcus ran over to her and said, 'Are you playing, Simone?' And she said, 'No. My dad said I can't play with you 'cause you're black.' I confronted this guy and asked him if he had said it and, calm as you like, he said, 'Yes, that's right.' It carries on through generations like that. I put it down to parents; they either follow their brothers or friends or parents. Some of the black parents tell them not to mix with white people, and the white parents tell their kids not to mix with blacks. People have said to me, 'Oh, I see you're going round with that nig-nog now.' They say they're not prejudiced, but when they say something like that, it shows they are. I never get any hassle around here from black guys. I'm not frightened to go out at night. And they don't all know I'm married to a black guy. If anybody hassles me, it's white blokes. I just laugh it off and carry on walking when they shout at me.

Marcus, then, would seem to inherit many of the problems of being literally neither black nor white. The problems are clearly seen by Mrs Beech, who states bluntly: 'I'd rather bring up two kids, a black and a white one, than one halfcaste kid; they're the hardest to bring up.' Marcus goes to the same school his father attended, and Horace remembers how 'Whites used to try to rule the school.' He used to have white friends, but they shunned him almost immediately after leaving school. Nowadays the school's roll has changed appreciably and this has created new tensions, as Mrs Beech points out:

Marcus is in a class of thirty-four, and there's got to be about thirty-one Pakistani kids. The others are black, pure black kids. Now, Marcus can get on with the black kids. He can't get on with Pakistanis, because they go round and they spit in your face; they swear at you; they try to teach you to talk Pakistani – which my son can do now! But Marcus tends to stay with the black kids. Every day black kids come and knock this door for Marcus to play. Even though he's halfcaste, they still like him. They don't say nothing about what the Pakistanis wear at school, yet my Marcus got told off for wearing leather shoes with steel tips 'cause they made a noise when he walked along the corridor. They're allowed to wear what they like. I've got a letter in my bag now telling me they're having a Divali at the school. I had to go and ask what Divali was. It's some sort of festival for Asians when they can all wear what they want. But all the others have to wear school uniform, which to me is stupid. They should all adapt to one way.

Asians annoy me. All the local shops are owned by Asians. You can go into a shop and they'll get it for you straight away. They talk and understand English as good as I do. Then you see the same parents at the school for a parents' evening; and if a teacher is saying something bad about their child, it's, 'Me no understand English.' Now if they're with a friend, they'll talk in their own language. A lot of people are against Asians because they come over here and they go out and buy BMWs and these big 3.5 Rovers. Horace's friend started off in the same school as Horace. That guy owns the supermarket now; the papers and everything are in his name. Horace says to him, 'How did you do it?' 'My dad bought it for me.' Now, we went to his house, and his house is, well, fabulous. He has got everything in that house that you could wish for: £500 for a good suite, shag pile carpet everywhere – even in the downstairs loo. And yet there's Horace's mum and dad, they've been working from the day they came over here, and their house is like this: just bare essentials.'

Mrs Harbourne adds her comments:

My dad's in CID in London, but when he comes over and sees me, we'll go through Handsworth, and he goes, 'You got your passport?' And this coloured bloke passed us in a BMW – A-reg, it was – and my dad looked and he said, 'God blimey, do you know I've slogged my guts out for this car?' He's got a Y-reg Rover. 'And they are on bloody Social and they've got an A-reg. bloody BMW!' He can't understand how they do it. He's not colour prejudiced, is he, Horace? [Horace stays silent.] He just wants to know what the art is in getting these expensive cars. What annoys me about the Indians and the Asians is that there's about three families live in one house; now, that bugs me. Why do they do it? When they've got the money to buy their own house, why do it? And they always build up enough money to bring somebody else over.

Mrs Beech returns with more grievances:

Horace knows quite a lot of Asian blokes well. Now, one of them passes the driving test, right? The others are 16, 17, 18. Now, he will go and do that test again, to get another driving licence. So there's two driving, but only one's passed the test. Horace knows three families that have done that, and there's fourteen boys in the one family, seven in another and three in the other, and they've all done that, because they've all got the last name Singh. And here's Horace having to pay out £24 a time. Well, luckily he passed first time. It's against the law, yet the Asians can do it and they can get away with it. Just after I'd had Marcus, I was in a ward with an Asian woman and I'd just gone for a fag in the coffee room. I never thought to look at the baby when I came back, but the doctor noticed when he came round: 'I would have sworn you had a little boy yesterday.' This woman had swapped my son! They don't like having baby girls; they love boys.

Interestingly, both Mrs Beech and Mrs Harbourne feel they articulate the views of the black community more than the white in their thoughts on Asians. They feel many whites are too preoccupied in lumping all ethnic groups together and labelling them all 'outsiders' to bother with the finer distinctions. They believe their involvements with black people have led them towards a mostly black perception. In maintaining their respective relationships, they were made to make certain decisions which ensured a near-isolation from whites, in social terms at least. When Mrs Beech moved into her present house, for example, her new neighbours greeted her with, 'Oh, hello, are you moving in next door? I hope you settle down OK.' But when they saw Horace, she says, 'it was no-go. They haven't spoken to us since.'

Even before that, when they lived temporarily in Handsworth, Mrs Beech's birthplace, she was continually unsettled. 'When I stepped out of the front door with my baby, the hassle I used to get from whites and blacks was terrible.' Her parents are, even now, distant: 'They've never got used to the idea of a black son-in-law.' She increasingly cut links with all but a very few whites and was eventually left with only Mrs Harbourne, whose position was very similar. Their perspectives are unusual, but insightful, for they grew up as white children, then became culturally black adults.

Like many other inhabitants of Newtown, Mrs Beech is compelled to be analytical about race relations. They affect her and her family in a way they don't – or at least don't appear to – affect Chelmsley residents. In Chelmsley, there is a more detached reliance on stereotypes and imagined fears; what amounts to a folk history of unpleasant, maybe frightening, experiences with blacks and Asians has worked its way into the shared beliefs of Chelmsley's middle range age group. Without direct personal experience, outercity dwellers persist with an unpleasant image of ethnics, and this in turn affects their contacts with the few that live in Chelmsley. The recommendations of people like Brian Eldridge, aged 41, are expressions of an antiethnic posture derived from heresay, suspicion and media stories: 'Push them all down to Southampton, give them a few quid and send them all back, then give their jobs to whites. I might even black my face and go myself for a thousand quid.'

The Newtown analysis cuts in a number of ways, sometimes revealing to residents what seems a ludicrous, unfair and damaging trend towards favouring ethnic groups in a number of areas, the most important one being council housing. Given that life in Newtown is a struggle at the best of times for many, some residents are inflamed at the idea of blacks and Asians being allocated accommodation and awarded grants. Mrs Fellows, aged 57, for example, stresses her sympathy with the ethnic minorities and resists saddling them with the responsibility for the many problems of the estate: 'My father was in the Great War and lost his legs. Yet I couldn't even get him a commode off the state. I think it's wrong that coloureds are getting grants all the time. It's the little items you read about in the paper like: "Mr Aswad given £10,000 to learn to play the tree trunks."' The analysis is a highly subjective one in that it measures current circumstances against personal experience. Sympathies are most readily drawn from those who have had disclosed to them at least some aspects of the ethnic experience perhaps via related processes. People like Mr Flanagan and Mrs Beech have a kind of vicarious comprehension. Working-class orientations to race are by and large forged by comparison. Groups assess the situations and progress of ethnic minorities by standing them alongside themselves. As we have seen, when they appear to be moving forward at a pace, resentment is stirred. Yet what of those groups who are sufficiently detached both physically and socially to make what should be a much more objective assessment? The middleclass will be the subject of the next chapter.

Chapter Three

A Loathing of Compulsion
– White Middleclass

Wearing blinkers

From a Teviot Tower flat in Newtown, race relations are a pressing social issue, massive in their consequences for all residents and craving the attention of politicians and policy makers. From a four-bedroomed, £90,000 house in Sir Harry's Road, Edgbaston, race relations are little more than a media invention.

'It's all been blown up, especially lately,' Stephen Miller insists. 'There's a lot of hypocrisy about today, with the media and do-gooders like yourself [E.C.] carrying on about coloureds. I think you create a problem where there isn't one by drawing attention to it. Things aren't too bad at the moment.'

Things are certainly not bad for Mr Miller. At 39, he is a successful chartered accountant, a director of two public companies, with a wife, two children who are being privately educated, two well-groomed Rottweilers, a BMW and a Peugeot. 'I'm fortunate,' he concedes. 'But I do get the feeling that, in both the unemployment situation and race relations, the media can be very powerful and tend to blow things out of perspective.' Mr Miller prefaces his reactions with the caveat that his views are 'based on the situation I happen to be in at the time and they may be simplistic'. The premiss of his argument is that the biggest difficulty in race relations is 'the natural conservatism of the English'.

When you have Europeans of any kind trying to integrate in the UK, whether it be in housing, education or religion, then you get new things thrust on the local inhabitants, and this creates difficulties. If you're coming into a country that's not yours by birth or by origin, then you've got to be prepared to do a bit of the local practice, a case of, 'When in Rome ...' Having said that, you're obviously entitled to practise your religion as you wish and to have your community style of life. But perhaps in Edgbaston we're spoilt; the type of people we have here are all professional people, and they expect others to make the effort to blend in. I find most people aware of the responsibility they have as foreign citizens to be sensible people and make a conscious effort.

During his formative years, Mr Miller was brought up in an atmosphere suffused with the Protestant ethic, that distinctive set of attitudes towards work, profit and consumption. His father, a solicitor, encouraged hard work, a steady accumulation of wealth and a willingness to defer gratification rather than squander one's resources. Mr Miller and his brother, a barrister, absorbed the lessons and profited from them. He is understandably slightly intolerant of those who are less rigorous in their application and less acquisitive in their approach. His Asian neighbours and colleagues measure up to his ideal much more than the other main ethnic minority does.

I have always considered the Asian mentality to be about hard work, applying oneself to making money – the sort of values one would associate with normal English and European-blooded people. Whereas, in general, the West Indian type of work has been more manual, perhaps needing less intelligence. Work-wise they haven't been in a position where they need to think things through in depth and they're therefore more easily politically manipulated. It could go back to the colonial influences, which have been in the Asian world longer than in the West Indian world. I'm not sure West Indians make the same efforts to integrate.

'Middle of the road' is how Mr Miller describes himself. He feels that the existing political and educational systems are adequate for handling race relations. The onus is on minority groups themselves to become more acceptable. So, for example, he sees little use in reorganizing education in such a way as to accommodate the needs and interests of ethnic minority pupils. 'In my eyes, any change would be retrogressive,' he observes; education, for him, should be designed simply 'to enable people to earn a living, or do something for the good of the country'. The danger in making changes in education, or in any other main social institution for that matter, is that 'you can *over-cope* for minorities'. Although he considers the educational system satisfactory as what he calls a 'means to an end' for minorities, Mr Miller chooses to send his own sons to a private school. 'I don't honestly think the schools in this particular area are of a standard that I would be proud of.'

Legislation is the other principal area in which Mr Miller thinks there might have been some 'over-coping'.

The motivation for race relations laws seems to have come from the political extremes. Either they tend to be vociferous minorities, about ten per cent, or they're manipulated by people for political gain who get associated with them by cosmetically appearing to sympathize with them and not actually doing so. This happens in other environments, of course, industrial strikes being an example.

The view is broadly consistent with Mr Miller's overall claim that the problematic features of race relations have been exaggerated. 'The majority of coloureds in this country are reasonably happy with their situation. You can make life *too* easy for minorities, you know. I think we should provide incentives for them to make the effort to integrate.'

'But the incentives – whatever they may be – do not necessarily appeal to everyone.

Then I would take one extreme view. Some of the people having no work prospects at all, who may be difficult citizens, who may have no intention of getting work anyway: for these I think some sort of repatriation programme is a necessity. I think there would be some merit in it. I don't think I'm usually that extreme, but I do think that at some point in time we've just got to encourage those jobless, English included, to move around the world a little more to make life a little bit better for the people in the areas where there is vast unemployment. I've got the same view of crime; if you've got persistent offenders I'd go back to slavery days and ship 'em out to where they came from.

Naïve? Well, Mr Miller readily admits this. 'I think my attitude is very naïve in a number of respects because I can only speak as I find. I appreciate that I live in a slightly cocooned environment in Edgbaston and I don't have to face up to all the problems that there are. One tends to treat the world as it finds you. I accept that this is wearing blinkers.'

Mr Miller isn't alone in wearing blinkers. We all to an extent have our vision limited by the boundaries of our immediate environment. In Edgbaston, people don't clamour for houses, and they don't line up in bus queues, let alone dole queues. Educated as Mr Miller is, he is unaware of the same kind of reality as a workingclass estate resident. Race relations are no big deal to him; conflicts don't impinge on his life. Riots are something he reads about in the newspaper and don't occur on his doorstep. Over-crowded schools are a problem, but not for him; his children are educated privately out of the area. He is, on his own admission, naïve, and this is revealed in his entire conception of ethnic relations. His endorsement of a repatriation programme betrays a misunderstanding of the full complexity of race relations. The unquestioning accept-ance of images of Asians as thrifty, hardworking capitalists and West Indians as 'lower-mentality' manual workers reveals a reliance on stereotypes rather than actual experience.

If this is racism, it is racism generated not by deprivation but by precisely the opposite: having sufficient resources to avoid confronting race relations. Mr Miller has capital, choice accommodation, access to good education for his children. This spares him the need for a scapegoat; he doesn't need to blame anyone else for his social condition – quite the opposite. His beliefs about and feelings towards ethnic minorities are of a qualitatively different order to those of his workingclass contemporaries in Newtown and Chelmsley Wood. So are his experiences. The mass media are Mr Miller's principal source of information about race relations; and what he reads, sees and hears often fails to square with his day-to-day realities. The Indians living in the house across the road seem perfectly decent folk. They are presentable and diligent, send their children to good schools and never make much noise. How could anyone have any trouble with the likes of them? He concludes that he cannot believe all he reads in the newspapers. So he scans selectively and reconstructs his own version of reality.

This is not to suggest that Mr Miller lives in a state of delusion. He knows as much about race relations as most people – except that he knows about them from his personal vantagepoint; he could argue that his vantage-point is as valid as anyone's. After all, just because he has not been a victim of some sort of oppression, or a participant in a conflict of one kind or another, does not mean his arguments are to be dismissed. On the contrary: one could contend that most, if not all, of the important decisions taken in relation to race and ethnic issues are designed and executed by people somewhat like Mr Miller in the sense that they do *not* live and struggle in the innercities and they have only very partial experience of and contact with ethnic minorities. This observation may help us understand why proponents of the 'official version' of race relations offer plans and perspectives that are often discrepant with the views of people who are directly affected by them.

The law of the jungle

Few things irritate the middleclass more than an ardent refusal to conform. Standards, values and principles exist for people to observe, not flagrantly ignore. 'I've no objection to the coloureds coming into my community,' remarks Peter Naylor. 'But if they do, then they must take my community on the terms on which they find it. They can't come and impose their rules on me and say, "I've come into your community; therefore you have got to accept my rules." ' Mr Naylor thinks he speaks for the whole white community when he expresses indignation at the way minority groups and their supporters have challenged existing norms which rest on the status quo and have pressed for changes to serve the needs of different cultural groups.

'Why the hell should a Sikh be allowed to ride a motor cycle in a turban?' Mr Naylor inquires rhetorically. 'If I do the same, I'd be straight down the nick. I've no objection to a Sikh riding a motor bike, but he's got a choice the same as I have: either wear a crash hat or don't ride. The choice is his. We're a free society.' This is a key tenet in an argument favoured by many middleclass whites; a 'free society' is one in which individual scope, ingenuity and endeavour are unconditionally encouraged. Everything is reducible to individual characteristics; after all, groups are no more than collections of individuals, according to this view. Great store is placed in the power of individuals to succeed in their chosen task, despite possibly adverse conditions.

If you go to Australia, or South Africa, or America, you have to take that country as you find it. You can't go and neither can coloureds go and scream, 'Race relations!' This is the only country where you can do that, and I think a great disservice has been done to the coloured community by making this so. In the fifties and sixties, there were a number of people who I would describe as 'do-gooders', who came along and said, 'You've got to take pity on these poor people.' That's where the resentment built up because the indigenous population said, 'No. Sod 'em. Why should I?'

As a solicitor, Mr Naylor, 44, is well acquainted with British law. This does not, however, prevent him from taking a detached, critical posture towards some areas. 'Most governments, of whatever political attitude, make decisions which have nothing to do with governing the community properly and everything to do with catching votes. I think race relations legislation was designed to catch the votes of the coloured community and I don't think that will necessarily win in the long term.' The reason for this is simply, in Mr Naylor's view, that 'It's an infringement of *my* human rights. They say to me that I can't discriminate, which immediately puts my hackles up, and I say, 'Why shouldn't I? It's a free country – or at least it used to be.'' '

The notion of the free country or society has several interpretations. Mr Naylor's view has a tinge of Darwin to it:

If you go back to primeval times, it's always been the law, not necessarily of the fittest, but of the largest number. You may say, 'How can you, a sophisticated twentieth-century man, go back to the law of the jungle?' But, at the end of the day, that is exactly the law that will operate: the law of the majority. Why should the majority be ruled by a minority? It's my belief that we have too much race relations rammed down our throats, which I don't think does anybody any good, because one of the inbred things in the British nature is that they don't like anybody imposing anything on them against their will. Hitler tried it; the Kaiser tried it; and they didn't get very far. Government by the majority works well because it's a consensus thing. But when people are told,

'You will take this coloured individual into your community', they say, 'If I like him, I will; if I don't, I don't want to know.' There are so many differences, and you're not going to change them overnight.

Mr Naylor's 'law of the jungle' approach is based on an obtuse utilitarian philosophy in which the will of a numerical majority is exercised at every turn. Happiness is maximized by following this simple rule. Minority interests and perhaps principles are necessary sacrifices in the pursuit of a longterm plan; when they are not sacrificed, this is seen – certainly by Mr Naylor – as a device simply to attract shortterm support. 'You're not going to educate anybody by pandering,' demurs Mr Naylor at attempts to usurp traditional education. 'You can't compel people to do things against their will; you've got to educate them.' He underlines what amounts to a middleclass dictum.

A school's fundamental object is to teach, to educate, and that is in terms of the laws by which we live. There are moves to work more social cultures into education; in my view they should be left to the particular community, if they want to preserve it. I don't care whether it's Indian dancing, African dialects, Welsh language, or Gaelic clog-dancing, the principle's the same. I don't think you can achieve any great results by arbitrarily imposing things and making the white population suffer. It may be very well to speak of 'the moral good', but the moral good of the community doesn't pay the rent and feed the baby.

There's too much interference of the wrong sort. Education is the front-runner, it must be, and I think that somewhere along the line we have to teach the immigrants what our basic morality is, rather than imposing on us their minority racial morality. It seems to me that if you have an immigrant community, then the principal thing to do is teach them. You can't go imposing different rules on different communities. For example, why should a coloured shopkeeper be allowed to open his shop on a Sunday, selling anything he wants, while a white shopkeeper has to give up that shop because he can't open it on a Sunday and therefore can't make enough money? The coloured community has to be educated into *our* morality and *our* laws.

Mr Naylor's appeal contrives to be both simplistic in its assumption that moral values are mutually commensurable and can be weighted numerically, and riven with contradictory crosscurrents of ideology. He believes in the state's minimal interference with individuals' rationally self interested activities, at the same time recommending a government role in promoting a single standard – technical, legal and moral – to which minorities must adapt. Patriotism is overshadowed by the potential development of individuals, although the good of society is ultimately maximized by encouraging the majority's pursuance of happiness and satisfaction. Consequently, no useful purpose would be served by restructuring admissions to the legal profession to allow more ethnic minority members to filter through. Mr Naylor is unimpressed by the argument that individual white casualties (those with qualifications who would be refused admission when an equally qualified minority member was granted preference) would be balanced out by the longterm benefits of the whole society. 'The reality of it is, you're not raising the standards of the community; you're lowering the standards of the profession. You wouldn't be improving the facilities that are available to the community at large, because professional standards would be lower.' Any attempt to modify the profession's basic competitive entry system, he presumes, will result in a slide in standards. The implication about ethnics is clear.

Like many middleclass members of his age group, Mr Naylor voices concern not only for his own future, which is reasonably secure (he has a successful city centre practice), but for that of his three children, all currently at school. He wants the 'free society' in which he has flourished maintained; he dreads further state intrusions into areas such as education and employment. His 'primary duty' as a solicitor is, as he defines it, 'to defend the individual against the state', and if instructed to implement something resembling US-style 'affirmative action' and to ensure a certain percentage of his employees were of ethnic origin, he would resist and 'go to gaol if necessary' (other views on this subject will be considered later in the chapter). There have been social changes, 'improvements', in Mr Naylor's view, over the past thirty or forty years, 'and it will probably take another thirty or forty before it improves much further'. What is more, he contends, those changes won't be precipitated by governments but by individuals willing to apply themselves. 'The coloured people I know who are happy are the people who've said, "Yes, we will take the local conditions and work within those conditions." ' He illustrates this with a propitious account of

one man I've acted for for ten or twelve years. He's a Kenyan Asian and he came in here with nothing. Now, he's a lot wealthier than I am simply because he's prepared to work harder. He's done it within the rules and he's achieved it because of greater efforts, greater application and greater dedication. He doesn't have to come in to me and say, 'Race relations!' He just says, 'What are the rules?' And then he works within those rules, or uses them to his advantage.

All this may suggest that Mr Naylor is ignorant of the manifold effects of racism and discrimination, but he insists that he is not: 'I admit that blacks and Asians don't get a fair deal in this country. But "fair under whose standards?" I ask. They're fair enough by our standards.'

We can distil three elements from Mr Naylor's argument: the stress on individual effort and achievement; the unyielding impulse to preserve values and standards; the resentment of government interference in affairs that should be governed in the last instance by individual actions. These characteristics are all integral to the middleclass perspective on race relations. Typically, the middleclass experience is one of progress and enterprise. Race relations will progress, but only through individual enterprise – not through a capitulation to ethnic needs, nor through government intervention.

Staying remote and analytical is often best accomplished when the object of attention is not exercising a tangible influence on one's own circumstances. Rex Johnson's statement would find agreement in the ranks of the middleclass: 'I look at things from the point of view of how it would affect me. A very selfish outlook, I know, but I think most people are bound to look at it from how it would affect them in their own particular business.' When considering race relations, one of the main middleclass characteristics is detachment from responsibility. An example from Mr Johnson:

Each individual, whatever business they run, must do their best to make a success of their business. We know that in our particular branch of business, which is dealing with what you might call the moneyed classes, they do not like being served by coloured or black people. And if we employed those people, we should lose a great deal of customers and prospective customers. On the other hand, we might gain a few people who agree that minorities should be encouraged. But, to begin with, you've got to find the people, the black or coloured population who are sufficiently well educated to do the work. Secondly, you've got to educate the customers to being served by these peoople.

Mr Johnson, a 40-year-old resident of Solihull, is the director of a chain of wholesale and retail jewellers. He considers himself totally free of any type of prejudice and expresses the wish to do as much as possible to improve race relations. But he reckons he can't: 'I wanted to employ a black girl. The first thing I had to do was ask the staff what their feeling was, because they're all normal white people and you can't simply turn to your staff and say, 'We're employing so-and-so. Blow to what you say.' The answer was, 'No.' They objected strongly; they didn't want her. *It wasn't me*. I was prepared to employ this girl.'

Mr Johnson is not alone in his views. Virtually every middleclass resident engaged in some kind of entrepreneurial enterprise agrees that staff and customer preferences have to take precedence over the more abstract objective of improving race relations. There is also unanimity about the ruinous consequences of any government attempt to introduce measures to force or, at least, influence employers' hands in appointing more ethnic minority employees. As Mr Johnson puts it:

In the same way as you have to pay your income tax because you've got to, if the government says you've got to employ coloured people, then you've got to do it. All I say is, it won't help race relations, because all you'll have is a feeling of 'I don't want those people, but I've *got* to have them.' If they're being forced on you, but your feeling is anti, it won't change your feeling. It would be detrimental in my business if we had to say to a customer, for instance, 'Well, Mr So-and-so, we hope you don't mind, but our salesman is black.' But, so far, it hasn't affected me, and consequently I haven't taken much interest in this particular area.

It may not have affected Mr Johnson directly, but he has still considered the possibility of ethnic employees in some detail.

When we've advertised a vacancy and we get letters applying, you can always tell which ones are black and which ones are not, even before interviewing them; you can judge pretty well from the replies. The quality of the ones we've had applying are not the quality of person whom one would want to employ. There are a small minority and they are different. It's mostly Asians in that category. West Indians' intelligence doesn't seem to rise to that degree. Don't ask me why, unless it's that their initial intelligence isn't sufficient to absorb what is required.

This impression leads Mr Johnson to conclude that problems lie ahead. 'We've lost control' he believes. 'It's rather like a weed that gets into a field; although you may prevent any other weeds getting in, what is in there will spread like wildfire. What you've got here is sufficient basis to produce a race of black people without any further immigration whatsoever. And you can't say they've got to go back somewhere; not once they're in. The problem will intensify.'

As a company director and employer of more than two hundred people, Mr Johnson is precisely the kind of person who does not feel personally affected by race relations, yet he can, in fact, affect race relations himself. Institutional racism prospers when employers exonerate themselves with phrases like 'It's not my fault.' Whose fault is it, then? The thoughts and influences behind employers' decisions not to take initiatives, but to let existing arrangements stand, are often based on racist images. Mr Johnson's impressions are shared by many others in middleclass areas, who may not personally encounter minority groups, but derive ideas from other sources.

I was told by quite an important member of the police force that, firstly, crime is a growth industry and, secondly, once a man turns to crime, they'll never break them of it. They're too lazy to work and they find that crime is an easy form of reward. In their defence, I'd say that blacks are in the minority of crime, but if you had three youths committing a crime, one would be black; about a third all the way through. I think blacks are more vicious in crime. They seem to have no compunction or compassion whatsoever, no sympathy even. They will do anything, it seems to me, to do a decent crime. They'll stick screwdrivers in people, that sort of thing. I only know what I read in the newspapers of course. I've always thought they should bring back capital punishment; if they don't, they ought to bring back the birch.

In addition to the propensity for violent crime he attributes to blacks, Mr Johnson has thoughts on their relationship to industry: 'They're unemployable, completely unemployable. First of all, I don't suppose they would stick to a job; secondly, it's not their fault, but is their intelligence sufficient to hold down any sort of job? It's a very serious problem.' It certainly is a serious problem and one to which the likes of Mr Johnson may well be contributing by clinging to pejorative notions and excluding ethnic minorities, especially blacks, from his workforce. Mr Johnson advocates compulsory state employment for those drawing state benefits, 'cleaning the streets' being the most appropriate form for blacks, he suggests, 'but that's a utopian idea'.

They'll never make the quantum jump to white

So far, three dominant themes have surfaced in the arguments of middleclass residents: (1) the resistance to any form of compulsion; (2) the need for ethnic minorities to assimilate to white cultural patterns; (3) the stress on individual potential and application as the way forward. There is additionally a reluctance to accept personal blame for the persistence of racism and, related in a contradictory way to this, a dependence on simplistic and superficial images of ethnic minorities. In all cases, there is a future orientation; thoughts revolve upon the implications of present actions. Immediate material conditions do not pose the problems; the future possibly does. By the year 2000 today's children will be in their twenties; the middleclass does not want its children growing up in an unrecognizable landscape in which traditional values and principles have been superseded and the state intrudes into previously private areas of life.

Prospects for the future involve the reorganization of education towards a multicultural model. Some middleclass members are relatively tolerant of the changes in education, although in most cases their children do not attend schools where such changes have been, or are about to be, implemented (see Chapter 11). At the other extreme

52

are those for whom any change to what is regarded as an honoured and functional system is anathema. This view is captured by Harvey Levine, 47, a Jewish company director from Edgbaston with two children: 'Nobody told me about the Holocaust. I didn't know about the Holocaust until much later in life, when I was able to understand it and appreciate it. So I don't think it warrants dislocating an entire educational system just because you haven't had your ethnic background explained to you.'

Hilary Smithson, a 39-year-old mother of two from Solihull, expands on the subject, acknowledging that some change is necessary, but not radical change:

I think there are so many things the children have to learn to equip them for life and these are not the same things that I was taught. It is nonsense to take up their days teaching them African Studies, or whatever the subject is which you include in the programme purely for racial reasons, and for no other reasons at all. I certainly wouldn't argue against an appreciation of other cultures and religions and things. If you were to tell me that the normal religious education programme was to be replaced by one which espoused all the different beliefs and customs of Buddhism and Hinduism and all the rest, I think I would be for it. But if they're all going to start learning to play steel drums instead of violins, then that's something else.

Mr Levine, Mrs Smithson and like-minded critics of multicultural initiatives would object strongly on the grounds that any attempt to improve the educational system by identifying what some call 'lowest common denominators' is bound to founder because of the supposed inadequacy of blacks. It may not have a genetic foundation to it, argues James Billig, 39, of Solihull: 'I can't go along with Eysenck and his lot at London University. But I suppose it's this thing called civilization. India is seen as being old, possibly an older civilization than our own. The West Indian is not; he is seen still as being very directly linked back to Africa and a lack of civilization. I always wonder how thin the veneer of civilization is.' And Howard Lyons, 39: 'A person may be 100 per cent black down to 12½ per cent, but they're always black. They never make the transition, the quantum jump to white.' The issue for those who believe that, despite all other changes, a residual and irremovable qualitative difference between blacks and whites remains is that education will experience a drop in standards. Hence the desire to enclose children in the sealed-in 'safety' of independent private schools, at least in the predominantly white schools of Edgbaston and Solihull.

Evelyn Wallington, 31 expects her daughter, now 12, to be married to a Conservative voting solicitor and be pregnant by the end of the century. Mrs Wallington is generally optimistic about her daughter's future, although she worries about such world problems as unemployment, starvation, crime, rape and nuclear power. There is another crisis she has anticipated.

I don't approve of mixed marriages. If my daughter brought a coloured home, I think both my husband and I would talk very seriously to them and point out the enormous difficulties that would be there. Marriage is a hard-working relationship, and our job, as parents, would be to point out what the pitfalls are. I think that it's difficult enough to mix things in marriage, even within two religions. I think that's difficult, although a lot of the children nowadays don't put as much emphasis on religion as older people. I really feel that it is as much the actual colour that it is not right. God intended people to be a certain colour, not half and half; if he had wanted to do that, then we would have had blacks and whites everywhere in the world.

Surgeon Daniel Kramer, 49, has three children, two married. He comes from what he describes as 'a middle-of-the-road Jewish family' which was collectively hostile to the prospect of his marrying outside the faith.

I think it's the same with mixed marriages between blacks, whites, khakis or whatever; they get criticized from all sides. Two people can't live in isolation. There's no real reason why a mixed marriage can't work satisfactorily, but within the context of Western civilization it's impossible. There is inevitably a feeling against the minority, like anti-Semitism, and from Jews anti-Gentile feeling. It's a *social* problem; the people, if they could live in isolation in a nice little island in the Pacific, would have nothing to worry about.

Mixed marriages are theoretically acceptable to Mr Kramer, although he sees social pressures, particularly from families, as militating against them in the future. He finds the Asian institution of arranged marriages 'barbaric', the element of compulsion jarring discordantly with him, as with most middleclass residents. Yet the middleclass emphasis on voluntarism, that is, freely willed action, seems to falter when the issue of mixed marriages arises. The idea is often that two young people may not know what is good for them, not having studied the implications of their decision. Some parents are horrified at the prospect of having their son or daughter wedded to an ethnic member (although less horrified by the thought of an Asian in-law than a West Indian). Most opt for a longer term perspective, pondering the problems faced by the children of such liaisons. The consensus view is that mixed marriages are neither advisable nor by any means as inevitable as many think; they will not burgeon amongst the middleclass in particular, it is speculated, if only because of social pressures to conform. Yet here is a culture that abhors the notion of arranged marriages in which conformity is paramount.

There are other future possibilities. Despite the many historical and demographic differences between the UK and USA, there are intriguing – and in some ways disturbing – similarities in the development of race relations on both sides of the Atlantic. Ethnic inequalities permeate both societies, and efforts to eradicate them have not been wholly successful. The US system of affirmative action embraces all forms of minority groups, including women and the disabled, but has affected ethnic minorities most crucially. Many members of the middleclass are aware of the US initiatives and cautiously scan the possibilities of their future adoption in the UK. 'Positive discrimination', as the UK equivalent of affirmative action is known, involves a type of reversal of racialism: singling out minority groups that have been discriminated against in the past and affording them preferential treatment. This can take many forms, such as making funds available exclusively to support ethnic businesses, specifying a quota for ethnic students on educational institutions' rolls, or possibly instructing companies to appoint and promote ethnic employees. Given the middleclass resistance to compulsion, the prospect of any kind of affirmative action is understandably unwelcome.

The aforementioned Mr Billig speaks as a company director:

We would be very unhappy if we were informed that we had got to take, whether we liked it or not, a certain proportion of applicants who were coloured, as we would if we were told to take a certain proportion of women. We must reserve the right to take on *merit*. I would be very unhappy if we should show any discrimination against people, but I don't see myself why we should positively discriminate in their favour.

Mr Billig searches for comparisons: 'The closest parallel I can think of was the disablement legislation which required you to employ 3 per cent of registered disabled. Our firm never used to come up to the quota. On the other hand, a lot of people never registered as disabled because they felt it a slur to be identified as such. It never worked, so you couldn't impose the same pattern on the immigrant population.'

The statement is consistent with the more general middleclass position which favours an unhindered market place and rewards for a combination of ability and application – in other words, 'merit'. But the middleclass believes in a meritocracy, a society in which, as Michael Young put it in his satirical novel *The Rise of Meritocracy*: 'You need intelligence rating, qualification, experience, application and a certain calibre to achieve status' (1965). Merit is the sole criterion of educational and occupational success: 'It is no longer enough to be somebody's nephew' (as Young's cover blurb puts it).

This is an exaggeration, for very few members of the middleclass believe that racism doesn't impede progress in society. Still, many underestimate the extent to which it can impede some groups. Nearly all believe the best way to overcome this is by doing as little as possible to interfere with market mechanisms: 'doing good by doing *nothing*', to adapt writer David Kirp's phrase (1979). Hilary Smithson, who has experience of affirmative action in the United States, points up what she feels are the more ludicrous implications of such a policy: 'Wherever a vacancy arose, we were always scratching around trying to come up with a minority group applicant. If we could have found a Spanish-speaking Negro of the Jewish faith, we would have paid him – or preferably her – whatever she wanted!'

Not even those who recognize some legitimacy in positive discrimination believe it could work without offending. Anna Wiley, 43, for instance, thinks:

It's morally justifiable, because if you don't give people the chance to be equal you've got to make it up to them. But I think it [positive discrimination] would be a bad thing, because I would be incensed if anybody got a job in preference to me or my children just because he happened to be some identified dis-advantaged group. It would give me fairly real feelings of aggression and resentment and wanting them out. It's morally OK but incompatible with people's sense of fair play.

Daniel Kramer's sense of fair play has been shattered in the past; so much so that he has little patience with any scheme to improve race relations. A Jew himself, Mr Kramer has learned to distrust attempts to elevate minorities through what he regards as 'artificial' means and favours a process of struggle. 'Nobody has ever made a point of saying that the Jew has been discriminated against over the years by almost every race in existence,' he argues.

Six million were annihilated, but no one says, 'Make places available for those who are left, so that they can progress along the road.' Nobody's done it to me, so why the hell should I feel any great sob story about doing it for anybody else? You might say it's selfish, but in life people are selfish. The Asian is not an oppressed person; he's not a poor little soul. He has a country of his own which he's opted to leave, so he's not in the same category as the Jew, who has always been evicted, for want of a better word. And, in spite of adversity, he's triumphed. This, I suspect, is due to having a greater number of neurons, being brighter and learning to overcome adversity.

Mr Kramer has three sons, whom he is eager to see progress in a society without the unnecessary restrictions he is sure any kind of affirmative action would bring. His attitude is: 'I've made it; so can others.'

Complementing this view is that of Glenda White, 42, an Edinburgh-born mother of two:

I'm a Scot. I don't have anyone up in Scotland going to a race relations board for me to say I'm refused entry to a club or place because Scots have a bad name in England. An employer, or anyone who owns somewhere, has the right to refuse admission to anyone. Everyone surely has the right. It is discrimination. Say I didn't approve of black people, I wouldn't have black people in my house, and no one would tell me I had to, because this is my house and it's up to me who comes in.

Clearly, the middleclass is set rigidly against any future arrangement in which the rights of owners, as they see them, are infringed. The ability to make individual decisions based on personal preferences is seen as crucially important. Ownership, whether of business or of property, confers this facility on people, and in the perception of the middleclass it must be preserved at all costs. The costs in question may be a continuing position of disadvantage for ethnic groups and an enduring pattern of discrimination; but the immorality of these, which is acknowledged, is outweighed by the greater immorality of depriving a person or group of the capacity to exercise freewill. The middle class is very ill at ease with a vision of the future in which its children will succeed in commerce or the professions only to have their autonomy threatened by government institutions seeking to impose priorities and limits.

The position of the middleclass in the 25 to 50 age range is consistent and comprehensible. It is bound together with a more general outlook in which the rights of the individual must not be violated and should never be subordinated to the less tangible rights of the group. Ownership or control were gained within a framework of rules and values and bring with them privileges that must be respected – by all. The middleclass is assured of the legitimacy of the existing framework and why not? It has served the class well. The commitment to it is unshakeable; hence the opposition to any attempt to modify important institutions, like those of education and employment, to cater for new needs and interests. New factors should adapt to the present system and not vice versa.

Whilst many believe the media have exaggerated race relations problems, few members of the middle class would deny the debilitating impact of racism on ethnic minorities. Equally, few would concede that, as individuals, they have played even a small part in the perpetuation of this situation through their own business and occupation practices. This is, after all, a market situation; if anything, the exigencies of supply and demand are to blame. Model agency director Pamela Parker, 32, distils the view with her hypothetical scene: 'I would put a black and a white model in a customer situation and see how the customer reacts to the two models going for the job. If there's some antagonism from the customer towards the black girl, then that would go against her, and the white girl would get the job.'

And so the cycle continues. 'Well, what would you expect?' asks Mrs Wiley. 'You can't wipe out in twenty or thirty years what's been inbred as a way of life over generations.' Some may call this conservatism, others complacency. Without exaggerating its representativeness, the middleclass is a source of moral values, capable as much of ameliorating as of worsening a culture in which racism is a norm. With its implicit notion of the free society and the inviolable right of the individual to make his or her own decisions, the middleclass is adding strength to chains that are already lashed about society. What is not, it seems, visible to the middleclass is the role it plays in perpetuating the injustices of this supposedly free society – which paradoxically encourages minority groups to participate whilst at the same time denying them the opportunity to do so. But again, as Mr Kramer and others readily acknowledge, it is a selfish society.

Chapter Four

Coming to Terms
– Ethnic Minorities

It's always at the back of your mind

Jane D'Costa had been living in Newtown for just six weeks. During that time, dirt and assorted rubbish had been pushed through her letterbox, a greeting reserved for the first black family in the street. Pellet holes peppered her front windows. At first, she thought the culprits were kids, but later it dawned on her that kids are not usually so persistent in their pranks. Perhaps her neighbours were to blame. This view was given more substance after a conversation with a neighbour, mother of the only other young girl in the road (Mrs D'Costa's daughter was just 2 years old, the same age as the neighbour's girl).

'There's no one for my Christine to play with around here,' Jane remembers the neighbour telling her. 'She's the only little girl on the street.'

An innocent mistake perhaps, but Mrs D'Costa drew another inference: 'She may not have meant it directly. Still, I knew what she was saying; my daughter wasn't to be counted 'cause she was black.'

The episode signified to Mrs D'Costa how little times had changed since she was a young girl. Her earliest recollections of England are of bus rides when white passengers used to change seats to avoid sitting next to her. This was 1963, just after she had arrived from St Kitts, at the age of 11.

There's something else that sticks in my mind as well. When I used to go into a shop to buy something, the shopkeepers didn't really like to touch me, so they used to drop the money into my hand. Then, at school, the kids used to shout 'golliwog' and 'wog' and 'go back to your own country'. But, honestly, the racial thing didn't occur to me. I thought it was just me looking different to them. I thought they'd get used to me in time. I just had to learn to live with it. It isn't that bad now, of course, so you just have to put it all behind you and take no notice. But it's still there. People don't show it, but it's still there; it's sort of swept under the carpet where nobody can see it. Look at my neighbours. They stick to each other; they won't have much to do with me. We're still the only black family in this street. I have to turn a blind eye to a lot of things. You can't condemn all whites for a few incidents that have happened to me. I judge one person at a time.

When I left school, I remember going for a few jobs but with no success. They were only shop jobs, and the money wasn't much good, but I needed work. I didn't suspect I wasn't getting the jobs because of my colour until I went for a shop assistant's job in a greengrocer's where they had a vacancy. I asked about it, and the girl in there went to a sort of office at the back of the shop where the owner was. He took one look round the office door at me and then shot back. I heard him say straight away, 'Tell her the job's gone.' He didn't even bother to talk to me. It put me off trying to get a job. You see, his idea must have been, 'Oh, I'll lose customers if they see a black girl working here touching the food.' I was naïve at the time about that, but it came to me just how deep the discrimination against blacks goes.

I don't think whites have been conditioned to employ blacks. They've thought blacks only capable of rubbishy work. At school, there used to be careers classes, and one day a woman from Marks and Sparks, I think it was, came to give us a talk. And she told all about the great opportunities for young people like us after we'd left school. I suppose I must have been about 15 at the time. I only really wanted to work in a shop, but she was going on about all the careers in buying and management and that. And it sounded really good. So some of the girls started asking questions about how you get in. The woman answered them all. Well, there was only me and two others who were black and I put my hand up first and asked something or other. And I can still remember how she went blood red as I spoke. Honestly, she tried to avoid the question. She stuttered and began to look around and she didn't want to say, but I knew that the message was that black girls weren't considered the same as whites.

This took place in 1967, the year before the second Race Relations Act, which extended the provisions of its 1965 predecessor and made acts of racial discrimination in such areas as employment, housing and financial services unlawful. The 1965 Act penalized discrimination only in places of public resort, like hotels, trains and restaurants. So it would have been perfectly legal for companies who actively engaged in recruitment in schools to operate with impunity policies that excluded blacks from their personnel.

At that stage, I didn't completely realize what was going on. As I say, it was when I overheard this guy in the greengrocer's telling his assistant to get rid of me that it all fitted into place. Call me a bit slow on the uptake. But in those days it wasn't the done thing to go shouting it from the rooftops, 'Racialist! Racialist! He won't give me a job 'cause I'm black.' It seems strange now, but no one said anything about it; it was as if black people knew they were being pushed out, but they were too scared to do anything about it.

At that age, 15, you go through all sorts of stages. You envy whites and want to do anything you can to be accepted, like straightening your hair or bleaching your skin so that you can pass as white. Then you have a few shocks and you turn nastier and resent whites. I can quite understand young black kids now getting frustrated and angry. In my young days, you had to accept the fact that you were going to be held back, but you thought that eventually whites would get used to us and treat us as equals. These kids today know better than that 'cause they've grown up staring it in the face. I'm 34, so I'm sort of between generations. I can remember my parents' generation being quiet and soaking it all up and I can see kids half my age becoming rebels and wanting to fight society. I can understand them, especially when I look around at my own neighbours and see how they keep themselves to themselves. I suppose I feel more for the kids, but I'm too secure now with my husband, Arnie, and the three kids to do anything. I turn a blind eye. But I can see it becoming more like America was in the 1960s with more and more riots. We've already seen it happen a matter of half a mile from here [Handsworth in 1985], so it's got to get worse.

Jamaican-born Arnie D'Costa, who is 37, has been silent while his wife of fifteen years articulates her views. He nods as if to endorse them, adding only this postscript:

I've had it all too. I've been refused jobs at places like Davenports Brewery 'cause they would employ no blacks. But I keep myself to myself most of the time. I take a man on how I see him. If he gives me respect, I give it back to him; if he makes a fool of me, I try to make a fool of him. I treat people as individuals. My mother and father, they still say to the white man, 'Yes, bwana.' But kids now talk to whites like human beings, not like in the past. The younger generation treat people the way they've been treated.

Jane D'Costa and her husband are old enough to remember the more blatant forms of racial discrimination in the 1960s, but young enough to share the perceptions of black youth, who recognize that racism manifests itself in much more subtle yet no less significant ways in the 1980s. 'It's always at the back of your mind,' says Mrs D'Costa. 'You don't get people *saying*, "We don't want blacks in this job" any more. But it doesn't stop them thinking it just the same.' She sees continuity where many others have seen change. She has grown up through successive pieces of legislation aimed at breaking down discrimination, and has seen her peers settle down in predominantly white neighbourhoods, something that would not have been probable fifteen years ago. Yet more recent events, like her neighbour's remarks, convince her that there is still plenty of resentment against blacks. And the number of unemployed black youths on the streets reinforces her belief that more civil disorder lies ahead. Despite the strength of her conviction, she is rather weak on ideas about what to do about it. In her estimation, the problem is a white problem; blacks can do little more than they already have, and the hostile stance adopted by young blacks is both predictable and reasonable, 'treating society the way it's treated them'.

Unless they want to be seen as foundry workers for ever

Others, however, have different visions of the future. Shokat Chokshi believes that ethnic minorities have to acquire the resilience to resist racialism without getting either disheartened or aggressive. A basic acceptance that society's institutional arrangements are biased against ethnic groups is a precondition of Mr Chokshi's argument.

'The only way we can change society is to change it from within,' he argues. 'It's no good attacking it or crying about it; you've got to accept the problem and work it out.'

A 42-year-old Bangladeshi and one of a very small Asian community in Chelmsley Wood, Mr Chokshi first gained evidence of what he considers institutional bias when he applied for council accommodation. 'If Asians keep getting denied houses by the council because they lack the residential qualifications – which is what happened to me – they have to keep trying until something gives, or go out and buy themselves a place. But you shouldn't just give in.'

Perhaps more importantly, he applies the principle to work:

When I first came to England twenty-five years ago, the only jobs you could get were in foundries. Very dirty, unpleasant work and not very good wages. Now, I could have kept doing that and thought, 'Well, it's all I can get, so I'll be satisfied with it.' But I wanted something better for my wife and family, so I decided to try to make my own business. And I did it. We're not rich people, but I'm happy being self-employed and I have no boss to answer to all the time.

As the owner of a clothing shop, Mr Chokshi has the kind of independence he feels is essential to the future of the Asian community in Britain.

It took the Jews more than one generation to establish themselves, so it will take Asian people longer than thirty or forty years. But it must be done. Asians have to follow the example and earn the respect of the host community. And I mean *earn*; it's up to them, unless they want to be seen as foundry workers for ever. All Asians have to work against this by improving themselves. It has to be worked at by individual efforts, in school, in work, in every part of society.

In Mr Chokshi's scheme, the onus is not so much on society to accommodate ethnic minorities, but on the ethnics themselves to make society accept them. He is as sharply aware as Mrs D'Costa of the severity of racialism. His experience when moving to Chelmsley six years ago almost duplicates Mrs D'Costa's, but with extra malice. Graffiti to the effect of 'Pakis go home' was scrawled across his front door; his windows were smashed six times in as many months; his Vauxhall car was damaged, and a dog was set upon his son for no reason. Although his wife wanted to move, Mr Chokshi refused to ask for a transfer. He required a four-bedroomed house (which is what he had at Chelmsley) for his family of five and was satisfied with it. Such properties are rare, and Mr Chokshi wanted to stay. Prior to moving to Chelmsley he had been physically attacked by three white youths when leaving his shop and in the mid-1970s he was routinely pushed about and spat at. The harassment simply fitted into a pattern, and he remained unmoved by what must have been a frightening sequence of incidents – although such incidents are frequently experienced by Asians even in the mid-1980s, as recent reports from both the City of Birmingham Housing Committee and the London Race and Housing Forum have indicated.

Mr Chokshi's stress on individual effort and achievement and his acceptance of existing social arrangements run through his general political views, which are to the right of Tory policy *circa* 1986:

The government is encouraging unemployment, and so the country is going down. People now don't want to work when they lead an easy life and pick up their money on the dole. Why work when the money's there for you every week? This Welfare State has gone too far. If you cut down the dole payments, you'd soon see people finding jobs. It's as simple as that; when you've got no money, you go out and earn it. That's what I did and my children will do the same. I wouldn't let them be on the dole.

Mr Chokshi's views and assessments contrast markedly with those of Mrs D'Costa. Yet despite their different backgrounds they have shared the experience of being migrants in a country they both felt rejected them. Neither is convinced by the argument that the rejection has subsided. In the opinion of both, racialism has just become less detectable. Hostility against ethnics has been a fact of life for both. Neither has managed to rise above it and become so successful that they are immune to hostility; as residents of council estates, they both live at the cutting edge. Mr Chokshi lives amidst a tiny Asian minority and is constantly aware that he is easy prey for racialists seeking vulnerable scapegoats. His defences are few. At least Mrs D'Costa has the comfort of a substantial black community about her, although racialist attacks on black women are not completely unknown in Newtown.

Drawing generalizations from these two cases is fraught with the usual problems of caricature. Neither Mrs D'Costa nor Mr Chokshi is typical of their respective ethnic groups, and it would be dangerous to make anything but tentative judgements on the basis of their testimonies. Yet Mr

Chokshi's clear intention to work inside the system rather than face it and criticize it is an ambition shared by many Asians (certainly by most of those interviewed in this project). The willingness to use discrimination as a spur, almost as a resource, is also widespread; being pushed out of the mainstream is no excuse for wallowing at the margins of society, contemplating its inequities. Instead, Mr Chokshi encourages finding alternative methods to succeed, self-employment being an obvious one. He cites Jews as the model for Asians' future development (and, as we saw in Chapter 3, some Jews approve of Asians' efforts). The capitalist spirit flourishes in people like Mr Chokshi.

Mrs D'Costa doesn't speak for the entire black community but she does express some widely held sentiments, especially about the endurance of racialism and the hollow rhetoric of 'equality of opportunity'. For her, the system stands obdurate and daunting. Careers lectures at school, rejections in greengrocers' and rubbish through the letterbox may be memories, but they are vivid for Mrs D'Costa. They remind her not of things past but of the present. Society has simply become more sophisticated over race; condemning racialism and making it unlawful are insufficient. Discrimination persists. The reasoning of young blacks who oppose society is clear enough to Mrs D'Costa and her husband; why should they try to work their way inside a system that has systematically worked to the detriment of black people? Her understanding of racism is much the same as Mr Chokshi's, although her conclusions on how to respond to it are diametrically opposed to his. There is, however, another response from blacks, as we will see next.

Middleclass and streetclass

Stoically, almost invisibly, making their way up in society

are black businessmen and women, teachers, academics and professionals, a black middleclass. Or is it?

'I've reached a certain stage and level of income and, in a sociological sense, I am middleclass,' concedes Ronnie Selwyn, 34, who lives alone in his Edgbaston home.

But I'd never describe myself as such. I say: I'm streetclass. There's not the same sort of class rigidity among blacks. Instead of working at my social standing, I'd feel more affinity with a street kid in Handsworth than with my nextdoor neighbour, who may live in the same kind of house to me, earn a similar salary and drive the same sort of car. I'm black first. All black people are part of one spectrum; I'm just at one end, and the kids who throw petrol bombs are at the other. We're all parts of the same community.

Living in a £90,000 house, wearing a pinstripe suit and driving a Rover 3 litre might entitle a successful black to claim membership of the middleclass; but in subjective terms, being black is the more relevant and profound status. Beneath the middleclass accoutrements are several layers of black identity.

Mr Selwyn's parents preceded him to Enlgand in 1956. He followed them from his native Jamaica a year later, when he was 5. His 3-year-old brother travelled with him. His father found a job at British Leyland's Longbridge plant, although his mother had difficulty in securing a teaching job – which had been her occupation in Jamaica – so she took a manual job in a bakery while she studied for more qualifications. Such was her resolve that, after several years of part-time study, she qualified and got a job as a secondary schoolteacher. 'We'd always been brought up to believe in the value of education,' observes Mr Selwyn. 'So there was a fear of letting my mother down that motivated me at school.'

Having passed the 11-plus examination, he progressed to grammar school, where he excelled not only in formal academic pursuits but in sports too, particularly in rugby.

On his arrival at the school, he found himself the sole black pupil, but a number of others filtered through until by the time he arrived at the fifth form there were half a dozen.

We were all aware that we were standing out as what we thought were stereotypes. Now, I realize that we didn't match up to the stereotypes at all, but were all in the top stream. I guess we all worked harder because we knew what people thought of us. You become aware of, you sense, others' feelings towards you, and it gets stronger as you get older. So you hang around with people who had similar experiences, and we blacks and a couple of Asians started to coagulate into our own groupings. As you grow older, you get to realize that there are certain segments of society that hate blacks, like to keep them in their place, controllable. This no doubt motivated me. So first there was my mother and, second, this other factor. I remember a Jewish kid at school saying to me, 'I'm either going to be top of the class or bottom.' That is, he was going to overcome prejudice against him, or just take a couldn't-care-less approach. Most black kids today are taking the second; but I wanted to overcome it all.

After leaving school with nine GCE O-levels and four As, he was poised for a spell at university: 'I'd decided I wanted to teach after university.' This plan was devastated when his mother died in 1970. 'I had to be the breadwinner of the family because my father wasn't any longer working at Longbridge. So I went to get a job.' Mr Selwyn took to his first series of interviews a largesse of qualifications and a buoyant approach. But there were obstacles, as he notes: 'I knew they were there, but it's still a big shock when you get there. Brummie accent, qualifications, positive attitude: everything over the telephone was fine 'till I got to the interview, and they'd see me in person. Then it was, "We don't think you're suitable." It was very, very disappointing for six months after I left school, trying to get a job.' Nevertheless he did get a job, as a trainee accountant. Since then he has progressed through two companies, leaving each one for advancement, and now holds a position as a computer analyst progammer at a large accounting systems company in the West Midlands that employs, he estimates, twenty-five blacks in a total staff of two thousand. He has recently negotiated a loan with which he has set up a property business, although even in this venture he has had to make provisions for anticipated barriers. 'If I try to set up business deals I know people won't deal with me because I'm black. So I have a white girl who fronts the organization and I do all the marketing behind the scenes.'

Mr Selwyn's approach evokes parallels with Daley Thompson, another successful black, albeit in athletics, not commerce. Like Mr Selwyn, the sports star has recognized the futility of protest or resignation. Researching the book *Black Sportsmen* (1982), I asked Thompson what he'd do if he encountered continual job rejections despite having the necessary paper qualifications.

'You can't resign yourself,' he replied. 'You've got to confront things. I'd get a degree and go back to the job which required two A-levels.'

Mr Selwyn's attitude is similar. He is prepared to make one backward step to take two forward. He couldn't generate sufficient business because of the racialist responses of clients, so he rethought the situation and took up a position behind the scenes, leaving the image management to a white person.

Integral to this approach is a striving for independence strengthened by the simple perception that 'nobody is going to give you anything; there's too many people fighting over the scraps'. The only way to succeed, then, is 'by individual effort'. In this respect Mr Selwyn shares the same outlook as his Edgbaston neighbours, who abhor government interference and encourage uninhibited individual enterprise. But although he is not prepared to place great store in government initiatives to break down institutional racism, particularly in the job market, Mr Selwyn does regard race relations laws as essential. 'There's got to be

71

accountability within certain sectors of the community, otherwise there's too much ambiguity. Things couldn't be left to their natural course because the natural course is discrimination. Racism will never end, so you can only hope to control it.' He is satisfied that existing race relations laws are adequate. Improvements in the overall position of the black community in Britain will come via black people's independent efforts.

First, however, Mr Selwyn contends, young blacks need to adjust their ways of seeing.

There's a misguided feeling amongst black kids in the ghettos. Bombing and street rioting may be inevitable, but they don't prove anything. The ambition for education isn't there, even now when you must have qualifications for even unskilled jobs. I thought the comprehensive system would solve it; in a good school, black kids should have kind of 'osmosed' to the higher level. But in the innercity schools there were too many black kids without enough parental motivation. Most black families here are originally from lower classes in the West Indies and probably didn't have too much education themselves. I despair of what's happening with exam results. I can see some of these guys never working and girls getting pregnant and just getting by off the state. When I went to the States recently I had my eyes opened; black kids over there work like crazy, much harder than here.

US-style affirmative action programmes have been mooted for the UK, although Mr Selwyn has reservations: 'Blacks actually resent these systems because, even if they are successful and get to the top in a company, there's always the suspicion that whites think you could only make it as part of a firm's quota of blacks. So I don't think it would work here.' He does see some mileage in government contract compliance strategies, in which state-controlled organizations and holders of government contracts are required to demonstrate that all possible steps are being taken to recruit and promote ethnic minorities: 'The problem then is that you'll get a concentration of blacks in public jobs, but few in the private sector. You just can't wait for government initiatives. It's got to be by individual motivation.'

There are a number of problems with this outlook, a chief one being the gulf that invariably exists between motivation and achievement. Sometimes the gulf is bridged by ability and application, but often the potential achiever disappears into an abyss. In a society founded on competition for a limited amount of rewards, casualties outnumber successes. Motivation rarely compensates for capability, and there are, as Mr Selwyn concedes, a large number of people of all colours who are not capable.

There's still only one way – be in there fighting. *Everyone* can't succeed, not to start with anyway. We can't all be Richard Bransons. But I think there's a vibrant young black intelligentsia, a proud section, not the 'we hate whites' brigade, but a strong section. These are going to be a black British culture, with no misguided feelings, but a desire to mix. I consider myself a part of this. I didn't realize how British I was until I went to the States and got to know some blacks there. Then, I discovered how different from them I was. I'm black first, but I'm still very British. In a sense, you have to be British to be successful. I have to be an integral part of my work and that means mixing, adopting different personae as you work your way around the labyrinth. You have to adapt to survive. You have to fit into every different group you find yourself in.

Although he recognizes large demographic and historical differences between the black experience in the USA and its UK counterpart, Mr Selwyn constantly refers to the black American model as the blueprint. Radical posturing, he believes, should cede place to a new spirit of negotiation. Blacks must be prepared to forget that society is not a perfect ideal with full equality of opportunity; they must accept it, warts and all, and work their ways through it – by stealth, if necessary.

In the United States many blacks did tread the path Mr

Selwyn welcomes. One result of this was that during the 1960s and 1970s a process of dissociation took place in which the most capable qualified blacks entered institutes of education and the professions at a rate comparable with whites, leaving the black majority behind to stagnate in the same old underclass. Because of a demand for education and highly skilled labour, the more able blacks were accommodated in the job market. Poorly educated, lowskill blacks were not. The result was a black bourgeoisie, whose interests had little to do with the overall interests of the majority of the US black population. It is possible that a development along the lines suggested by Mr Selwyn might have similar consequences in the UK.

This is not an argument to cut ice with those sections of the black community which are foraging either to progress in the professions or to establish businesses. The fact that more and more are opting for the entrepreneurial route to success may be a reflection on a society which blocks other roads to advancement, in commerce and industry, but it is also a statement of a new sense of urgency and self-reliance. Mr Selwyn's ambitions do not end with his present company: apart from his property venture, he has several other business deals in the offing and eventually hopes to manage his own business full-time. 'I'm patient. It may take several years, but if you look at the really successful businesses, they rarely happen overnight. Look at the Asian community; it's got a bit more business history than the black community, but it's moving.'

Asians, especially those who travelled to the UK via East Africa, have made admirable progress in the business sphere, while West Indians have lagged behind. One of the reasons for this is the difficulty potential black entrepreneurs encounter, first in securing loans, and second in appealing to a wider market. A Runnymede Trust report on the subject, published in 1983, pointed out the problems, suggesting that black businesses typically have trouble with local authorities over planning permission and with finance companies over loans. They also seem to depend on strictly ethnic markets (Caribbean foods, Afro hair and beauty products, etc.). Still, the attractiveness of a lucrative independence and at least a partial escape from the more obvious obstacles strewn before ethnic minorities is sufficient to lure more blacks towards entrepreneurship. Whether they are on the same course as their US equivalents is not yet known, although people like Mr Selwyn are too preoccupied trying to be successful to worry about the historical consequences of their actions. He argues, plausibly, that by working the system rather than barking at it, he is acting rationally.

Part Two

Visions of Youth

Chapter Five

Posing New Problems
– White Workingclass

It's not a case of 'they've come to steal our jobs' any more

'Some of these people round here are racists through and through and they'll take their views with them to the grave,' asserts Karen Forster with some conviction. She's a Commission for Racial Equality officer who is familiar with Newtown, having had more than four years' experience with the community. 'You might as well concentrate all your efforts on the younger generation, for the future; the old ones won't change now.'

Is she right? Is the 'younger generation' easier to influence than its elders, while older generations remain stuck with their ideas, however inaccurate? Newtown has its fair share of hard-bitten racists. They are often over 50 and have seen substantial changes in their environment. Blacks and Asians populate areas that were once all white; businesses that used to employ hundreds or even thousands of people have shut down; dole queues have lengthened and multiplied. But to the generation born amidst the affluence of the 1960s, these changes seem to be of no consequence; the people of this generation can't compare life now with life in the 1950s, and should be unable to conclude that Britain's social and economic decline is, in large measure, caused by blacks and Asians. Yet this is precisely what many of them say. In this chapter I want to express how they are able to believe this and, perhaps more relevantly, *why* they believe it.

Talking in terms of the 'younger generation', as Ms Forster does, can sometimes be misleading. Not all youths share an identity of response and views about issues and events, because they do not necessarily experience the same problems. There are some difficulties of adjustment that all adolescents and young adults have to face, but there are many other types of problem that affect some youths and not others. Unemployment is one. About 40 per cent of Britain's unemployed are under the age of 25, and nearly a million of these are betweeen the school-leaving age of 16 and 19. This has consequences not only for the material lifestyles of the people concerned. As Mike O'Donnell writes: 'The overshadowing possibility of unemployment has affected the thinking and attitudes of a generation' (1985, pp. 112–13).

Those youths for whom unemployment is not a possibility, or at least only an extremely unlikely one, would not have similar thoughts and attitudes. So, for example, a 16-year-old Silhillian may be thinking ahead to a university place, followed by postgraduate or vocational study and a future profession. He or she will think differently to a Chelmsley school-leaver whose best hope of constructive paid activity is a Youth Training Scheme placement. Not surprisingly, they will have divergent thoughts on race issues. The Chelmsley youth who grows up in an area where there are few ethnic minority youths may think differently from a young person who is flanked by black and Asian contemporaries each time he lines up at the Newtown Jobcentre.

John Wilkinson, whose opinions are perhaps the exception rather than the rule, goes to that very Jobcentre. He has been attending for the past eighteen months since he was made redundant by a Birmingham wholesale firm that employed him as a storeman. He is 20 and has spent his last seven years in the Newtown area, four of them with his parents. If you believed most of the standard sociology textbooks, you might expect John to make a scapegoat of the ethnic minorities, to blame them as the causes of all his own problems. The classic '3 million unemployed = 3 million blacks and Asians' equation might be expected to appeal in John's situation. Textbooks would lead us to predict that he is exactly the kind of character who would turn racist, blaming others in his immediate surroundings for problems that have nothing to do with them and for which they can have no possible solution. But John intuitively sets up a different argument:

How many blacks are there in Britain? About three million. Out of three million unemployed, you take the amount of blacks that are unemployed and they shouldn't make much of a dent on the job opportunities for anybody else. Out of fairness, I would like to think that, if I went to their country, I could be accepted there and given social security if I needed it; or that I could get a work permit quite easily. It's not a case of 'They've come into this country to steal our jobs' any more.

Still, John is aware that this is precisely the belief of some of his not-too-distant neighbours, especially ones older than himself.

I was in a pub in town the other night and there was a guy stood at the bar. And an Asian guy walked in, bought himself a drink and went and sat down. I heard this guy at the bar muttering something or other. So I turned to him and said, 'What was that, then?' He said, 'Them black bastards all ought to be shipped off. I'd shoot 'em all.' So I said, 'Oh, you'd shoot people, would you? Do you like shooting people?' He said, 'I shot a few in the war, I can tell you. I shot a couple.' I said, 'You really shot people?' And he looked quite pleased about that and said, 'Yes.' I said, 'Christ, man, you're sick.'

A lot of people in my family, as well, talk about 'wogs' and 'niggers' and are racist to a certain degree. But when the first immigrants started coming in, before 1968, they were the younger generation. Probably, the older generation at that time was even worse, even more 'patriotic'. 'No, we can't have blacks here' and all that type of attitude. Blacks have stopped coming in so much, and those who are here are getting involved in the culture, the British way of life. So I should imagine it'll get easier. Because I'm sure all the stick the older generation took has influenced the youngsters in their lives; they've been taught by their parents, but youngsters of today, black and white, are becoming more liberal as time goes by.

There is an appreciation bordering on empathy in John's words.

What was the real reason for the riots in the eighties? In Bristol, it was police harassment in certain black areas, like St Paul's. What was it in Birmingham and London? Has anybody asked the people involved in it why they were rioting? They're the ones who should know. They weren't going out doing criminal damage just for gain. I would have thought that a mass riot like that, where there was a hell of a lot of people going out and wrecking places, smashing windows, stealing things, looting, wasn't just 'cause all those people wanted new hi-fi systems, or videos.

It was probably because of the sort of areas they live in. I don't know whether it's a deliberate ploy by the council, but blacks seem to be all put together in council estates in cities. I'm sure they prefer it that way at the moment, but in the future, hopefully, they'll be more integrated. In the black areas I'm familiar with I haven't seen any improvement in the last three years: improvements in the look of the place, renovation of the place, money being put into the area to create jobs. So we might see other riots, but not just involving blacks. I mean whites as well. Perhaps that's what's needed.

John envisages a mass demonstration involving whites, blacks and Asians in their thousands. He senses that there is a lot of racism in Newtown, but equally he thinks it is on the decline. 'I think we're getting closer together, and attitudes will become better.' For him, it is not just a case of whites abandoning their prejudices, however. 'It's difficult to make friends with coloureds,' he admits, adding his own credible explanation: 'They tend to be on their guard; they've experienced racism all their lives in different ways. They get a lot of stick, so they probably start to feel most whites are the same.' Sheer familiarity and an apprehension of shared social conditions seem to foster a kind of mental assonance. John, like many other white Newtown youths, is a conscious thinker about his own problems and sees no advantage in simply – and blindly – blaming his peers who have sat next to him at school and line up with him in dole queues. The 'stealing our jobs' scenario is implausible to him, although he understands the reasons for its credence amongst his elders.

John is unaffected by the worries of an Asian takeover of Newtown's shops, which seems to preoccupy his parents' generation. He has no fear of the stereotype black mugger who allegedly prowls the estate. First-hand experience tells him a different story: 'It's a struggle for us all, black, white, or blue, as far as I'm concerned.' His contact with members of the ethnic minorities obviates the need to resort to the stereotyped images so central to racism. He looks for alternative explanations of, and possible solutions to, the problems he confronts. 'I'd like to see less money spent on arms and things like that and more put into industry to create more jobs for everybody.'

In figuring out his own version of the causes and solutions to problems of unemployment, he has arrived at a theory of racism. 'If people have got no money and live in a dump estate like this, then they're going to get depressed and probably aggressive at times. And if you get that way, it's quite easy to take aggression out on anything. You could become a thief and go out robbing. You could become a racist.' (Maybe John has read the sociology texts after all!)

'But, if life was a bit easier, if people had jobs, had a better standard of living, they wouldn't need to be a racist. Or vice versa: black guys could do the same. It's pretty shitty in Britain when the average wage is about £110, and the government says, "These arseholes on the dole are only worth £22."' John has become aware of the bankruptcy of racism in understanding the problems he so evidently shares with other members of his neighbourhood, generation and, perhaps, class. But for many others who, in profile, have the same conditions of life as John, the awareness doesn't register; they are drawn to a different interpretation.

I'd shoot women who went with blacks – and the blacks with them

'This is a white country. Or it's supposed to be. But there must be 30 million blacks over here now. They're taking over, and I think they're trying to get back at us for when we had them as slaves. And they ain't got no right, no; if they would have overpowered us, we would have been slaves to them. So it was survival of the fittest.'

This is how Kevin Fiske approaches the issue. Like John Wilkinson he is unemployed, although his explanation of this opposes John's:

They [the ethnic minorities] do affect employment a lot. They'll do all the shitty jobs for a start. Then they stick together and they'll buy a shop. Then they'll get enough money from that to buy another shop. And they're knocking all our shops out of business. They're taking over the country, aren't they, the Pakis? You'll find a bloke will come over here and get a job and he'll send for his missus and kids and bring them across. If you threw all the blacks out of the country, the jobs that we've got now would pay more.

Born in the Black Country town of Dudley, Kevin moved to Birmingham with his parents when he was 4, then followed them to Chelmsley when 9. He is now 19 and recently completed a three-month spell in a detention centre for burglary. Before that, he worked in a butcher's shop in Chelmsley's central shopping precinct. Nowadays he drifts aimlessly around the precinct, 'having a laugh', as he put it, although Kevin seems a singularly humourless person and offers some unfunny proposals.

We've got to kick them all out. That's their tough luck, isn't it? If you don't, we're going to be overpopulated. Then there's crime; I saw it on tv not long ago that said more blacks are committing crime than the whites. But you'll get some nig-nogs who'll get away easy. I don't know whether it's the judges that are frightened of them, I don't know. There's a few people that are frightened of blacks, all right. We should get rid of them all: pakis and nig-nogs. I class them all the same – they're all a different colour. I was going to join the National Front, but I didn't 'cause somebody told me that if they were in power and the government gives an order you have to do it, and I don't fancy that. If they were just going to chuck the blacks out, I'd have gone with them.

If I'd got a business, I wouldn't employ a black; they cause too much hassle. Say if you've got a factory of about three hundred people, say two hundred are whites and a hundred blacks, then you're going to get all the niggers creating. When the wenches go past, they're going to keep whistling. Then you're going to get all the white chaps saying, 'Oi, that's my missus; pack in!' But, 'cause they can't keep to their own colour, they have to keep going for our women. I'd shoot women who went with blacks. I class them as slags. And I'd shoot the blacks with them. It's because I think blacks should mate with blacks and whites should be whites and not half-castes.

Kevin's views are not, of course, based on any analysis of social changes (30 million blacks and Asians?) nor are they based on close familiarity with members of ethnic groups. Rather, he operates with a limited repertoire of stereotypes of 'pakis' – referring to all those of South Asian origin or descent – and blacks, or 'nig-nogs' as Kevin calls them.

I just don't like Pakis. They stink. Pakis really reek; you can tell one in the street a mile away. Blacks stink of sweat and a lot of them are pimps. If a white wench went with a black, he could put her on the street. They'll pick them up and say, 'I'll give you a flat.' And the wenches will think, 'Oh, great, I'm all right here.' And they get shoved on the streets to work for the pimps.

Kevin's conceptions of ethnic minorities contrast vividly with John's. Yet they have broadly similar circumstances: both between 19 and 20, unemployed, unskilled, few qualifications and limited occupational experience. Their fathers are both blue-collar workers, John's being a machine presser (now redundant), Kevin's a car assembly worker; both mothers are housewives. Add to this the fact that both sets of parents seemed to have compatible views on ethnic issues. 'A lot of people in my family are racist to a certain degree,' to repeat John. Kevin reports: 'My dad don't like 'em, blacks or Pakis.' One might assemble the data about their lives and make a reasonable prediction that their perspectives would be similar. But no. Why not?

Basically the answer is that their actual experiences with blacks and Asians are different. John has grown up on an estate with a full multiethnic mix, while Kevin's interpersonal contacts have been restricted to a short — and, as it turned out, fiery — period in Birmingham with a black family as neighbours ('the old man ended up having a fight with the bloke') and a stretch in detention:

There was some hassle in there. We had two or three blacks, one who seemed to be drugged up all the time. There was another nigger who used to dance about, saying, 'Nobody mess me about, man; I kick their bloody heads in.' There was no reason for him to shout his mouth off. So we gave him a right going over. When I first got there, the others said, 'Do you like pakis?' And I said, 'No.' So they'd say, 'We'll give you a test. Get a brick and put it through the dorm window, where they sleep.' I said, 'Course.' Whenever we wanted a bit of fun, we used to put bricks or bottles or mugs through their windows. We'd throw bottles down from our window at them as well.

For the most part, Kevin has lived in areas where there are few opportunities to sustain relationships with ethnic minorities. Accordingly, his knowledge of them is not firsthand or direct but drawn from media images, like blacks throwing firebombs in Tottenham or headlines about 'Indian draws £300 a week dole money'; or from his father, who 'don't like 'em'. Because of his own personal geography he has not been able to test out this knowledge, except in the detention centre, where associating with blacks or Asians would have earned him the kind of unhealthy stigma that would have made his stay less comfortable than it already was.

Consider whether just living near ethnic groups has a marked effect on one's attitudes towards and beliefs about them. It appears an uncertain foundation on which to rest an argument. Mere physical proximity surely cannot produce a social formula for the elimination of racism. Indeed, the textbook writers would suggest that, in times of stress and economic insecurity, living close to visibly different groups would promote rather than prohibit racism. This seems to be true for those over the age of, say, 45. But here we are interested in the children born in the affluence of the late 1950s and early 1960s, when well paying jobs proliferated and washingmachines ceased to be the exclusive property of the middleclass. Fifteen or twenty years later, half a generation finds itself in a position summed up in the title of one of my previous books, *No Future* (1983).

The parents of those children growing up in innercity estates like Newtown may have witnessed dramatic changes in their environment; adjustments would have been forced on them. Maybe they disliked the idea of a black family next door after thirty-odd years in an allwhite street, but they had to get used to it just the same. Children accept the beliefs of their parents, often unquestioningly, until confronted by alternative, more credible beliefs. For instance, Sally Twinning, 18, of Newtown remembers how her father told her that all blacks had tails and she didn't question this until her observations in gym class suggested differently! Even if most parents don't fill their kids' heads with such ludicrous nonsense, many teach their children ideas that are racist in implication, if not in content. In Newtown there is ample opportunity to explore an alternative reality to the one envisaged by many older residents; and children, as they grow and develop, are likely to question critically and probably abandon the more untenable ideas of their parents. Over at Chelmsley, alternatives are not so widely available. Had Sally lived here and not had any ethnic minority children in her gym class, for how long would she have believed they had tails? People like Kevin, who have grown up without evidence to contradict their parents' and the media's perspectives, are more likely to internalize them. Children discard beliefs about humans with tails, as they do those about Santa Claus, but they cling to some of the more plausible ones, such as those concerning white superiority, the 3 million jobs equation and the inevitability of conflict. What is more, they find supporting evidence of this in the views and testimonies of peers, who are similarly deprived of personal contact with ethnic group members. There is simply not enough raw material to suggest anomalies in their parents' arguments. In Newtown and other multiethnic innercity areas, however, enough material exists to stimulate critical reflection on parental perspectives.

They want to do to us what we did to them

Theresa Samuels is 19 and has been exposed to ethnic

variety enough to be able to reflect on her parents', particularly her father's, views.

My dad's got the attitude that, if you know somebody personally who's black or Asian, they're a very nice person. But as a mass he can't stand them. He thinks they shouldn't be here. You know the kind of thing: taking white men's jobs. He thinks that if the country hadn't started all this immigration they wouldn't be here. He reckoned he was going to vote National Front, and I told him, 'Well, you're an immigrant as well; just because you're white doesn't make any difference. They're anti-Jews as well as anti-black, and when they've done with them, the Irish come next on the list – and that means you.' But it doesn't seem to make much difference.

He's OK to people who live in the street. He'll say 'Hello' to them and help them out, lending them the lawnmower and whatever. But when they mention it on telly, he goes sort of nutty: 'Bloody blacks shouldn't be here; they ought to be sent home.' Yet he'll come in and say, 'That bloke down the road, he's a nice bloke, isn't he? I was just chatting to him.' He doesn't seem to connect that. If people are nice to him, he's nice back; but if a bloke comes on telly with anything to do with race or immigration, he forgets he knows these people and just sees an enormous black population taking over Britain and getting everywhere. They're all blacks to him. He doesn't distinguish between West Indians or Asians. But he's not bigoted or prejudiced enough not to talk to them at all.

Theresa was born in London but moved to Birmingham with her parents when she was 12. Initially, the family lived in Lozells, the densely Asian district adjacent to Newtown. She has lived on the Chelmsley estate for five years, although at present she is saving what she can from her job as a secretary in Birmingham so as to afford to move to her own flat – 'just to get away from my parents, more than anything'.

I found that when I was a lot younger, me and my friends found the blacks a lot more aggressive; the Asians are a lot quieter. In the bus queues coming home from school, you'd push in front of someone who was Asian, knowing that they wouldn't say anything. But you wouldn't push in front of any blacks 'cause you might get a smack in the face, or they'd push you back. Being younger in that situation you noticed it most; Indians are quieter. You'd feel safer with them because you could tell them to fuck off if you wanted to.

I went to a Catholic school, so there was only about ten blacks out of two hundred of us. I suppose they played up at times; they got into this rasta stuff and went off and wouldn't speak to anyone else. But they improve. If you sit around and talk about race with a few different people, Asian people and black people, you realize everyone's got feelings on it; it's not just one group thinking about another. When I did my secretarial course, there were quite a few black girls, so we were all doing the same thing, and you get to know them. Having said that, the majority of my friends are still white, though everyone around here has got black friends and everyone goes to the same places. If you've grown up with friends who are mostly white, you don't suddenly go out and find some black friends as well. And if you've grown up with blacks, you don't just drop them. Though with all this unemployment and things like drop-in centres you can go to during the day, and certain youth clubs, most of the people who go are black, and perhaps they start to stick together more then. I mean, if you're a black bloke who's unemployed all your mates who're unemployed will tend to be black. And you might go and play pool all day; and you're all together. If a white happened to walk in, that'd be odd, not because it's a bad feeling but because the place has sort of been adopted or taken over by one group of people. It's not a strong anti-white feeling, but whites might feel they're not welcome – maybe they're not.

My dad would be absolutely bloody mad if I started going seriously with a friend who I've known for quite a long time who happens to be black. He's not West Indian; he's Malaysian. Now when he comes to the house, my dad says, 'He's a nice bloke.' But my friend's dad won't let him in the house. If he goes round, he says, 'That darky's at the door for you', and he won't let him in. My dad isn't like that. Knowing the person, he says he's all right. So if I brought a black guy home I think he'd be quiet, but he'd run off and complain to my mum. 'Have you seen what she's come home with now?' I think he'd be quite shocked 'cause none of the blokes I've ever come home with before has actually been black.

It is not just a generation that separates Theresa's views from those of her parents; it is a conception. At school, college and work, Theresa has experienced first-hand relations with ethnic minorities. She also realizes that her father thinks the way he does precisely because he lacks that first-hand experience. 'When you think about it, he's 60 and he's never really known any blacks or Asians. So you can't expect much from him.'

However, let us not exaggerate the idea of proximity as a recipe for ethnic harmony. Newtown is not the idyll that, after listening to the testimonies of youths who have chosen to reject the prejudices of their parents, one might suppose. Familiarity with ethnic minorities is often not sufficient to stabilize relations; and although Newtown has not undergone any serious interethnic disturbances, cleavages amongst the young certainly exist – significantly, however, not amongst the unemployed.

Those youths who feel no commonality with their ethnic peers perceive what they take to be black racism. 'I think they want to do to us what we did to them, like in *Roots*,' James Tyne believes. 'I know a lot of black kids around here, and we get on all right, but if new black kids come in from another area, they start on you. Even your mates who you'd get on OK with at school will side with the black causing the trouble. So you end up fighting your own friends.' James's version of events is that, at school, black, Asian and white children mix without inhibition, not recognizing differences of colour or culture. As they approach school-leaving age, or perhaps just after, clusterings seem to occur with ethnicity becoming more of a factor than mere friendship. 'Asians keep themselves to themselves, and blacks start to stick together and have nothing to do with whites.' Contact still remains, but ethnic loyalties supersede all others, and this is illuminated in flashpoints such as moments of conflict. In James's example, the entry of a new black youth into the neighbourhood created a necessity to take sides, and black former schoolfriends affiliated with the new youth. 'I still talk to them, but I don't treat them as mates any more,' he says:

I think that they think, 'We're above white kinds. We're new in this country and we can do what we like.' But they've got to look at it this way; it's not our fault what happened in the past. White kids are not angels, though. They do cause a lot of trouble. Whites say it's all black kids' fault for being prejudiced. But it works both ways. Some are always causing trouble; they don't like blacks or any coloureds; they're into things like the APL – the Anti-Paki League.

James reckons that the splintering into groups around school leaving time is precipitated by a broadening of black consciousness. Youths become aware that they share problems and difficulties that are not always experienced by their white counterparts. They learn from various sources, including their own observations, that their black-ness will make a difference to their future, that making progress in society is more difficult for a black person. They ask why and, according to James, find answers in the *Roots*-type of scenario, a reminder of the enslavement and transportation to the Americas of West Africans – as depicted in Alex Haley's book. This leads them to reject white friends and peers and form new patterns of associa-tion with other blacks. Amongst Asians this process is not nearly so pronounced, although they tend to isolate them-selves more after leaving school. This stimulates whites to reciprocate and cleavages form.

This is only one version. Others might add that whites develop exclusivist tendencies independently of blacks; they deliberately exclude ethnic peers from their groups and thus reinforce the divisions. The reasons for the whites' actions are difficult to determine. We know that in all probability they have picked up racist ideas from their parents. Many studies indicate that media stories and portrayals are full of racist undertones. Only since the mid-1970s have schools become sensitive to the requirements of education in a multicultural society, and even in the mid-1980s teachers on the four estates express views which veer dangerously towards racism – as we will see in Chapter 11. So the sources of racist ideas are plainly there. And if blacks either start a clustering into ethnic groups or perhaps respond to whites' clustering, then racism receives further impetus. Divisons harden as white youths see visible confirmation that blacks and Asians do not 'belong'.

In a tightly packed area like Newtown where a dense ethnic population and a high unemployment rate virtually guarantee daily personal contact, the divisions are under some pressure. Racism is often replaced by a sense of mutual tolerance or even camaraderie. 'We're all suffering because of this government,' is the sound of the unemployed of Newtown. In an area like Chelmsley, however, the reverse is true; the absence of daily contacts leaves the divisions intact and, indeed, creates the basis for open conflict, as Chris Balsall, 20, illustrates:

There was this skinhead type standing at the bar of a local pub, and this good-looking black woman went past him. He grabbed her arse as she went by, and so she turned round to him, and he head-butted her straight in the face. Her nose is still squashed today. Well, this black guy saw this and he went over to the white kid and knocked him out.

The next thing: some white punks and skins from the next bar came running in to get this black guy, who was with his mates – all black. Well, the bar just cleared, and this battle started. I saw one guy smash a bottle and start stabbing this black guy with it. The police arrived, but nothing happened. That night there was loads of vans and cars full of white kids driving around armed with axes and chains. The blacks and even Asians, who weren't involved in the first fight, were tooled up; the Indians had hockey sticks. Anyway, this went on for ages. There wasn't like open war in the streets, but blacks started staying away from the pub and sticking to their own.

Conflicts of this kind are common in Chelmsley. Ethnic gangs, including gangs of Asian youths who are mobilized and ready for action, are commonplace. Less so in Newtown, where the atmosphere, although hardly tranquil, is less turbulent. Cultures clash, but rarely do broken bottles. Old ideas might prompt those over 40 to regard all dark-skinned people as life's bearers, servants and 'shitworkers', but new ideas spring from a vague coalition – not a strong coalition admittedly, but one arising from a perception of common conditions and, possibly, shared destinies. The ledge on which Newtown youths stand may not be any higher than that of Chelmsley youths, but it affords them a different vantage point. They can see certain flaws and errors in their parents' views.

There are, then, good arguments to support the suggestion that living in the innercity amidst multiethnic populations has an appreciable effect on how you order your perceptions of, and organize your relationships with, ethnic groups. It would seem that sharing a condition of relative deprivation leads to an empathy, even to a sense of unity amongst ethnic groups. But what of youths in areas that have no material deprivations to talk of? Middleclass areas, by definition, have no housing or employment problems comparable with those of Newtown and Chelmsley, so the youth of those areas grow up with different sets of influences, as we will see in Chapter 6.

Chapter Six

The Keys to Tomorrow
– White Middleclass

I don't think there's any deep discrimination

As part of its General Studies programme, the lower sixth form of Lordswood Boys School in Edgbaston staged a mock general election. The poll included the entire pupil population of the school, totalling seven hundred. Pupils were asked to vote for any of the main political parties. The result surprised and embarrassed teaching staff: the National Front party was elected with a 35 per cent share of the total vote.

'It was only casual racism,' explained a staff member with some vagueness, presumably referring to the fact that pupils voted in a 'knee-jerk' response after listening to ideas from the media and their families but without having thoroughly examined the underpinnings of the ideas. By 1983, when the school election was staged, the National Front (NF) was in a state of electoral decline. Its impact on the adult voting population of the UK was nugatory, although its blatantly racist platform and provocative campaign strategies drew inordinate coverage from all the national media.

What limited electoral success the NF did have in the early 1970s came in such workingclass areas as West Bromwich and Leicester, both in the Midlands, and its impact in traditional Tory constituencies was *nil*. Why, then, were the pupils of a school in a predominantly middleclass catchment area like Edgbaston attracted to a discredited party that based its electoral philosophy on an unyielding anti-Semitism and an outrageous, impracticable plan to repatriate nonwhites? To answer this, we need to look closely at middleclass youth, to reach some understanding of the emergent middleclass mentality.

It could be suggested that this mentality is the single most important aspect of race relations; after all, the middleclass youth of today will be the decision-makers of tomorrow. The power to implement changes of any magnitude and consequence will in all probability not rest with people currently living on council estates. More likely it will pass to those currently enjoying the benefits of a comfortable home life, a quality education and the material advantages of socio-economic success. Just because middle-class youths don't display 'APL' tatoos on their arms or rove the streets picking on Asians does not mean that they are paragons of neighbourly tolerance, harbouring no prejudices. The Lordswood School 'election' might have been a joke to most of the voters, but it indicates if nothing else a willingness to countenance an openly racist political approach. And remember: about 14 per cent of the school's roll is from ethnic minority groups (mainly South Asian).

Richard Parkins did not vote NF at the school election and he laughs at the fact that many others did. 'The whole thing was a farce, anyway,' he says. 'I for one didn't take it too seriously.' He believes that the NF vote was an antiauthority display, pupils cocking a snook at the school system by refusing to vote for one of the established main political parties. He cannot accept that it was a vote for racism, because he does not think racism is that prevalent: 'I think there *is* prejudice about, but it's not as bad as they say, certainly not in this area.' Richard has lived in Edgbaston for all of his seventeen years. His father is an estate agent, his mother a full-time housewife. With eight GCE O-levels under his belt, Richard is aiming at four A-levels and then wants to go on to university, 'probably to do business studies'.

His perception of race relations differs only slightly from that of many older residents of Edgbaston. For example, he believes that too much has been made of the conflict between whites and ethnic minorities. 'Most people, black and white, get on fine. It's only isolated incidents, when it's blown out of all proportion, that give the impression that black and white people aren't getting on – when, really, they are.' His views on the 1985 riots bear this out; they oppose almost diametrically the perceptions of John Wilkinson of Newtown, who, in Chapter 5, argued that the motivation of the rioters was not the desire to accumulate material possessions, like videos and hi-fis. Richard contends: 'The disturbances hadn't anything to do with race relations. It was just black and white kids against the police. It had more to do with the frustration of unemployment than race. I think they used the race idea as an *excuse* for those riots. I don't think they were racially motivated; kids were just breaking windows to steal.' For Richard, the rioting of black and white youths was a product of the feelings of aggression which accompany the frustration of being out of work and the longing for goods denied them because of their lack of money. Generally, however, he feels that 'relationships between blacks and whites have got better over the past three or four years'.

There seems to be a consensus in Edgbaston and, for that matter, Solihull over the role of the media in enlarging race relations to the proportions of a major social issue. Richard puts it this way:

You get one or two things happening and then you get headlines like, 'Police are racialists'. It's the same with the way West Indians are portrayed; you might get one or two that cause trouble, but the majority will just leave you alone and cause no trouble. You seem to hear more about West Indian kids doing it. It's probably equal between black and white, but you always hear about it when a black kid is involved. I think the media give black people a bad image by blowing up everything. You get on with your life and let them get on with theirs. A few will get the others a bad name.

Those 'few', according to Richard, are totally unrepresentative of the majority of blacks and Asians in the UK. The majority have little or nothing to complain about, he says. Access to council housing is 'about the same' for whites and for ethnic minorities. Young blacks may find it marginally harder than the equivalently qualified white to get a job: 'An employer is likely to pick the white kid because he thinks the West Indian is more likely to give trouble.' Again, Richard feels the West Indian image has suffered because of the media's sensationalistic coverage, although he admits: 'I don't really know any black kids, only Asians. But I think we should learn to respect their different ways and attempt to learn more about them.'

John Hornby, Richard's classmate, was one of those who voted for the NF and is not particularly impressed by the motive to respect and learn: 'It's *they* who have to respect that they're in somebody else's country. They [minorities] should mould into our way of living. It does bother me when you go into a shop or on the bus and Asians are talking in their own language. It makes me feel as if they're talking about me. I think they should talk English if they're living here.' John, the son of an architect, is 17 and intends to pursue a career in advertising; he has nine O-levels. 'I don't think there's any deep discrimination against [blacks and Asians]', he opines:

In fact, my father reckons they've got a better deal than most whites, with all this race relations law and whatnot. What makes me angry is the way they seem to get things done for them, like housing. Also, all these children they have and get benefit for them. What about white people who have worked for the country all their lives? Coloureds haven't worked here all their lives. We only get benefits from what we've paid in; they haven't paid anything. OK, they should get something to keep them going, but not luxuries. I mean, blacks are on the dole and that and have videos and all sorts. Even though there are some whites who have luxuries and hang around doing nothing, at least they've paid into the system. I think the same about Australians and Canadians as well, although I might prefer them to West Indians and Asians. This isn't their country just the same.

Why the preference?

I just hang around with people who hate blacks and Asians, and eventually it becomes embedded in you, and you get not to like them. It started because I used to go around with them, and they just became arrogant towards us. It was all right at junior school, where there was a few, and when I got here I thought it would be the same. But somehow it isn't; I think they're prejudiced against us, hanging around together and not really getting near us.

John speculates on the reason for this: 'Perhaps it's because we treated them bad when they first came over here.'

Richard and John agree that the amount and intensity of racism and discrimination have been inflated, mostly by the media, but also by bodies like the Commission for Racial Equality, which, as John puts it, 'picks on isolated incidents and makes them into huge affairs just to give a false impression'. Richard regards himself as a liberal, while John refuses to categorize himself, arguing without intending to be sardonic that his views are simply based on 'what's right'.

The positions they hold are hardly extremes. They differ in the sense that Richard acknowledges the existence of a certain degree of prejudice and wants to allow for some adjustment to accommodate cultural differences, while John downplays prejudice and believes in a 'moulding' of ethnic cultures to more traditional Anglo ways. Coming from middleclass homes and living in Edgbaston, neither youth has much opportunity to experience the diversity of ethnic life; and for all their condemnation of the media, they rely on them as their main source of information. They merely infer that the media exaggerate, preferring to think that the situation is not as gross as newspapers and television would have us believe. Should they need to supplement their knowledge, parents can supply additional information, as Richard points out:

My father is an estate agent and he buys and sells houses for Asians. He doesn't mind them at all; but my mother doesn't like the way they hoard their money. They've got all their money underneath the carpets. But she doesn't understand how they've got their money. My dad says it's just because they're prepared to work on Sunday mornings; they open their shops while everybody else is lying in bed.

Two intelligent young men: seventeen O-levels between them and a possible eight A-levels in the pipeline. University educations beckon both, and their families will if necessary support them in their future studies. After that, although career plans have a habit of going wrong, it seems a reasonable bet that both youths will progress to secure, well-paying, high-status occupations. In the process they may well have their horizons stretched, but at present they are both labouring with the middleclass malady of under-exposure. They just have not seen or absorbed enough of the world outside of Edgbaston to establish much of a perspective. So they accept ideas and images rather than think them through – or, where they *do* think them through, they have only a limited amount of raw material to work with. This will become more evident when we consider the youths of the next section.

Their own fault

One of the interesting features of middleclass youths is the heavy emphasis laid on individual motives. Little weight is given to social background, material circumstances, or physical conditions as influences on people's thoughts and behaviour; ultimate responsibility is held to lie with the individual. This line of reasoning is fully consistent with the Protestant-capitalist ethos, with its stress on individual application and industry as the keys to achievement. And it translates roughly into an analysis of race relations, once filtered through the school experiences of young people.

'We should like them, but they don't help by being so arrogant,' says Hilary Jencks, 18, a resident of Edgbaston.

At the junior school I went to, I went around with a lot of blacks. I can't remember thinking of them as black; but once you get into secondary school, everybody started saying, 'Oh, we hate blacks.' And when you thought about it, you thought, 'Yeah, they are horrible.' Why? Because they keep themselves totally separate and don't mix. The Asians are more like us, even if they have their own customs, but the blacks are just so arrogant. I think this division occurs because they have older brothers and sisters expressing their opinions. When I was in junior school, there weren't many anyway. But now the numbers are more, a lot of people hate them.

Hilary admits to hating blacks, but puts the blame on them: 'It's their own fault, wanting to be different and separate. They bring it on themselves.' Nor have Asians helped engineer their acceptance: 'They've built their own mosques and temples and that makes them stand out.' Being different, for Hilary, is an aggravating influence on race relations: 'It makes people look at them differently, and that creates tension.' She reflects on how, in situations where being visibly but not culturally different was possible, there were few problems:

There weren't many coloureds in my last school, so we [whites] were in a majority. So they had to fit in with our ways. But as the numbers grew, so the hatred did as well. I think it's people's cultures that lead to prejudice. When they want to be different from the majority, then the majority turns against them. I think, with culture, it should be give and take. As an example: at one of my uncle's factories, there was an Indian worker who had to break every so often to pray on work's time. My uncle had to wait for this guy to get changed, wash his feet and then after he'd finished, get changed again. Well, I don't think that's right. He should have come to some sort of arrangement where, if he wants to pray, then it comes off his wages. This guy eventually had to stop. It needs more give and take.

For 'give and take' read 'assimilation'. What Hilary alludes to is a process whereby ethnic groups who have distinctive beliefs, customs, practices, appearances and lifestyles conform to more familiar Anglo ways. If this involves abandoning elements of the ethnic culture, then this is a sacrifice that has to be made in the interests of good race relations. It is by now a familiar cry from middle-class areas; the middle-class of all ages believes that might is right. If the majority have one way of doing things and minorities have others, then the minority should change accordingly. 'Enough is enough,' says Hilary:

Take the police force: Asians are already allowed to go in and wear turbans. But our women police officers aren't even allowed to dye their hair pink, or even tint it. I object to that. Where's the logic of it? If they can do it, why can't our own people?

When the situation's reversed and Asians are in control of things, they don't do whites favours. They employ whites on very low wages. I worked for one once, and he paid me 80 pence an hour for working in his shop. Woolworth's pay about £1.40 an hour. It's a reversal of roles; years ago we employed them as cheap labour. I suppose you can't blame them for turning it back on us. Mind you, it's their own fault. They didn't *have* to come over and work for cheap wages, did they? The way I look at it is that the reason they came over was they were virtually dying through poverty.

Hilary's argument turns on the fact that the cause of the race relations conflicts is usually the ethnic minority group. The group, instead of dutifully changing its culture to suit the requirements of white society, tends to cling to its traditional lifestyle. This in itself, according to Hilary, is no great problem; it becomes a problem when the group grows confident enough to want to promote its cultural distinctiveness. This heightens visibility and creates resentment. She gives the example of West Indians:

When they first came over, they were all Jesus-loving Christians, the same religion as us. They tried to blend in and I don't think there was too much trouble about. But it's the second generation who are going over to rasta that wants to cause trouble. And that's where the lines become crossed. Asians have got their own community, but keep themselves to themselves to a great extent. Rasta kids want to cause trouble; they're arrogant.

Hilary's arguments reveal three concerns. The first is that the prime mover of race relations is the motivation of the minority group; to be more accurate, it is the *lack* of motivation to try to anglicize lifestyles and assimilate cultures. Second is the seemingly ever-present division between 'us' and 'them': 'their own community', 'their own fault'; 'our ways', 'the same religion as us'. Hilary, in her own eyes, stands on one side of a fence along with other whites, while ethnic minorities stand on the other side; no amount of 'give and take' can remove the fence. Third is the resentment that emerges when roles are reversed, which she feels is occurring: Asian workers taking time off to pray; police officers being permitted to wear turbans. In her view, whites resent the apparent favouritism of these and other strategies designed to improve race relations, which, in reality, worsen them.

It is surely significant that young people like Hilary, living amidst the prosperity of middleclass areas which afford a degree of protection from the more corrosive elements of innercity life, have a benign and simplistic conception of race relations. The idea that the problem is much less than the media say it is; the willingness to apportion blame on the ethnics themselves as opposed to the system in which they operate; the unflinching dogmatism in defending the 'British way of life' as the norm to be adapted to, rather than a cultural process liable to change – all these are platitudes. In the absence of any meaningful, sustained social intercourse, at school or after, middleclass youth are bound to rely on wornout notions that are never tested out on reality. Their workingclass counterparts can and, as we have seen, do test their views out. Middleclass youths in the innercity have at least some contact with Asians and, to a lesser degree, with blacks, yet *meaningful* intercourse still seems absent. Perhaps this is because ideas inherited from parents work as a deterrent to relationships. Parental values and assumptions transmit readily from one generation to the next amongst middleclass sectors, where the availability of competing values and assumptions is scarce – less readily where there is a prevalence of encounters and experiences that jar discordantly with what parents regard as common knowledge.

Edgbaston has a relatively high ethnic profile for a middleclass area, although it suffers from what social scientists call 'sampling error': its quota of ethnics is wholly unrepresentative of the population as a whole. The prohibitively high cost of property in the area alone acts as a screen, allowing in only the affluent sections of the ethnic community, typically Asian business people and professionals. It seems a reasonable supposition that many of the ethnics already in Egbaston have, to some degree, assimilated, since the very fact of their material and professional success – in medicine, law, commerce and industry – indicates a preparedness to negotiate in a world populated by whites and dominated by white assumptions. A retention of ethnic identity and values is possible, especially if a Jekyll-and-Hyde existence is pursued; but the suggestion arising from this project is that the more successful, socially mobile ethnics are often the ones who have assimilated, sometimes consciously, to gain acceptance in their career sphere.

Edgbaston youth, therefore, typically encounter ethnic youths already disposed to some sort of assimilation, if only because of the example of their parents. If anything, this reinforces their original conceptions. Young people like Hilary can square what limited experience they have with their own views. 'See, the ones who are prepared to be like us are getting on fine in society,' she might argue, with ample justification. But what of middleclass white youths who lack the support of experience with their ethnic contemporaries? The ethnic content of Solihull is negligible, so one might expect the perceptions and attitudes of youth in that area to have a sort of textbook attitude, flavoured with guesswork. In fact, Solihull youth are cocksure about their theories of race relations, as we will now see.

The educated are more prejudiced

Most innercity children are, by their very location, forced to adapt to social changes more rapidly than their peers living out of the city. Solihull may not be an island, but one would be forgiven for mistaking it as such. Isolation, exclusivity and continuity: these are the key elements of life in Solihull. The area is tucked safely away from the vortex of Birmingham city. Access to Solihull dwellings is rigorously controlled by a most effective market mechanism: high prices. And residents like the stability and order this affords both them and their children. So there is an almost timeless quality about the area, where one generation succeeds another in a smooth progression, uninterrupted by the bumps and jolts that innercity folk have to endure.

Kate Cargill and Charles Webber, both 18, are awaiting the results of their A-levels. Kate has ten O-levels, Charles eight. She has a place at Durham University, while he looks forward to Cambridge. Both their fathers are company directors with sufficient resources to pay for their private education, yet they disagree on the relationship between education and racism.

'I do think if you've had little education you're more likely to be prejudiced,' Charles believes.

Kate objects: 'I don't think so. I think the educated are more prejudiced. I went to a private school and it was terrible; they were really prejudiced because there wasn't so many people around who were black or Asian.'

Because?

'Well, because there was just a few, they tended to stick together and congregate at break-time, so you didn't have too much to do with them.'

Charles still disagrees: 'The worse the school, the worse the racism.'

For Charles, 'questions of colour', as he puts it, are irrelevant:

I don't see colour. I see people, and to me they are all the same. One day you wear black trousers, the next day, brown. That's how irrelevant it is to me. Colour means nothing. I don't understand all this race relations stuff. OK, you get white people who hate black people and blacks who hate whites; but it could be for so many reasons, not just colour. There are blacks living in poverty and whites living in poverty. I know white people in some areas who have no hot water, and politicians come along and say, 'Oh, the reason why there are so many problems is that the black and white people hate each other', which is just a load of rubbish. I've been over to Handsworth in Birmingham quite a lot, and to me the riots there and in Brixton had nothing to do with colour. Yet the politicians go on about race. It's because people can't get jobs and decent houses and that.

Black and white people are together in Handsworth. I've no doubt about that. I've been over there to blues and most people there have a good time until the police come on the scene and something starts. And then people start saying, 'The blacks attacked the police', when, in fact, it was probably caused by the police. It's the easiest thing in the world to blame the blacks, to hide the real situation. Very few people actually are in a position to do anything about it. If you're poor and you're black, there is no way you can say, 'I'm in this 'cause you put me here.' Even if they do say that, they've no way they can change it 'cause it's the people who're in power who are ignorant, who are letting the country carry on the way it is.'

Kate is less sure about this: 'I think in some ways it's easier for blacks to get housing.' Charles smiles at what he takes to be her naïveté, but she continues:

They all seem to be in the same area, like Balsall Heath all seems to be Pakistan people. And it always seems to be those areas getting grants. So I think they're not deprived by the government. Maybe to get a job is more difficult, but not as far as housing and things go. OK, I will admit that there are bad areas, so perhaps they need more grants and things, but I don't think the people who live there have a much harder time.

It's not just a question of all the white people picking on all the coloured people. It's difficult with Asians because they're so much into their own religions, with things they can and can't do; with West Indians, they don't seem so different. But a lot of the time you can't get near them. I think we're moving more towards a multicultural society. There are a lot of multicultural areas, like Sparkbrook and Sparkhill, and people accept them, now.

Charles does not envisage a transition to a multicultural society:

There are areas which are no way multicultural; like here, or Hall Green, there's only about three or four families who are Asian or black. The only way you're going to get a wholly multicultural society is if coloured people are evenly distributed where they live. Those that are born here, as they get better educated and better jobs, they'll probably move into other areas. But it will take a long time happening. Asians will probably be first. They've taken on certain of our values. In fact, they've built up businesses. They take on a credibility. A lot of them are really successful business men, and that's why they fit in – because our society revolves around business and making money.

'On the other hand,' Kate interjects, 'I've heard a lot of people say, "I can't stand Pakis." I think they resent them because a lot of Asians tend to work harder and are more intelligent generally. People resent that 'cause they're not where they think they should be, and that's when they start saying, "They're taking our jobs", and that sort of thing.'

Charles concurs.

Kate continues: 'A lot of old white people live in these areas and have lived in a certain way. When they see these different people moving into the area, who are a different colour and behave differently, they're shocked. People are ignorant of each other's culture and just don't accept them as people, and so the trouble starts.'

Charles believes that the non-acceptance of cultures is epiphenomenal, a mere secondary symptom of a deeper cause. That cause is power. Racism, he thinks, is not such a momentous issue. He takes a 'colour-blind' approach and refuses to accept that others, especially those living in high ethnic density areas, can generate hatred for each other simply because of skin colour or cultural differences. For him, the 'colour problem' is manufactured so as to divert the media's and public's attention away from problems of material deprivation. The argument is insufficiently developed to account for what would appear to be a fairly arbitrary distinction between groups. A marxist would probably want to add to Charles's basic premiss the 'divide-and-rule' principle by which ruling élites hold on to their positions of political and economic power by perpetuating divisions and internecine conflicts amongst the workingclass. Whites are covertly encouraged to see their different-coloured neighbours as potential competitors in the job and housing markets and therefore to regard such people's interests as incompatible with their own.

It is interesting that someone in Charles's comfortable and relatively insulated position can arrive at his conclusion. The reason he is able to do so is simple: detachment.

Charles has lived his eighteen years mostly in the seclusion of a district that neither blacks nor Asians have penetrated. He is intelligent and well educated enough to be sharply aware of important social issues, and strong-minded enough not to absorb unquestioningly the popular wisdom. So when he reads or hears of 'racial tension' or 'the colour problem', his mind goes into critical mode and he questions whether the alleged race issue is a real one at all. Racism is not a reality that Charles can readily apprehend; he simply has too little direct, or even indirect, experience of it for it to register. As a consequence he cannot comprehend that it is anything more than a convenient fabrication of the police force to tighten its grip on certain areas, or just a phantom of a headline writer's imagination. Yet in a roundabout way Charles's ruminations have led him to a rough-hewn theory that would gain the endorsement of some Newtowners (featured in Chapter 6), as well as of many marxist commentators, to whom Charles' class, the bourgeoisie, is the genuine enemy of ethnic minorities. The middleclass reaps the rewards of workingclass racist antagonisms by exploiting the divisions. If racism did not exist, then the divisions would dissolve, and the white workingclass might enjoin its fellow black and Asian comrades in opposing their true exploiters.

Kate's background is similar to Charles's, but she seems to accept the basic parameters of race relations. Her parents are, in her words, 'more racist than I am . . . They contradict themselves all the time.' She means that they express racist ideas without ever meeting blacks or Asians. Racism and racialist conflict, in her view, are produced by culture clashes, lack of familiarity and the resentment that germinates from poor material conditions. Hers is a more conventional argument, as is her prognosis: 'For older people, like our parents, it was hard for them to accept because immigration and black people were new, strange. But for the next generation it [racism] won't be a problem.'

Neither Charles's nor Kate's view is exactly typical of Solihull youth, but between them they represent many elements shared by Silhillians under 20. The sheer pressure of living on workingclass estates is absent in Solihull; and youths, their wits sharpened by a good education, encouraging families and salubrious circumstances, are able to take a back seat and coolly analyse the situation in far-away Birmingham and other centres of alleged disharmony. Kate has encountered racism at school; Charles dismisses it. Whereas, as we saw earlier in the chapter, racism is a closer reality for the middleclass youth of Edgbaston, who live nearer to Birmingham's innercity estates, in Solihull young people rarely see ethnic minorities, less still think too much about them. Yet, ironically, their arguments are cogent, consistent and analytical. It seems that detachment does not necessarily lead to a reliance on the perspectives of elders, but can spur youths on to greater objectivity in their appraisals. Solihull youth are not preoccupied with race, and because of this fact they are able to develop their own version of reality, which complements almost bizarrely that of many young Newtowners.

Chapter Seven

Crawlers No More
– Ethnic Minorities

Blacks against blacks

There is a sort of composite picture of black youth in the mind of white council estate tenants over the age of 35. The typical black youth is unemployed, perhaps of his or her own accord, involved in some kind of illegal activity, whether it be street crime or living off immoral earnings, and extremely reluctant to integrate into society. Hence the penchant to pursue an 'alternative lifestyle' based on hanging around pool halls, going to loud all night parties and taking drugs. Maybe not only the white workingclass have such an image. A good deal of older blacks and members of the middleclass have similar ideas. If there was a scale of disreputability, black youth would rank right at the bottom.

In the 1980s black youth has become the social problem *par excellence*: centrally implicated in the chain of events that led to the urban uprisings of 1981 and 1985, disproportionately represented in the unemployment statistics and consistent underachievers at school. These were some of the factors that led Barry Troyna and myself to entitle our book on the subject *Black Youth in Crisis* (1982), and the crisis has surely not yet passed. No other ethnic group has proved so perpetually troublesome in establishing dialogue.

Black youth have their own theories on why it is regarded as a source of social problems, and the theories are not derived from a view of themselves as congenital misfits, prone to long spells of idleness and a talent for the criminal life. Young blacks question the whole validity of the 'social problem' perspective. To them the real problem is a transparent discrimination that is rarely officially acknowledged, but which works systematically at one level to deprive them of the chance to gain constructive employment and, at another, to emasculate them as black people. The theories favoured by many young blacks have as their inspiration a rastafarian perspective. According to the rasta vision of history, the present, and, indeed, the future, white colonial capitalists have sought, over a period of four hundred years, to enslave blacks, to exploit their labour and to suppress their potential. After the abolition of slavery in 1865, whites no longer had the legal right of ownership over black slaves, so they had to devise less obvious methods of control. Racism and discrimination fitted the bill and effectively served to maintain blacks in their subservience.

Leon Brewster fits many people's idea of black youth: 19, unemployed, a couple of spells in detention centre and prison, and dreadlocks. He speaks in an eclectic mixture of Jamaican patois and Brummie as he sets his views in historical context:

The reason the present situation has come about goes back to the days of slavery. The white men were slave traders; they sell blacks. Blacks have been property, so they've got no roots, no culture, and they've been 'evil' all the way through history. So when they confront whites, these things matter. At school it's the teacher; it's a white man who's educating them, who's actually turning blacks against themselves. At that age you're all sort of loving and pure. Nothing matters to you at all. And your parents and teachers are putting this stuff in your head that black is this and white is this. You adopt everything they tell you.

Educated in Tyseley and Newtown, where he still lives, Leon left school at 16 with 'two low-grade CSEs'. He worked as a trainee in the catering industry for twelve months before he left: 'I could have stayed there, but it would've meant that I'd be washing up and cleaning and I didn't want that.' But the drop in income posed problems, as he already had a motorcycle and a car and suddenly could not afford to run them. In addition, his parents, with whom he lived, began to put pressure on him to find work and earn his keep. 'So I became a drop-out and started stealing cars with a mate; changing the plates, changing the colour – he showed me how to do it. I found there was no money in stealing cars, so I started taking bits off them, like wheels, bucket seats, head rests, anything. I kept nicking to earn money for myself.' So started Leon's passage into thieving. Not a very successful one, either: he had already served two sentences by the time of our meeting, and if his own thoughts are anything to go by, he reckons he may be returning to prison. His reason for thinking this stem from his general impression of blacks' role in a society geared to suppress them rather than offer them scope for development.

The white man doesn't like to do the dirty work. He likes the better jobs; he likes sitting behind his desk or driving his car. Let the Asians and blacks do the dirty work, let them scrub the factories and produce what he wants. That's why blacks are kept in the dark, not brought into the limelight. As soon as a black gets a full realization and starts to be better off, somethings happens to him, and he's wiped out. It's a trick. For instance, when they give a black policeman promotion, they only want him so he can give information about what's happening on the black scene because they can't get to it themselves; so they've got to get it by other means. And as soon as a black man starts rising, straight away other blacks turn against him and they'll try to bring him down. A black businessman, for instance: he's going to be thinking so much like a white businessman that he'll want nothing to do with other drop-out blacks. It's just through their ignorance more than anything else. If a black man has got a shop, black people are going to go into that shop to try to get things on credit. When he turns round and says, 'Look, I'm trying to run a business', they're going to avoid him. They'll always rip their own off.

Leon argues that the conspicuous lack of black success in business is in one sense their own fault, but in another, perhaps more serious sense it is the fault of an historical system that has fostered competition and disunity amongst blacks. 'They don't see this as against whites,' says Leon. 'It's blacks against blacks.' This means that blacks have to contend with two adversaries: other blacks, with whom they compete for status and material success, and whites, who have a kind of in-built resistance to blacks, as Leon explains:

You'll get white guys who mix with blacks, but then again, they're drop-outs. But no sooner are you mates with them, than they turn round and say, 'Black cunt!' I don't think there's any such thing as a true, solid friendship between blacks and whites because somewhere inside there's a little bit of prejudice. I came across this when I went to prison. It's a frightening experience. There's a lot of friction between blacks and whites. You'll get a group of white guys who stick to themselves and who usually call themselves some stupid name. And straight away they'll say, 'This black guy, so-and-so, said this and that about you.' Then they'll go and say the same thing to other black guys. So there's strong friction in the air, and something's got to go off. The screws know it's going on and they turn a blind eye to it. Blacks always end up fighting black. I don't just mean in prison either; for some unknown reason they always seem to charge on their own instead of all getting together and saying, 'Look, we're all black brothers; white men are our enemy.' They've got to realize what's going on.

This is what's going on now: they're getting together and they're getting whites together. And even if it's not becoming a friendship, at least everything is getting closer; all the gaps are closing up; blacks and whites are moving into a group. Around here they are, anyway. Even in Moseley and Handsworth, where there are clubs designed for blacks and only blacks use them, whites are beginning to use them. Whites are going to blues, their parties, smoking their weed and getting in on the scene. Everything is coming good. But the police don't like it. They know it's happening and they will continue their harassment. They'll see a black guy and white guy driving along in a car and they'll think, 'Oh, they're up to something; they can't be friends, black and white.' They want to see black stay with black and white be against black. There's no such thing as a fair cop. They're always trying to get blacks in prison or out of the country or putting them under constant pressure. That's why, when I see a black police-man around here – and there are quite a few now – I wouldn't utter a word to him. If he was to talk to me, I'd just blank him out 'cause he should never have allowed himself to be caught up in a system like this one. As I say, they're just there to give information on the black scene; they're used.

The 'system' Leon refers to is what many young blacks call Babylon, to denote captivity and repression. They feel that the present system is virtually the same as the one that began when an African was blessed by a fifteenth-century Portuguese cleric and sent away in chains to the Americas for a life of servitude. The immense changes that have improved the general social condition of blacks do not overly impress many critically minded youths, for one reason: power. The basic power relationship between blacks and whites has remained intact for years; whites have it, blacks don't.

'But you have to realize what people are like, and not all whites are bastards,' stresses Leon. 'Not all white men hate us or are against all blacks. But *most* of them will play you false, being like they're your friend either 'cause you can defend yourself, or are providing them with something. It's a false friendship because they're under a lot of mental pressure from their normal crowd. This is how the system works to make whites prejudiced against you.'

The divide-and-rule principle operates to split members

of the workingclass, black and white, and to set them against each other, yielding a conveniently fragmented army of underlings who are easy prey for exploitative white capitalists. 'They use colour as a way of making money,' Leon observes. 'The workingclass mind will never change from what it thinks about blacks because that thought's always been there. There's always been continued harassment, and even if it isn't barefaced, it will be in another form.' Contradictions run through Leon's argument, for whilst his premiss is that whites, even those with the most liberal leanings, can never rid themselves of some trace of racism (because they are as much a part of the Babylon system as anyone else), his latest observations are of a unification: 'It's in downgraded areas like this [Newtown] where this is happening, but it could happen in other places.'

For some, Leon's arguments sound like one hand clapping: one party to an arrangement vigorously trying to contact an absent partner. If, as he suggests, most whites are still possessed of a racism – although, for some, a residual racism – then any kind of unification built on a perception of common interests would be unlikely. He gives the example of a white acquaintance:

All he ever used to talk was black talk and he used to talk about black and have his hair locksed. Then we were both in the Green [Winson Green Prison] together, and I saw him, and he'd had all his locks cut off. Still, I recognized him, walking with his mates, all white, round the exercise yard. And it was incredible; it was like he'd never mixed with blacks. When he saw me, he sneaked away from them and talk black talk. He'd never let on to his mates that we really knew each other.

Leon's perspective on Newtown youth seems to undermine the one suggested by John Wilkinson in Chapter 5. The rough-hewn alliance between white and other ethnic groups is, in Leon's view, visible and developing but it has limits. Those limits are defined by a system that encourages and feeds off disunity amongst the workingclass. Some may feel that Leon's arguments are based less on a vivid imagination and more on essence: racism does flourish amongst the white workingclass, and capitalism as an economic system does sustain itself by perpetuating class and race inequality. As Leon puts it: 'It's a big ladder, and when you get to the top, there's always a white man there.' This kind of perception of life is the result of experience, not of reading history books and *Das Kapital*. 'What I am today is the outcome of living in a rough area,' Leon reflects. 'There's a lot of fighting: good crowds, bad crowds, skinheads, blacks, NFs, all sorts. You have to think about why it all happens, especially if you've been chased by gangs of whites – as I have on several occasions.'

For all the negative stereotypes of black youth, it is they, more than any other single group in society, who face a tough time ahead. In this sense, they are victims rather than villains. As Jeremy Seabrook writes: 'Theirs has been a long experience of historical dislocation, a story of driven restlessness and uprooting. They have far less securely anchored resources with which to resist the continuing epic of dispossession to which they are heirs' (1983, p. 63). As if persistently attaining less at school than one's peers was not handicap enough, black youths, especially males, have to confront routine discrimination when they apply for jobs in what is already a viciously competitive employment market. As Leon says: 'We're classed as troublemakers, louts, layabouts, pickpockets and thieves.' It could be that being excluded, one could say dislocated, from the job market forces black youths into positions where the alternatives to playing up to others' negative expectations are few. And police attention is usually sharply focused on black youth: 'We get the most hassle from the police; they'll even admit themselves that they're racist.' The street is the likely site for 'hassle', and when you're unemployed a considerable amount of your waking hours are spent precisely there: on the street.

Set against this background, the views Leon shares with many other young blacks in Newtown become plausible. The job that people tell him to chase is never there. The prejudice they tell him does not exist confronts him like a brick wall at every turn; and the affinity he is meant to share with white members of his class never seems to materialize. So he follows a different path, working out a different version of his predicament; in this version racism is an integral part of a great historical process that has been fine-tuned to the material interests of white élites. Every piece of racist aggravation he encounters is but a small manifestation of the wider system of Babylon.

Such a view has gained currency since the emergence of the rastafarian movement in Britain's innercities. Adherents organize their ambitions around a mass exodus of blacks to Africa, their cultural 'fatherland', and take Haile Selassie, the late emperor of Ethiopia, as their spiritual guide, inspiration and redeemer. The theory of Babylon defines a loose theological structure for rastas' interpretation of history, in particular the history of slavery, and nowadays the concept has purchase for a great many black youths apart from those accepting the full rastafarian doctrine. Even white innercity youths grasp the significance of Babylon – although, Leon might add, they can never fully appreciate the effects it has on blacks. Beyond this, he exhorts everybody, black and white, to look critically at their environment: 'The truth is there for everybody to see it; then they can all get together. It's not a hard thing to do, it's straightforward.' It is anything *but* straightforward and the hint of mockery in Leon's tone as he speaks reveals that he knows only too well that this is so.

It is difficult to start from the position zero and actually get worse, but people like Leon are doing precisely that. His parents came to England from Jamaica unqualified in the

1960s and struggled for twenty-odd years without making any significant progress. They still live in a council flat; they have no savings, and the only luxury they can afford, Leon says, is a rented colour television. Leon himself left school with nothing to show for his contributions apart from a couple of tawdry trophies earned with the school's football team. He worked briefly, although the majority of his time has been spent either in the streets or behind bars. His criminal record is hardly going to help when he comes to applying for jobs – if he ever does apply for a job. Measured in objective terms, Leon has slid down the scale from the position established by his parents. He lacks even the very limited status and material possessions of his parents' hard-won gains after more than two decades of persistence.

To gain equal status, Asians have to crawl to whites

Renu Khadar comes from an entirely different family background to Leon and she doesn't intend to fall short of the high expectations her parents have of her. Both parents encourage her to study for her A-levels and then continue to university (she has seven O-levels). After that, they would like to see her succeed in a professional career. Renu's parents migrated to England in 1966. Her father had qualified as a doctor in India and set up in general practice in Birmingham; her mother had also studied medicine, but gave up her career to concentrate on her four children, of whom Renu, at 17 is the second eldest.

As a successful GP, Renu's father was able to afford the material benefits so obviously lacking in Leon's life. Again unlike Leon, who was virtually consigned to the streets before the age of 10, Renu was not allowed out unaccompanied until near her teens; one of her parents used to escort her even to school. The Khadar family lives in a spacious four-bedroomed house in Edgbaston. The eldest

119

sister is at Bradford University; the younger sister lives at home and goes to a nearby independent school, and the only brother is a boarder at Warwick School.

Despite their different backgrounds, Renu and Leon share experiences. 'I've been pretty sheltered,' Renu concedes:

It's the way my parents wanted me brought up, the way they wanted me educated, never leaving me to go out alone unless it was absolutely necessary. So I don't suppose I've had the chance to come into contact with racism. But the fact is, I have. And that shows how big the problem is. The first time I was in touch with it was when I was at nursery school. I still remember this; it's weird. I was standing in this little boy's way and he goes, 'Get out of the way, blackie!' At the time I couldn't understand it because it hadn't touched me before. But after that I didn't want to go to school, and nobody could understand why. So I told them, and they said, 'Ah, who said this?' And they found the boy, but they didn't expel him or anything. I don't suppose I was more than 5 at that stage, but just to show that things don't change, I was in school a couple of weeks ago. I do fencing after school on Fridays and I'd just had a fight with this girl who'd gouged my hand. So I had blood everywhere. And the teacher came over, all concerned, and he goes, 'My God! You've got red blood just like the rest of us.' It's not the first time he's said things like that. Perhaps he doesn't realize what he's saying is so insulting. Maybe he's not a racist: maybe he is. I just don't know, but it's pretty disturbing.

It's lying there inside people. It's not on show all the time, but it's definitely there. I think that a lot of people, especially middle class people, they'd be disgusted at the idea of racism itself. But they wouldn't realize that, inside, they did have racist feelings. They'd be quite shocked and horrified if it was put to them that they were racist. Ask a white woman what would happen if one of her daughters came home with a black kid.

Unlike Leon, Renu's immediate contacts have been with the middleclass, but she agrees with him that there is a kind of sediment of racism in whites when you drain off all the liberal pretensions.

My best friend: we've been friends for about nine years. And then, last year, we were having this discussion about immigration policy and what Thatcher's doing. My friend's really Tory and she was saying, 'Yes, you have to have restrictions. You don't want to be swamped.' And I thought, 'What are you talking about, *swamped*?' Something like that hitting you after nine years when you thought you had a friend really shakes you up. I always thought that kids rebelled against ideas which their parents have, so I would have thought that, if the parents were racist, the kids would automatically go against that. I can't understand how these kids can really adopt these ideas from their parents.

Edgbaston is no hotbed of racism as far as Renu is concerned, but she is reminded, sometimes quite gently, that white residents do regard her as 'different', even if they make allowances for her personally and except her from their generalizations. At school she participated in a discussion in which black people, as she puts it, 'were being put down in a derogatory way'. 'Hold it, I'm black,' she interrupted, to be told: 'Yeah, but you're different, aren't you.' 'No,' she replied, 'everybody's like me!'

The cumulative effect of such remarks is, in Renu's opinion, the development of a kind of inverse racism, which she sees in both her parents and in a different way in her elder sister:

You have to take into account that my parents were brought up and educated in India. They'd lived in India most of their lives before they came here. So they wouldn't like me to have boyfriends. Full stop. If I came home with a white boy and introduced him to Mother, I think they'd be pretty shook up. They'd be even more shook up if that boy was black, as in Negro. So my parents are racist and they'd probably admit to that. But you have to understand that they've been brought up in a really strict way with their own religion, their own culture. Then to have one of the family going with a white person is a big thing. So it's to do with background, really.

That's the elder generation, but the new Asian generation is coming up and they've been restricted. When you grow up and

121

you're at college people seem to be level headed and rational and they realize that if they get hassled by the police, they shouldn't just smile and take it. They're more willing to fight for their rights, and we should all try to unite against this racist thing. So the new generation is very different from the old. At my sister's university I found quite a few people who really hated whites for the way they'd been treated by them. It was exactly the same kind of feeling that the National Front has for black people. I don't know if it's a way of trying to get back, saying, 'Yeah, we can hate too.' They're getting an almost racist instinct in them too, so they've got to be careful of this.

But at least I'm happier with those kind of people than with my parents and their Asian friends. When I'm made to go to parties with them, I see these people who're so pseudo: they would creep to any white person, even if he was a racist. It's because they've come up in the world; they've got a bit of money together and they think their money will give them equal status with a white person. To gain equal status, they need to crawl to white people to make them like them. That's what I find in Edgbaston, Solihull, that kind of place. That makes me angry; there are times when I hate being Asian because that's the kind of image I see in front of me and I think, 'God, is that what Asians are really like?' And when I see my sister's friends, I think, 'Yeah, this is more like it.'

You get people who are educated or partially educated here, and they're willing to see the problem from a more radical point of view. The elders are used to divisions and prejudices because they believe in the caste system. Unfortunately, the leaders of the Indian community here are probably high caste people from well-to-do families in certain parts of India. So they're not really equipped to be responsible for many people. Some of them are only in for the status they get out of it. But you get that everywhere; you get MPs like that, don't you? The leaders of the communities in the next ten years are going to have more sense.

She means that, while today's Asian leaders are too preoccupied with gaining acceptance to mount any constructive attacks on racism, tomorrow's will share her perspective and want to make stronger efforts without worrying too much about preserving the image of passivity.

She admits that being enclosed in the middleclass seclusion of Edgbaston is hardly an ideal training ground for a would-be ethnic radical, but the fragments of racism she has inferred from an admittedly limited series of encounters has prompted her to align herself with her sister's approach rather than with that of her parents. The longterm answer, she argues, is to forestall racism; for as soon as it gets 'inside people', as she puts it, it is virtually impossible to expurgate.

If they're going to start teaching kids about race and different cultures, they've got to start when the kids are really young, not just starting bringing it into secondary schools. Also, they've got to take a look again at school textbooks, 'cause they can affect a kid's mind. If it's done at an early age, then the kids aren't really going to have any racist views to begin with. So, if you carry it on through infants and in secondary school – maybe with more adult things, like learning about different cultures, not just Asian ones or black ones, but everywhere – it would make people appreciate others' cultures, others' views. I just can't see any other solution. I mean, introducing legislation to give minorities an advantage makes the barriers higher, really. It might be something to protect black people, but it means that white people might think, 'Why should they have extra protection?' It works both ways.

Renu reasons that, if she can pick up hints of racism in a 'nice' area like Edgbaston, life in the workingclass inner city must be every bit as bad as some of her peers say it is. The way she gleans her information is entirely different to Leon's method. She hasn't been chased and beaten by skinheads, rejected by prospective employers, or given a hard time in Winson Green. The threads of her tapestry come through teachers' remarks and schoolfriends' 'give-away' comments, her parents' fawning deference to whites and her sisters' critiques. But the conclusions are in broad agreement; racism is rife, irrespective of area, class, or generation.

When the chips are down, I'm not white, and that's all that matters

Leon and Renu are sharply conscious of the fact that racism has affected their lives and will continue to do so. Their own efforts to neutralize the effects are in a way irrelevant: they come from ethnic minority backgrounds, and whatever they do to improve their status will not remove this. Renu is permanently different in the eyes of many and no quantity of paper qualifications, nor perfectly modulated English accent (which she has) can change that. She is Indian and knows that, for many others, she will always be regarded as inferior in some way. On the positive side, it could be argued that people like Leon and Renu know what they are up against; like other black and Asian youngsters, they have been made aware of the evaluations placed on their backgrounds, cultures and colour and will strive to organize their thoughts and behaviour around that. Their judgements, based on past experience, are that they will forever be recognized as different. Whether or not this will prove the case is debatable – but here we are primarily concerned with how *they* view their present and future.

What of those youths who, unlike Leon and Renu, don't know what they are up against – those who can identify strongly with neither the white majority nor an ethnic minority?

'In about forty or fifty years the world will be full of quarter castes and half castes,' Sanjay Thakrar comforts himself. 'Most white English people aren't pure anyway; they've got a bit of German in them, or something. And a good deal of blacks are partly white.' Born in the Irish Republic twenty years ago, Sanjay has an Irish mother. His father is Indian, an ex-seaman, originally from Karachi. They moved from Dublin to the Midlands when Sanjay was 18 months old. Balsall Heath, a district to the south-west of Birmingham's city centre, was the family's first stop. But after his parents separated, Sanjay moved to Chelmsley with his mother; he was 14.

I never thought about my colour at all until I left junior school. I went to a different school, and of course all the kids were older. I thought everything would be the same as before, but I found that the Indian and other Asian lads stuck together and they'd stay in one corner, and the English lads and blacks seemed to get on all right and communicated on the same level and they stuck together. So I thought to myself 'Where do *I* go?' And, to be honest, I still don't know today. To people who want to think that way, I'm a black bastard. To Indians, I'm not truly Indian 'cause I don't think like an Indian – I speak a bit, but I can't write it or anything. And to most people I'm just, well, you know, nothing in particular: a misfit, I suppose.

So I never did figure out which gang or group I was meant to be in at school. I didn't feel I fitted with the Asian kids; you know, Indians must be the most prejudiced people in the world. To tell you the truth, my dad's prejudiced right through. They'll stick together, but they think, 'Oh, we're a lot better than anyone else.' But they're not better; they're just more intellectual. I mean, when you're a kid and it's your birthday, most kids expect toys and things. But Indian kids get dictionaries and encyclopaedias and anything to do with study. English people think Indians always doss about, but it's because, when they're in the house, they're always reading and writing; they don't get to watch tv or anything.

Indians won't mix; they see others as a threat. You see, a lot of Indians believe the only way to get back at somebody who's ruined your life and got you down is to go to school, study and get your qualifications. You can't beat people physically, but you can beat them when it really hurts. All these shops and mini-markets: this is how they start. Then they get into factories, usually clothing, and try to monopolize the industry, to take over. And this is what the English are looking at. When you're young, an Indian lad might get a white girl as his girlfriend. But as they get older, the girl will realize what her dad's trying to tell her: 'It's hard to explain, but they're taking over a lot of our business and they're not doing us whites any good.' And the girl will look for herself and think he's right. It's what parents say to kids. I've known kids whose parents aren't racist and they aren't racist either. But I've known lads whose parents have said, 'Oh, well, he's all right. He's Irish. We can explain it to him.' And they'll tell me about how they did National Service and how, 'When I got out, I could get a job, I could go from job to job, but because of these people coming into our country, our sons can't get a job.' And the son's sitting there thinking, 'God, yeah man, let's get out and kick the bastards' heads in.' But sometimes they don't see I'm one of the ones who gets his head kicked in. Like, one night when I was with this white girl and we was just coming out of the Chinese take-away, and there was a gang of white guys, and one of them says, 'What are you doing with that dirty black bastard?' It ended up in a fight and I was the one who got charged with causing an affray.

On the other side, you've got Indians who live like English people, but underneath they're very aggressive to anyone who isn't coloured. They'll be friendly to you, but if you cross them they'll sort you out, get somebody to beat you up. They're always the same; that's why I don't get on with coloureds very well at all. Because I know a load of them and they're all the same: they look after themselves and don't look out for anybody else: they're selfish, looking after number one and doing anything for money.

Sanjay can look through both ends of the telescope. He sees what it is like to be an ethnic group member and an object of racist attacks and, at the same time, is privy to some of the racist thoughts harboured by his white peers and their parents, thoughts that inspire resentment and maybe hostility. But Sanjay has no time for those who depict him as 'straddling two worlds' or experiencing a 'crisis of identity'.

I read about the so-called problems of kids like me, half castes, but most of it's bullshit. I know who I am and I'm not ashamed. All right, so you get accepted more by white kids, and as I'm not so dark I can almost pass as white. But who wants to, really? I can see why the hardliners don't like blacks or anybody who's not white, but I can't agree to what they do. You see, when the chips are down, I'm not white, and that's all that matters. I still think Indians are prejudiced against anybody who isn't their own, mind, and they're as violent as anybody when they want to be. In the area I came from before here, an English lad'll get his head kicked in if they found out he'd mugged one of us. Where I am now there's not really enough Asian kids, so they have to try to stay out of trouble. I just keep in touch with them, but that's all. I don't hang around with them. It's not so much blacks against whites over here, though; it doesn't matter what colour you are, you get done. There are whites, coloureds and Indians in these gangs. It depends more on how you're dressed. It used to be blacks and whites, but you get coloured kids who beat other coloureds up, now. Thinking about it, it might be just their way of surviving.

According to Sanjay, whites are in such a commanding majority in Chelmsley that any attempts to mobilize, even as a defensive manoeuvre, are fated to fail. If you belong to a stigmatized majority group, as Sanjay feels he does despite (and perhaps partially because of) his Irish ancestry, then there is little room for retaliation. As Sanjay expresses it: 'You get the shit kicked out of you.' One result of this is a number of ethnic youths deliberately not identifying with their own minority and instead forging allegiances with white youths. Survival takes priority over ethnic loyalties when the odds are impossible.

The Indians I used to know over Balsall Health used to talk to me 'cause they know my dad was Indian and so they classed me as Indian. Not over here, though. I don't have no loyalties, anyway. Why should I? A mate of mine – his old man was from Pakistan – he's the opposite: hates 'em. His mum was a white woman. He used to knock around with a bunch of real hard-liners; 'APL' tattooed on his fingers and everything. I suppose it was 'cause his old man left him and his mum when he was young. At any rate, he hates pakis. I can understand how this happens; you feel as if everybody's sticking to their own sort, so you want to stick to something. I've always been in between, but it's never really bothered me too much. I've taken a few beatings, but I've dished out a few when the need cropped up. I've not thought of myself as Indian, but I think I know what it's like to be Indian: it's hard. But, as I say, they're prejudiced themselves, so they don't help themselves by not mixing. Perhaps they think they're too good to mix.

Sanjay is hardly obsessed by the injustices spoken of by some ethnic leaders. His is a balanced view that manages to look at the situation from two different perspectives. He sees the exacerbating factors, such as the Asian penchant for an insularity that borders on élitism, and the white characteristics of finding scapegoats and venting frustrations on any available group. He has taken stick from both groups, but mostly from whites. Like Leon and Renu, Sanjay observes that 'Colour is always at the back of whites' minds. You might get a bunch of black and white kids who hang around together and then they'll split up, and the white kids will always stick together. They'll get round to thinking it eventually: "We aren't the same colour". It's always there.'

The collective thoughts of the three ethnic youths whose perspectives comprise this chapter would provide little comfort for those who place their faith in the future. The youths have all, in their own way, tasted the medicine of racism and have all arrived at more or less the same conclusion: it will not fade away. Despite their very different origins, experiences and, indeed, futures, they all believe that racism is not in decline. It may have become less visible, but it still lurks not too deeply below the surface. Under suitable conditions, racism will manifest – because it is instilled in whites in early childhood; and, as Renu argued, it has to be combated from the word 'go' – before the parents' views have a chance to assume credibility.

If we were to choose a gauge of racism, we could do worse than settle for the perception of ethnic youths. After all, their vision is not coloured by decades of hatred and abuse. Their opinions are not fouled up by sheer dogmatism. Their arguments are reasonably well informed by the current debates and their ambitions are fresh enough to make them want to overcome obstacles instead of laying down before them (as they feel their parents may have done). The testimonies of the three youths are neither dramatic nor exceptional. Each has a different interpretation of his or her own and others' situations, each insists that racism will prove an influential factor in the future. Whether one accepts their judgements and prognostications is a matter of interpretation. Some may accuse them of exaggeration, or of a selective use of data. Still, these are forgivable sins when committed by groups which have been victims of history, especially when in the attempt not to become victims of the future. If nothing else, their arguments are the authentic material out of which we should be building that future.

Part Three

Perspectives in Later Life

Chapter Eight

As Communities Crumble – White Workingclass

It only takes one

Forget the conventional wisdom that age brings with it tolerance, temperance and disinterest. There is no more vocal, active and opinionated group in the innercities than the elderly. Perhaps this is because they have witnessed dramatic changes in their lifetimes. Not only have the elderly had to assimilate the devastation and carnage of a world war, but they have had to adjust to what they understand to be a complete ruination of their neighbourhoods since the 1930s. The rebuilding programmes that gave rise to places like Newtown were intended to modernize cities by improving their physical structure, but they simultaneously destroyed the intangible spirit of working class community that had been so integral to the lives of many who had lived through the war years. Those under, say, 50 have grown into a world populated by self-seeking individuals, competitively trying to accumulate the housing points which will give them a case when they push for a move, and insulating themselves from neighbours with the aid of video recorders that encourage home centredness. The body of sentiment and feeling of collectivity that once ran through the streets of the innercity – before it was even called 'the innercity' – may linger on in some small traditional neighbourhoods, but not in the new estates that have proliferated since the 1960s. These are sites of abrasive individuality.

Newtown's councillor, Frank Lester, speaks lyrically of the new estates: 'Vertical streets; that's what the tower blocks are. There's no reason why the old values and feelings should die just because the streets are built upwards instead of sidewards.' Perhaps not *just* because – but certainly the very physical shape of life has contributed towards the erasing of those traditional values and feelings. Older people, especially, have seen their back gardens disappear; they have lost the familiarity with neighbours fostered by living almost flush to each other, and have had to reckon with the inconvenience of traipsing up and down flights of stairs when the tower blocks lifts are out of use. Many cannot even handle the concept of having their home in such an impersonal environment. In fact, the final ambition of many of the older residents is simply to move out to a more satisfactory dwelling, to less noise and they hope to a place more congenial to the more traditional way of life.

Housing is a central concern of estate residents, young and old alike, but it has a special primacy for older folk. The unsatisfactory nature of where they live seems to symbolize their general condition. Standards of space and amenities may be better than in the 1930s, but everything else is worse. For them, the area has disintegrated, and these older residents often see ethnic minorities as key agents in this destructive process.

'The place started deteriorating about ten years ago, and over the last five years it's got really bad,' reflects Jean Dobbs:

What's happened is that the people who moved in in the 1960s have either moved on or died off and been replaced by single parents and coloureds. You can't say it's all coloured 'cause there are a good few whites that need shaking up. I mean we've got a block of maisonettes, and the stairs are a disgrace, disgusting, and there are no coloureds there. And there's Mr Needham at the top; he's black, and you can't say he's not respectable, and his house and children are the same. We find that the trouble comes from the young: noise, mostly, nuisance and vandalism.

Mrs Dobbs is 57 and has lived on the Newtown estate for the past fifteen years, at first in a two-bedroomed flat and now in a three-bedroomed house. Popular amongst older people but seen as a 'stirrer' by younger residents, she maintains a reasonably high profile in the area, making it her business, as she would put it, to ensure standards are upheld by all residents. She deliberately makes a pain of herself to the Housing Department and is virtually a one-woman pressure group for Councillor Lester. The estate's residents' association is her creation and seems to feed off her energy. When she speaks, she speaks for the entire white population of Newtown – or so she believes: 'A lot of them are just too scared to speak up.' This condition is not specific to Newtown residents, according to Mrs Dobbs, but a general state of affairs.

I think they're frightened of the coloureds. I was up at the DHSS office with my two daughters the other day. I sat there for three hours 'cause my youngest had been offered a job at a hairdresser's, and they wanted her to buy some new clothes, so I said, 'We'll go and ask for a grant.' Well, there was a coloured woman sitting next to us, and I overheard her talking and I was reckoning up the cheques she said she was getting every week: about £300. She said, 'Don't tell them the truth; tell them a load of lies.' Then an Irish woman came in and started shouting, 'I ain't leaving here till you give me some so-and-so money!' Well, by the time I got to the counter I was up to here listening to all this. They told us that my daughter had got to go back the next day. I explained the position about her not having enough money to buy clothes for the job, and they just said, 'We don't hand out clothing grants.' So I lost my cool and said, 'If I'd have come over here on a banana boat, I'd have the money handed to me on a plate!

Mrs Dobbs is far from alone in believing that ethnic minorities hold distinct advantages over whites in key areas. In housing allocation and social security benefits especially, she thinks ethnics have reaped a rich harvest and, at the same time have severely undermined whites' standard of living, peace of mind and sense of morality.

We had a coloured unmarried mother move in over the road, and for six months she'd got no curtains up. She whitewashed her windows and wrote for all to read 'fuck off'. They can spell good English. So of course the neighbours, a decent lot, petitioned. I gets a letter back from the housing department: 'She's an unmarried mother and she's waiting for her voucher to come, and the DHSS will be supplying her with furniture and curtains.' The next thing was: beautiful net curtains up, furniture brought round. She had a deep-freeze, colour television, carpeted from top to bottom. Then, what do we have to listen to? Taxis pulling up at all hours of the night. We knew what was going on. A coloured bloke started turning up and shouting up, and she'd be on the balcony in a dressing gown. 'The pimp' we used to call him. She and about three or four mates move in. She used to go out at midnight and leave the kids on their own until six in the morning. *And* they get on better than we do; they can get their electric and gas paid for, as well. I blame Social Security for handing out grants and encouraging them. They're better off than some of these old age pensioners who've worked all their lives; they get nowt. Try saying that to the DHSS, and they say, 'You're surmising things.' But you don't surmise when you see it with your own eyes.

Because of her involvement with Newtown, Mrs Dobbs has a special relationship with the area. Her two daughters live within a couple of miles, and she is concerned that they will be affected, possibly more than her, by the environmental and moral rot that has set in.

My daughter lives in a maisonette block round here, and when she moved in, it was four white families and two coloureds. Fair enough. One girl, a white girl, was evicted when she couldn't pay her rent, so they moved a coloured unmarried mother in. Now, she performed right, left and centre. She plays loud music, and her boyfriends are coming and going all the while. Doors are being kicked and banged; back windows have been smashed in. On top of that, my daughter's had one break-in and two attempted break-ins in the last twelve months. Now they've moved another coloured in next to her; she seems quite a decent person, but it's the one who causes all the harassment. It only takes one.

My daughter won't let her kids out the back to play, neither. I asked her why, and she took me out the back garden. And there we are in the garden, just looking round and the next minute: 'Hey you fucker!' I went, 'Uh?' and I'm looking all round. I couldn't believe my ears. 'I am talking to you, fucker.' And my daughter says, 'Look up.' There he was, a little kid, 3 or 4 years of age, shouting from an upstairs window − no chain on it − from the coloured woman's place. Now, you're not going to tell me that a child of his age is going to say things like that on his own. So I said to my daughter, 'Tell the kids to play and ignore him.' But she says she can't. So I say, 'I'm going round to see her.' She says, 'Please don't Mum', 'cause she's frightened of some of the blokes who go round to see her. It's the same with the parking: the coloured woman has got a garage, but she rents it out and so she and her men park on my daughter's forecourt. And when my daughter asked her to move, she said, 'You can't do a fucking thing about it. Fetch the police if you like.' But my daughter's frightened to.'

Mrs Dobbs's inferences are to be taken seriously. She has been a resident of Newtown for fifteen years and has had her opinions formed out of experience rather than conjecture. She does not examine the complexities of the social security benefits system, but hears through the Newtown grapevine about colour tvs and fitted carpets. In her position as self appointed moral watchdog, she hears the residents' complaints of prostitution, rackets and noise. She is convinced that, contrary to the 'official version', existing institutional arrangements favour ethnic minorities over whites, and she cites three examples of this. First:

James Hunte from Handsworth and Councillor Edge say, 'The poor ethnic groups, they can't get jobs and they can't open businesses.' All I can say is that they want to go to a good optician's. You walk up Handsworth and they call it 'Burma Road'. It's the same up Lozells Road. You'll be lucky if you see three whites' shops. You go to Newtown precinct and the majority of shops are coloured. Down the main road, the warehouses are coloured, and the factories that have closed down have been opened up by coloureds. Now they're talking about putting money on one side for black businesses. That's discrimination straight away against whites. What about if a white factory owner needed £1,000 to keep his business going? We've watched factories round here close one after another.

Second, she cites changes in laws and rules to accommodate ethnic religious strictures. 'Let's take them with the bad heads [Sikhs]. Their turbans might be as safe as a crash helmet when they ride a motorbike. But what annoyed me was when my daughter was at school up the road, where they'd got to wear school uniform. She couldn't wear trousers. Yet you get these other girls, Muslims, who can wear trousers. My daughter was sent home for wearing a black skirt. The coloureds were going to school in striped skirts, brown jackets and everything, and nothing was said to them.

Her third point is more general. 'They're on about the young ones can't get jobs, but I was down the shops the other day and I saw them pouring out of the government training centre. I saw one white lad in the lot of them. Now where's the discrimination? I think it's gone too far and it's up to people to make a stand, or it's going to be the white man who will be the black man's slave.'

Mrs Dobbs blames both ethnic minorities for obstinately remaining different and refusing to adopt to English lifestyles, *and* state authorities for allowing them to do so without sanction:

They come over here and don't even make an effort to learn English. We've got a family of Pakistanis in Gray Tower. They don't speak a word of English – only 'money'. When they first moved in, they were throwing their rubbish over the balcony. We had to get the councillor in to explain to them not to do it. And I don't think you can blame education because there's more attention paid to them than there is to our own children; it's got to be because they've got to have the attention before our children get it. If you've got a class of forty and about three whites in it, who's going to suffer? The three whites, because the teachers have got to concentrate on teaching the others. I say the parents should make the effort to understand English if they want to live in this country; they should abide by our rules. If you go to their country, you've got to abide by their rules.

Mrs Dobbs is full of examples of how ethnics have, in a thoughtlessly provocative way, failed to conform and set in train a long series of conflicts. Newtown, in common with other innercity estates, has a conflictual saga of almost epic proportions; it concerns the penchant of black youths to play loud music, sometimes for the entire night. Intolerance of white neighbours? No: Mrs Dobbs thinks white residents are reasonably tolerant people with a legitimate complaint.

Bump, bump, bump, go the jungle drums. It's enough to send you demented. It's like a Chinese torture, where they lock somebody in a cell and keep playing this loud noise. We've had meetings with the police and the Chief Inspector turned round and said, 'If you knocked the door and asked them politely, they won't play the music.' I know a pensioner, 78, who had to get out of bed at one in the morning to ask them to turn the noise down. 'Please, please,' she said to the chap. 'Let me have a bit of peace.' He told her to fuck off. He was took to court three times.

The black tenant was eventually evicted; and, encouraged by the result, Mrs Dobbs has pursued this tactic, although she is convinced that it is an unnecessarily long and burdensome procedure to have to go through just to secure some tranquility at night. She feels that white residents will grow frustrated at the bureaucracy and resort to more immediate measures.

I know that if nothing is sorted out with this one coloured family in particular, there is talk of vigilantes. They're saying, 'The police reckon they can't do nothing; the Housing don't want to know; the Department of the Environment don't want to know, so what's next?' We're going to end up like America. They're going to take the law into their own hands. If the law isn't altered soon, something will blow, not only in Newtown, but all over the place. The other week there was a party, and somebody went up there and threatened 'em with a shotgun.

People like Mrs Dobbs – and she has a veritable army of admirers, mostly over-fifties – do not accept the inevitable. They don't see conflict of the kind witnessed in Newtown as grinding on inexorably; 'something will blow' before too long. But they are still hopeful that commonsense will prevail, and this will mean public housing administrators and police taking greater consideration of the needs of white tenants, who have progressively been relegated to a second-class status over the past fifteen years. The honourable traditions, complete with comradeship, that held communities together before the 1960s have been shattered. Mrs Dobbs knows they cannot be restored. She does not pine for a past golden age, but simply wants to recover some of the better qualities that used to unify areas. All she sees nowdays is divisive arguments over an apparently unfair housing allocation system, unkempt dwellings, noisy and immoral neighbours and rude kids. The general outcome is sour neighbourly relations, which she hates. She thinks back to the sound community spirit up to, during and just after the Second World War and wonders what exactly happened. Her conclusion is that the onset of immigration from the New Commonwealth coincided with the beginning of the decline of traditional workingclass life. She had never heard the cries of 'white bastard' or 'black bastard' before the late 1950s. That is when the conflicts began and in her view they have grown more intense as the council estates have accommodated more and more black and Asian tenants. Are they the causes of the trouble? Not entirely, Mrs Dobbs reasons: as the host society, British people had a role to play. The role was not to make life as pleasant as possible for the newcomers, but to ensure a total equality of treatment. Britain's failure to play that role has led, Mrs Dobbs firmly believes, to the white workingclass being reduced to impotent recipients of continual aggravation without any recourse to the procedures available to ethnic minorities, such as the Commission for Racial Equality – the 'Race Relations Board', as Mrs Dobbs still chooses to call it. As we will see next, Mrs Dobbs has allies.

This isn't England

'Am I safe?' asks Mrs Adams. 'Do *you* think I am?' She turns her head to stare out of her first-floor window at the street below. 'And this is the good part of Newtown.' She means no stripped-down cars at the roadside, nor too much litter, with the nearest highrises being four streets away. Mrs Adams worries over her personal safety. 'I've lived in Newtown for twenty years and I've seen it when there was hardly any race trouble; you could go out at night. But lately things have gone from bad to worse.' Mrs Adams's outlook is inspired by fear. It is a fear that resonates around Newtown; white residents especially those like Mrs Adams over the age of 50, are unsettled by what they consider to be a constant, and possibly inevitable, tension between blacks and white.

It was 1949, Mrs Adams remembers, when she first saw a black person. 'He was a harmless little bloke. I can remember my mother pointing him out. We used to call him "Spider".' She was 14 then, and although the Newtown estate had not yet been created, the area surrounding it was, as Mrs Adams put it, 'a slum'; but 'people had pride in the area . . . I remember my mother taking pleasure in cleaning her windows and polishing the front step. Things were hard. It was back-to-back houses, and you had to run ten yards to the outside toilet. No fun in the middle of the night.'

When Newtown was built, Mrs Adams moved into a new flat with her parents. Later, aged 32, she married and moved into another flat. The marriage lasted eight years before her husband went off, leaving her with three children. Her assessment of Newtown until the late 1960s is good; after that, she says, the older folk died and their places were taken by blacks and Asians. 'That's when the noise and the mugging started, and people were living like thieves.'

Such was her attachment to the area, even after the death of her father, that she refused to move out of Newtown. Still, she pleaded for move after move, complaining to the Housing Department that her neighbours were causing her anxiety. In a way she regrets leaving her last home; in another way she had no choice.

I used to live in a lovely house, beautiful it was. It was like a palace compared to this place [a maisonette]. But I had to move out. What happened was that blacks started to move in the street. I had a West Indian family on the one side and an Asian family on the other and another opposite. Well, I had noise all the time from the West Indians, and there was fighting going on between the two Asian families. They say *we're* prejudiced, but we're not so prejudiced as they are against themselves. These two families used to throw stones and bricks at each other. And, of course, they used to miss, and I was in the middle. I couldn't stand it any longer. The Asians were filthy; you know, the home was just dirty. I'll tell you something; the woman next door's husband died and she came round to me to see if I would help her. Well, I went in the house and I couldn't see him anywhere, so I said, 'Where is he?' Do you know where they'd put him? In the deep bloody freeze! He'd been dead for five days.

It wasn't just that that made me leave. One day, my second eldest son, Brian, was having a wash and he heard a noise. He thought it was Julie [her daughter]. Julie had heard the noise and thought it was Brian. Anyway, Bri heard it again and went to

142

investigate and he saw these blacks leaving the house with a radio-cassette, tv and some other things. They'd got a passkey, opened the door as calm as you like and just walked in. Brian gave chase and ran after them, but one turned round, hit him, and that was that.

A load of people saw it happen, but nobody would say anything because most of them were blacks as well and they all stick together. Even my few black friends: I know that, one minute you can be talking to them and they're OK, and the next minute they're against you. They put other blacks in front of their friends. So, the area I used to live in became virtually all-black, and I just moved out. Not because it was black, but because of what they're like. I couldn't feel safe. I exchanged my house with a black woman. Mind you, only a black woman would take it.

It could be argued that Mrs Adams's flight from one dwelling to the next is an irrational one. Only about 14 per cent of Newtown's residents are of New Commonwealth background or descent, and although there are signs that their presence is increasing, Mrs Adams's judgement seems based on a highly selective perception. But her views, like those of the other residents in this book, have to be understood in terms of her life experience: a traditional white workingclass background, geographical immobility (moving in a radius of only three miles), employed until marriage at the nearby Lucas factory.

During the decade of her twenties, she witnessed appreciable changes in the ethnic composition of her neighbourhood – and she still believes it is *her* neighbourhood. 'Spider' was no longer a unique character, a social curio, but a member of a growing legion of blacks who filtered into Newtown to be quickly followed by Asians. By the time she was 30 the ethnic minority residents of Newtown were well in evidence. By the time she was 40 the stores where she shopped were owned by Asians; the small businesses in the area were run by Asians; the private flats where her friends lived had Asian landlords. All the buses she rode seemed to be manned by black drivers and conductors. More urgently, she saw her children attending schools that were very different to the ones she had been to. Whenever she lost a neighbour, the replacement seemed to be black or Asian. The changes engendered a sense of insecurity which was, and still is, compounded by first-hand experience.

The other day a woman round here noticed two West Indians coming out of a house with a television set in a wheelbarrow. The woman asked them what they were doing and one turned round and said, 'You'd better keep your fucking mouth shut, or we'll be back for you.' They just live off thieving. People are scared to report them half the time for fear of their own lives.

I went to visit my friend the other night and a woman told me the buses were on strike, so I decided to walk; it was only a fifteen minute walk. Anyway, I noticed this black kid on a bike behind me, watching me. There was a subway up ahead and there was no way I was going under there. So I crossed the road and he came running up to me, grabbed hold of me and pushed me against the wall. He said, 'Give us your bag; I don't want to hit you!' Well, I was ready for him, so I hit him across the face and ran off. He ran after me. I arrived at my friend's and told her what had happened. She said she'd heard in the pub that the same thing had happened three times already in that week alone.

There's not many white youths left in Newtown – and they daren't go out. All the clubs are dominated by blacks and, if you want a game of snooker, they won't let you on. You only need to go down the chip shop at night to see all those West Indians stood around. You can't walk past them without them sticking their legs out and swearing at you. And if you're a woman they say things like, 'Come and get a bit of black, you white pussy.' My son was stabbed on his way home the other night. He had my cigarettes and some cans of beer. Some blacks stopped him and said, 'Give us them.' When he said no, they just slashed at him with a knife.

It's just as bad at the schools. Take Holte School: my mother works there, and they had to lock her and the other staff in a room because a gang of black lads were running wild and smashing everything. What happened was that a black lad had hit a teacher and another teacher had come to his assistance, and the black lad was smashed. Well, that day, blacks throughout the school and from other schools came down and ran wild. The Holte School is too full of blacks in my opinion, and they don't live round here all of them.

At my son's school, St George's, blacks were running a protection racket. My son used to ask me for 20 pence extra every day. I found out he was giving it to some black lads; there was one big black lad in particular called Big Red. I went to the school to see the headmaster, and he didn't accept what I was saying was happening in his school. So I told him I bloody *knew* what was going on and even told him Big Red's name. Well, you know what the stupid bugger did? After I left, he called my son and Big Red into the room together. Well, my son got a good pummelling afterwards. After that, I kept my son away from school for the next twelve months. He was in hospital for weeks. The doctor said he was lucky to live 'cause he was kicked down below. One black gang around here is called The Firm, but it's not just West Indians; the Asians have got their own gangs. They got some white kid the other night and cut off his hair with a knife. I'll tell you what's going to happen in the future. I've heard through the grapevine that the few white kids that are left are going to get together and arm themselves.

The problem nowadays is that everybody's scared of the blacks. You can hardly get a job, and some of the Asians have got firms and they only employ other Asians. If whites were to do that, they'd get called prejudiced. Blacks all stick together too; they have a system for everything, even things like queuing up for each other at the Social Security. The people behind the counter know they do it when they're not supposed to, but they're frightened to do anything against the blacks in case they're accused of discriminating against them. That's why they can have so many in one house and make a noise. If we did that sort of thing, people would complain, and we'd get evicted. But they wouldn't do that to blacks. The authorities are scared. My mother and me would have loved one of those houses over the road, but all the blacks have got them. They get first choice 'cause they kick up a fuss, and the Housing Department backs down. I don't know why they bunch all the blacks together, though. Eventually all the whites, including me, are going to move out.

Anxiety over personal safety is but one level of a general workingclass *Angst* that pervades Newtown. In common with other innercity council estates, Newtown has been affected by housing shortages, unemployment and education cuts; these issues have an immediate impact on workingclass residents. So it seems logical that they feel insecure, threatened by the changing complexion of the neighbourhood. Sure, Mrs Adams has misconceptions; but they are understandable ones. She has little inclination to study the history of British colonialism and the post-war shortage of labour which drew migrants from former colonies to urban centres like Birmingham where work lay in abundance. All she knows is that she seems to be followed by black and Asian neighbours. Nor does Mrs Adams fully comprehend the often obscure housing allocation policy operated by Birmingham City Council's Housing Department. Again, all she knows is confined to her immediate environment: her and her mother seeming to lose out on the more desirable properties, while blacks in particular seem to get priority. In her eyes, ethnic minority residents have grabbed a better deal than her. What is more, they have done so at *her* cost. After all, Newtown was where she was raised; she has barely ventured out of the area. Like her mother before her, she took pride in the area. Now every advancement gained by blacks and Asians appears to be paid for by the likes of her. Why? 'Because they're frightened to upset the blacks, 'cause they might get called prejudiced or whatever; so they take it out of whites. I shouldn't think they care. We can't claim prejudice.'

Whatever the facts – and Mrs Adams is too preoccupied with her own life to worry about them – inequalities reveal themselves differently to different social groups. Mrs Adams belongs to a group which has had it rough. She is working class, a lone parent, a woman and a resident of an area that is physically disintegrating. She is immune to arguments that ethnic minorities often have an even more raw deal than herself. 'Don't make me laugh', she smiles mockingly. 'This isn't England any more.'

I'd pay a higher rent to help them go back

Fewer than 9 per cent of Chelmsley's 14,000 residents are of pensionable age. The great majority of these elderly people would have spent most of their lives in Birmingham (where 17.4 per cent of the population is of pensionable age). As workingclass people, they would have lived in areas like Lozells, Hockley and Aston, where the Newtown estate now stands, and their experiences prior to moving east in the mid-1970s would have been broadly similar to those of older Newtown folk. Coming from the innercity, they would have witnessed the changes in ethnic composition that cause such concerns to Newtowners. But whereas Newtown residents are still trying to get to grips with the changes, people in Chelmsley can detach themselves and attempt to appraise things more analytically. As we have seen in previous chapters, issues confront Chemsley dwellers with less immediacy than they have for Newtowners; practical solutions to problems of noise, housing scarcity, morality and so on do not preoccupy them. These problems are all seen as in some way related to race in Newtown. In Chelmsley, by contrast, they are not considered issues at all. Nevertheless, the elderly residents of Chelmsley are interested, albeit in a rather academic way, in race relations. Indeed, many of them opted for a move away from Birmingham for precisely this reason, as Mrs Forge, 60, explains:

I originally came from Acocks Green and then Hockley on the outskirts of the city. But they started moving the coloureds in, and that created problems. Then the area began deteriorating and places was used for immoral purposes, and there were problems that will never die out. I don't think coloured people should live in a white man's country. So I got an exchange and moved over here. It was quite nice at first as well.

Mr Chapman, who is 67, moved over to Chelmsley on his retirement. His purpose was not to escape the reputed problems of the innercity, merely to break away from the industrial surroundings in which he had spent all of his working life. Now that he has moved, however, he admits a certain relief at being distanced from the city. He reflects that

Twenty-five years ago, we had no coloureds at work. After ten or fifteen years, half the firm was coloured. We had no problem at work, mind; the problem was housing. I had a sister living in Small Heath and a coloured family moved in at the end of the road. In twelve months the whole lot had left, and all coloured had moved in. This is where you get your problems. One family moves in, whites move out and, naturally, the houses are let to coloured again. Over here, this problem doesn't arise.

'The problem' of white flight – white families fleeing areas, leaving vacancies to be filled by black and Asian tenants – does not affect suburban areas like Chelmsley. Ethnic families have tended not to move from the inner cities, partly because of council house allocation policies, partly because of the relative cheapness of privately rented and owner occupied accommodation in the cities and partly because of a desire to remain in an ethnic community. As a result, areas like Chelmsley have attracted few ethnic minority families and just 2.1 per cent of Chelmsley's total population comes from the New Commonwealth. Most elderly whites there have seen the process of white flight and, either wittingly or unwittingly, joined in, accelerating the scattering of white families to the newly created suburbs. They can look back on their past life in Birmingham from the 'safety' of their present home. The question to be answered is: does living at this 'safe' distance affect one's understanding of the main issues? After all, the elderly of Chelmsley come from more or less the same background as their Newtown counterparts. But the decision to move to Chelmsley was not a totally voluntary one, so it could not be argued that those fearing and loathing ethnic minorities worst moved to Chelmsley. The options to move are granted by Birmingham's Housing Department and are established by reference to complicated and frequently confusing criteria. People opt to move when the opportunity arises. Racist fears may or may not be a motivating factor.

The abiding difference in the orientations of the elderly is that Chelmsley views are not inspired by fear. Residents are not alarmed by the threat, real or imagined, of a takeover of shops and businesses; they are not apprehensive about the rumoured preferential treatment for black and Asian families operated by the Housing Department and, although they worry about the moral decline of the area, they do not apportion the blame for this to the ethnic communities. Mrs Forge, in fact, would not object to having ethnic minority neighbours although, as she stresses, nor would she exactly welcome the prospect. 'If I'd got to have them living next door to me, then I wouldn't object. Provided the people were like myself, I wouldn't mind.' *Like myself?*

From the experience I've had, I think West Indians are more likely to adapt to our ways than the Asians; they're prepared to mix it more. With West Indians, you'll see a lot of the children going to our schools, and the parents don't care what education they get. But the Asians tend to think we should educate them as if they were being educated back in Pakistan; and I think that if that's the way they feel, they should stay over in Pakistan and see they are educated in that way.

Mr Chapman believes:

They don't seem to have the same values. Now, I'm not against coloured; I've worked with hundreds of 'em before I retired, and their values are very funny. At one time, I was a shop steward, and we were having a bit of an argument so we went round to see what people thought. A few told and I got a coloured chap who'd worked for us for a couple of years. 'No ask me,' he says. 'Me black man. You ask white man.' Now, I'd never thought anything about this: he could have been a green man or a Chinaman for all I cared. I didn't ask him what his colour was. *They* started this business. They've got a chip on their shoulder; we never created this chip. They seem to regret being coloured in a way. With the labour problems being as they are now, night after night, you read in the paper about robberies and muggings and it's nearly all the coloureds. I've been in the centre of Birmingham years ago at twelve o'clock, one o'clock in the morning. I wouldn't go there at ten o'clock today, not for anybody.

I'm not arguing that there's no discrimination, 'cause there is, in my opinion. You'll get firms that will set a white man on, but they won't set a coloured man on. They do do it. They didn't at my firm: before I retired, there were more coloureds than whites; but it goes on. It's obvious why. At least, I think it's obvious. We know more about things than they do; they haven't had the education; it's their education that's the trouble. Now they're here, their children are getting the education, but it's no good to them, is it? They still can't get a job. That's why they go for these robberies. It's quite logical.

While Mr Chapman thinks that discrimination in employment stems from an educational deficiency amongst the ethnic minorities, Mrs Forge believes that this wrongly attributes them with the responsibility for their own failure:

As far as white people are concerned, especially of my generation, they've always been made to feel that the coloured races are inferior to white. You've got other immigrants who come here, Irish, Poles, Germans; they're all white. There's not a lot said about them, is there? And yet a lot of those people are infinitely more undesirable than the coloureds. But because they're white, like us, they're not considered an inferior race. That's why we tend to disagree with the coloured people being here. I think back to when we were kids and we'd see jungle films; these people would be like animals. So when they came over here, we thought they were the same as we'd seen years before. But they're human — they've got to be the same as we are, obviously.

Mr Chapman's reasoning follows a different line: 'When they first came over, they had a chance. Opportunities existed. They had freedom; they were accepted as someone who was a different colour but "he's a good bloke at this" or "she's a good woman at that". But now we've been overrun, swamped. Just look at our schools: in some of them, there's over 80 per cent blacks.'

The problem, for Mr Chapman, is primarily one of number, compounded by an attitude that ranges from indifference to downright arrogance. He cites a former workmate, Hardy, as a typical West Indian:

He was like a bull, and you'd tell him what you wanted and you'd get it the next day. *But* only if you pushed, pushed, pushed him. You'd got to push him or he didn't bother. My greatest sympathy went to Hardy because, when I first knew him, we used to go to a pub every night after work for a drink. He worked hard and he was entitled to spend his money how he wished. In due course, circumstances became such that he wouldn't go to this pub because he was threatened by other blacks. You see, he got made a foreman, and there were fifty blokes on the floor, mostly white. But his own mates, West Indians, were getting at him: 'You're a foreman, get us a job.' And eventually he had too much pressure, so that, although we had a unity of purpose at work, we had very little outside. They will cling together.

Mr Chapman agrees with Mrs Forge that West Indians have a greater propensity to assimilate than Asians, but adds that this tendency is crushed by the sheer weight of numbers. Thus even the individuals who can readily adapt and gain acceptance of some order are pressured into a more oppositional posture by fellow, more embittered ethnics, those who have chips on their shoulders.

Although Mrs Forge reasons that white prejudice – in the literal sense of the word: judgements formed prior to experience – was the central cause of much conflict, she confirms Mr Chapman's belief that numbers aggravated the problem. 'I think politicians are to blame for this,' she says.

'When the British took over the colonies, they told their people they were British subjects and they were entitled to come to England. That was wrong because those countries had far more folks and far more space and by allowing them in here, they've taken a lot of the houses, a lot of the jobs, and we're becoming overpopulated.'

Mr Chapman thinks similarly:

I've lived through six decades and I hate the people who did it to our country and, don't forget, to the people most concerned, the immigrants. They did it to people like Hardy. Wilson brought them in because he wanted the country to be socialist for ever. Heath I blame for not stopping them when he came in. Those are the two people who've got this country in the state it's in, and I'd shoot both of them for what they've done.

His passion rises as he goes on:

We can't only talk about what's in the country now. You can add another ten or twenty thousand on top of that because they breed quicker than us. I say that because I worked with two brothers and one had eleven children and the other had nine and they were only just over 40, these two. Their children are going to grow up and get married and they'll have children. By the next century, it'll be half and half – and then we'll see the trouble. It's not when they come into the country that matters: it's when they get like they do in South Africa. I shan't be here, but that's not the point. They'll be telling the government, 'We want representation in Parliament. Our numbers are 20 million out of 55 million.'

Even though Mrs Forge agrees that the UK has not been as rigorous as it should in immigration control and that 'they just shouldn't be living in a white man's country', she does not share Mr Chapman's despondency and says that 'This younger generation doesn't think of coloureds as inferior in the same way as we used to, so they'll be more tolerant because they've grown up with them.' But she concedes that she will never learn to accept and tolerate in the same way: 'I'd appreciate it if a lot were given the money to go back home. I think a lot want to, but haven't got the money. In fact, I wouldn't mind paying a higher rent to help them go back. But I wouldn't force them.'

Failing a 'voluntary repatriation' programme, Mrs Forge would encourage geographical segregation: 'If they would allocate one big area where the majority of coloureds would all live together, it'd work out better than putting them next to whites. Then they would have their own shops, doctors and things like that.'

Mr Chapman disagrees: 'I'd thin them out. I think that's the answer. You've got about 3 million living here now and we've got about 60 million in the country. If they were spread out and become part of the country there'd be a massive change in attitudes.'

Between them Mrs Forge and Mr Chapman pose the central dilemma of housing policy in regard to ethnic groups. You can attempt to disperse populations, possibly against their will (as Birmingham City Council did in 1969, housing black families in a 1:6 set ratio to whites in council dwellings; the policy was formally abandoned in 1975); or you can attempt to herd ethnic group members together in one single area (as the US city of St Louis did in the early 1950s with its Pruitt-Igoe project; twelve years after opening, it was demolished). Both policies have potentially disastrous consequences, the first because it fails to consider the element of choice, the second because it encourages the kind of segregation that sustains racism.

Living away from the innercity appears not to have diminished the power of Mrs Forge's and Mr Chapman's views. Despite the different premises and conclusions of their arguments, they are both fervent believers in the sanctity of British culture. Both have resigned themselves to a future in which the way of life they were brought up in has disappeared. Neither moved from the innercity solely because of what Mrs Forge calls 'the invasions', although both acknowledge that this was a contributory factor. As Mr

Chapman points out: 'When things don't touch you personally, you don't care. Take any Prime Minister – Thatcher, Callaghan, Heath, or Wilson. You put a coloured family next to them and see what happens. They'd sell their houses and move out to somewhere where there wasn't any. It's all right for *them* to talk about the ethnic population.'

Things have touched Mr Chapman personally and he did indeed move out. It would be fair to say that many over-sixties in Chelmsley were motivated, at least partially, by similar concerns. As a result, their views have not significantly altered. They don't rub shoulders with ethnic minorities every day and their information is nowadays based on media reports and the testimonies of relatives who might remain in Birmingham. What they have acquired in their comparative seclusion is an understanding of sorts of the origins of conflict and an outlook on the future.

Like the other elderly residents in this chapter, Mrs Forge and Mr Chapman have been through the momentous changes forced on them by war. The postwar period, particularly the 1950s, brought with it another series of changes, not nearly so dire in their consequences but serious enough in the eyes of many to prompt concern. The presence of migrants is in itself no cause for concern, especially when jobs are plentiful. As Mrs Forge remembers: 'When I was a child, you never saw a coloured person. If you did, it was a marvellous thing. "Ooh, I've just seen a coloured man!" It was an amazing thing to see.' The 'coloured man', of course, was not meant to be an equal – not quite. He was thought to match up to Edgar Wallace's *Sanders of the River* image, a breast-beating savage more used to mud huts than back-to-backs and more suited to tropical Africa than steely Birmingham.

The occasional sight of a curio, like Mrs Adams's 'Spider', became less occasional. As more migrants from the West Indies and South Asia were attracted by the lure of work to UK cities, the sight of a black person became less a source of wonderment, more a source of concern. The concern manifested in 1958 with serious conflicts in the Midlands city of Nottingham and the London Notting Hill district. Attacks on blacks and Asians became commonplace thereafter. The people considered in this chapter would have been in their thirties at this stage, stabilized after the trauma of war and no doubt hopeful of a sustained life of relative affluence ahead. And here was the country they had fought and paid dearly for being, as Mrs Forge puts it, 'invaded' by 'inferiors'. In the eyes of Mr Chapman and the others, migrants were acceptable up to a point. But that point had been exceeded when half the workforce of his factory was black and when he had to strain to find a white face in the playground of his local school. For Mrs Forge, the crunch came when housing became scarce and black and Asian families began to appear in the streets: 'Some of the neighbours would look at the coloured woman and think, "She shouldn't be here. She's a nice person, but what's she doing here? She's living in a house that should be given to our people".'

'Our people', the white workingclass were seen to be unwilling participants in a struggle for jobs, housing and, later, places in schools. And yet this was the class that had given most, in terms of both life and effort, in the war, now being pitched into competition with a group 'our people' had been taught to regard as inferior. The racism that had been propounded in a somewhat academic way, through books, newspapers, film and other media, was given an additional relevance as Robeson's burlesque black chief of the Wallace novel left 'darkest Africa' and moved in next door. Such was the impact of the changes in the 1950s, that, thirty years on, people like Mrs Forge, who lives on a pension, would still gladly pay a levy on their rent to be used to repatriate West Indians and Asians.

Housing, jobs and, to a more limited extent, education are the three major issues that have aggravated racism amongst the elderly workingclass. Competing with people they have regarded as inferiors and have difficulty seeing any other way has sustained a subdued but ever present resentment. As far as those still living in the innercities are concerned, they are perpetually locked into the struggle. Those who have moved have become detached and try to think through the problems; they no longer make the ethnic minorities their scapegoats, but blame the political parties for being too lax in immigration control.

What, however, of those groups whose standard of living has not been felt as under threat by the incursions of migrants? The elderly members of the middleclass have not had their lives seriously disrupted by the migrations of the postwar years – certainly not to the same extent as the workingclass. Chapter 8 will look at the reactions and reflections of these better-off elderly people.

Chapter Nine

A Natural Equilibrium
– White Middleclass

We've bent over backwards for them

Eric Hemmings was pondering the developments in British race relations since the mid-1950s. 'Recently, I was discussing the effects of the French Revolution with a Chinaman, and he said, "I think it's too early to say." You see the point? Thirty years is a very short time in which to make an assessment; one hundred and thirty more like.' In his maturity – he is now 61 – Mr Hemmings, a retired architect, feels he has acquired the quality of patience. 'The problem of race will disappear almost certainly, but probably not in my lifetime. These things do have a time effect; it's just a matter of getting used to people.'

The elderly middleclass sees virtue in forbearance. Its members live in a comfortable world of steady patterns, a composed, predictable existence in which breaks and disturbances are unwelcome. They perceive the issues relating to racism and ethnicity with a sharp clarity, at the same time stressing the way in which any kind of interference, including that prompted by writers like myself, can serve only to impede what is regarded as a natural progression. Their favoured model is one of imperturbable equilibrium. Of course, there will be conflicts, mostly the outcome of misunderstanding and unfamiliarity; but these are as inevitable as the four seasons. The bitter winter we are now having to brave will be followed inexorably by a calmer spring and a joyous summer. Alarm over present conditions betrays a misconception of the logic of history and may even pervert the logic.

Former company director Charles Pride has his own version of the theory of natural progression.

The expectation of the man in the street I'm not able to speak for, but I know myself, from a fairly wide study of history in all countries, that civilization takes about a thousand years; and we should have no expectations, if we're sensible, that the immigrant population will be assimilated in less than several generations. Take your reading back to when the Edict of Nantes [which made Protestantism illegal in France in the seventeenth century] caused the Huguenots to quit France and settle here. Admittedly, they had less difficulty, apart from language, than immigrants with different-colour skin, but they were assimilated in this country and we benefited from their expertise. But assimilation cannot be a rapid process, particularly if the different appearance of the coloured man alters relationships, and intermarriage between the different communities is slow.

These remarks provide a general theoretical perspective in which to view the elderly middleclass. Mr Pride has lived in Solihull for most of his seventy years, but worked in central Birmingham, where he owned and ran a printing company. He envisages a gradual but inevitable assimilating process in which ethnic minorities abandon the distinctive features of their cultures, such as language, dress, religion and custom, and become similar to the majority of the population. There is no room for diversity in Mr Pride's conception, and attempts to provide space for the integration of different cultures are doomed, as the experience of United States blacks seems to illustrate.

Jesse Jackson is the hope of the Negro population to perhaps one day become President of the United States. I listened to a speech of his recently and was both surprised and disappointed to find that a man who'd been born in America and is as American as anyone can claim to be was speaking like a Negro. Here is a man who is asking for equal treatment but is keeping alive that strange formation of words and speech, wilfully, that marks him off from the ordinary American. Do they want to be equal or don't they? I'm sure they do, so why don't they stand back a few steps and see themselves as other Americans see them? They have nothing to lose. I have no patience or sympathy with people who will not assimilate when they find themselves in a minority. You go back to the Roman Empire; now, *there* must be a mixture of races which cannot be exceeded by any example in history. And they used to say, 'When in Rome, do as the Romans do.' That's not a harsh dictum; its a commonsense one. Dame Nature is a wonderful dissolver of objections and rooted habits; everything will be assimilated in the end, and the distinctions we have now will disappear. Race relations is a new study but, I believe, a misguided one. One may slightly hasten the processes, but this won't materially change things.

Many elderly residents of Solihull and Edgbaston, although they may not have thought through theories with Mr Pride's thoroughness, would agree with the central tenets of the model: that present difficulties will resolve themselves in due course, that interference is both un-necessary and undesirable and that the conformity to majority standards is a matter of 'commonsense' rather than an intolerance of diversity. What problems race relations have thrown up have been caused by the resistance of ethnic groups to the natural process of assimilation, by a residual conservatism of whites to change, however inevit-able, and by a hopelessly misconceived government strategy to introduce legal measures aimed at improving race relations. Inducing better race relations is impossible: it just happens.

This is the consensus view of the elderly middleclass, and it reflects the members' own backgrounds to an extent. Exactly how will be evident after considering a number of

159

other perspectives. For example, that of John Armitt: he trained as a toolmaker, served in the armed forces, started a light engineering company in 1952 and helped it prosper in the 1960s and 1970s. Until quite recently, he insisted on keeping a space at his old workbench, even though most of his commitments were on the managerial side. He's now 58 and plans an early retirement in two years' time, when his three sons will continue the business:

My parents were English but they were in America when I was born. I lived in Detroit until I was 6. My father tended to run with the herd and when black faces appeared at the end of your road, everybody popped off and moved a few miles out of the city centre. A few years ago I went back to try to trace the place where I used to live, but I was told not to go there as it was a black ghetto now. As a 6-year old you don't have many opinions, but I got quite a few by talking to my parents.

I'm in business in West Bromwich and, in the past, have employed West Indian girls in the office – I must admit, without success. Without any prejudice whatsoever, they appear to suddenly get a chip on their shoulder and they leave. We thought we were getting on well; being a small firm, we have to work cheek by jowl and then it was as if a screen came down. Both girls left of their own accord. Having said that, the Indians are good business people. You've only got to look around to see that; they're opening businesses left, right and centre. But possibly for their own race: although you do see some whites working there, they tend to keep it for their own community. In this respect, I think they hold up integration. I mean, we've got some Sikhs next door and some more around the corner, so they do try to integrate; but they keep themselves to themselves very much. Possibly, we haven't given them a chance to get closer around here. I don't force myself on them and neither do I expect them to do it to me.

It's because of this that my main contacts with immigrants have been at work, rather than at home. My impression is that the Asians are much more ready to assimilate, possibly because they're more like us to start with. West Indians don't have a lot between the ears, in my experience. My impression of West

Indians is that they are lazy layabouts, in my honest opinion. A more tactful way of putting it would be: they don't seem to have any urge or drive, whether they're capable or not. There's a further problem in that they're going to produce children who will be educated by the state system and, if they've got the wherewithal to rise through the system, are they going to meet with resistance? Let's just say that West Indians' life standard is somewhat lower than ours, unfortunately. But that's probably only the people who arrived here as adults. What I'm suggesting is that the bigger problem will come when their children get educated and want to climb on to the better things that are on offer in this country. That, I think, is when one might see real trouble. The Indian community are moving up and out. The Indian's got more drive than the average Englishman, I should think. Their outlook seems to be more European. But very few West Indians go into business. But, then again, that leaves behind one thing: they must toe the line. If Sikhs or any other weird religious sects or nationalities come over here, I don't want to be told they can't possibly wear safety hats at work or crash helmets on motor cycles because it's against their beliefs. I feel that, if they want to live over here, they must toe the line.

They do enjoy all the benefits available to any British person. They've got health care from the National Health system, welfare benefits and so on. And I'm still sure that a lot of people don't want to integrate. For example, there's a very sizeable Chinese population living in Birmingham, but you never see them around; only the children at school. They keep themselves pretty much to themselves. With West Indians, their physical characteristics put most people's backs up to start with, and they seem to aggravate the situation by their outrageous dress and hair-dos, even the children. And you know how cruel children are; cruel children become cruel adults and the whole process goes on. They look different; they will always look different and providing they stay in their own ethnic group, you'll never change them.

I don't know what the good Lord was thinking about when he messed about with different colours. Slight differences in shape one can deal with; it's the skin colour that gets you every time. Colour will hold the second and third generations back. White people don't like blacks. They've got to live long after I'm gone.

We're on course for trouble because the communities don't mix. I sometimes think we bend over backwards too much to help. I don't mind them being here – they're not influencing my life directly – but we should have made it harder for them to come here, insisted that they contribute something at the outset. Even now I think we should deport those who consistently fail to find work, the unemployable.

I think we've got to the point where *we*, in our own British way, are being discriminated against in all sorts of subtle ways. Otherwise why would these laws have come out discriminating against us – virtually saying to the indigenous population that we must be good and we must do this and we mustn't do that against the immigrants? If you want to sell your house, and a black man comes along, you could in deference to your neighbours say, 'No', even though they may be perfectly OK. But now you can't: laws against this aggravate the situation. Nobody's going to tell a British person that he's got to be nice to that black man. You can pass laws till you're blue in the face, but if the white person A doesn't want to do something with black person B, you can't legislate him to do it. I deem it my own right to sell my house to whoever I want to sell it to. If Mr Black comes along with all the money, I can still tell him, 'No, I don't wish to sell the house.' That is only an example of how we do vent our feelings against these people. Other than that, I've got to the point where if I go from Edgbaston to Birmingham I'm always cheek by jowl, so they don't worry me particularly.

There are aspects of Mr Armitt's view to which many middleclass residents of Solihull and Edgbaston would take exception. Some, for example, would object to this crude image of West Indians having 'little between the ears', which he attributes to 'something genetic'. Others would endorse this stereotype. Yet the tone and thrust of Mr Armitt's argument speak in a general sense for the middle-class. The emphasis on the individual ethnic groups as perpetuators of their own problems reveals a faith in the power of minorities to modify themselves and lift themselves out of abjection, if only they have the 'urge and drive'. Seen in this light, anyone can bootstrap their way up the social ladder. It is as if we should acknowledge the obstacles erected by white racism – which Mr Armitt fully recognizes – yet never concede that they can impair a minority's progress. The only true impairment, the reasoning goes, lies within the group itself.

That impairment, simply stated, is an intransigence. By standing their ground and attempting to retain elements of their culture, certain minorities are demonstrating an unwillingness to become parts of mainstream society. As a condition of acceptance, they must become similar to whites. The opinion is common amongst the middleclass. Diversity is discouraged; success is often seen as contingent on conformity, 'toeing the line'. Asians have made incursions into commercial sectors on their own initiative, according to Mr Armitt. But they must break with traditions before prejudices against them will dissolve.

The dissolution, for Mr Armitt, cannot be accelerated by race relations laws that erode civil liberties, such as the freedom to choose to whom one sells one's property. The obverse idea that a black person with sufficient funds wishing to buy the house of his or her choice may have civil liberties denied them by racist sellers does not enter into this argument. Mr Armitt goes further in suggesting that firms such as his own would rather risk prosecution and operate a discriminatory policy than upset white members of the labour force who may object to working alongside ethnic minorities:

There's a lot of antipathy amongst white workers to sharing facilities with blacks, even things like toilets. You've got to keep your workers happy and, if the law takes your decisions away from you, you could be put in a dangerous position of taking on workers who you know are going to be rejected. A lot of the time, the employer wouldn't discriminate; it's his workers who won't accept the blacks.

This final strand of the argument gains the virtually

unanimous approval of the middleclass; civil liberty is sacrosanct, and legislation designed to diminish racial discrimination constitutes an attack on it. Any measure by which an individual's decision making facility is trammelled by government interference is wholeheartedly rejected. Those who have made their careers in commerce and industry are especially forceful in their arguments on this subject, which appears to them to be of critical importance to race relations in the UK. A great deal of their success is, they believe, based on fine judgement and sound decision-making. Discretion is therefore essential. Once the capacity to exercise this is compromised, then the basis of business success is threatened.

If you don't like it, go to Moscow, or the States

Arthur Mossley emphatically agrees with Mr Armitt's criticism of race relations laws and, indeed, of any legislation that interferes with a person's ability to discriminate: 'In fact, I'd go as far as to say that the only person who has no rights now is the white English male. You can't complain you're discriminated against. Everyone else has legislation to protect them.' A resident of Edgbaston, Mr Mossley is the managing director of a West Midlands business consultancy. In his fifty-six years he has worked in South Africa and Australia, and he has actively tried to adapt each time: 'I didn't stick it out and say, "I'm English and I'm going to have it my way." If you want to get anywhere you can't please yourself.'

As one might expect with this background, Mr Mossley is intolerant of groups which he regards as 'traditional': 'I think you have to be absorbed by the place you go to and I would hope that the coloured community will gradually be absorbed into the community as a whole.' Race relations laws have, in Mr Mossley's view, struck hard and damaging blows against this ideal. He outlines his reasoning:

The Race Relations Acts [1965, 1968, 1976] have not done anything. You can't compel people not to be prejudiced. You merely underline the fact that you have a problem; and the more you underline it, the worse it gets, because people are conscious of the problem. If you got rid of the Acts, I don't think the problem would be any worse.

If I was interviewing for an apprenticeship, and there was a white lad and a coloured and I wanted the white boy, I'd be thinking, 'How am I going to cover myself so that the coloured boy can't hit me with the Race Relations Act?' I wouldn't be picking the other lad because he was white, but because he was best. But I'd be worried of the effects of the Act; it makes people conscious of colour. If I'd got the choice of three equally suited people, I'd be hard put to choose between the Asian and the white man. I feel that, at a certain educational level, the Asian will probably pull ahead of the white person. I probably feel in my heart of hearts that someone of West Indian extraction is likely to be less educated and to have achieved a lower standard of living. Whether it's their own fault or ours I don't know. If I was looking for purely physical capabilities, I'd choose the West Indian because they're capable of superb physical work. Generally, if I was looking for a labourer, I'd go for the black man. For the skilled job, for the Asian or the white.

People such as Mr Mossley and Mr Armitt were in their mid-thirties or forties at the time of the first Race Relations Act and were established in business or private practice. Then new 'rules' were pushed before them. They were, no doubt, aware of the growing ethnic minority presence and the new debates it was prompting. Yet only at this point did it seem to affect them, and even then none too directly. The fact remained: they had, through their application and industry (and possibly a little family push), made a mark for themselves. It seems plausible to infer that, in the process of establishing themselves, they acquired some allegiance to the system of free enterprise. Their progress had been unfettered by the type of obligation the government was now forcing on them. Any constraint was unwelcome. So one which involved a command not to discriminate against groups that were, to many, deserving of discrimination was likely to be particularly unwelcome. It was almost a case of habits of a lifetime being bludgeoned to appease a few soppy liberals in the House of Commons. Yet there is a certain contradiction in the views of many of the elderly middleclass; for despite the undiluted criticism of race relations laws, there is an equally consensual agreement on the need for more restrictive legislation in the area of immigration control. 'Special circumstances' were thought to have arisen in the 1950s and 1960s, and – admittedly with the advantage of hindsight – many elderly middleclass whites feel that successive governments were excessively generous in regard to immigration policy. Whilst adhering to an unconditional *laissez-faire* philosophy in other areas of government, the elderly middleclass make an exception for immigration law. Eric Hemmings, quoted at the start of this chapter, supplies some background:

I think we've got ourselves in an impossible situation. Historically, everybody had British passports as a result of our empire. This is the price we paid. We had the policy in the 1950s of encouraging immigration, principally of West Indians; if you went to the West Indies in 1950, you'd have found they were actually advertising for people to come over and do the jobs we didn't want. That was wrong for an overcrowded island. Short term, good idea; long term, disastrous idea.

Keith Wark, however, thinks the idea was wrong even in the short term. 'We shouldn't have had immigrants in. I don't care whether they're ex-countries we ruled over in the British Empire,' asserts Mr Wark, still a company director at 71:

We gave them hell in the empire; but just because they had no freedom then doesn't mean they can have freedom in a different way now. They've become members of the Commonwealth, and all we should have done is have people who really wanted to get education, educated them and then said, 'Right, now go back to your own country and implement those things we've taught you. And, if you don't like it, fine; go to Moscow, or the States, or wherever you like. Don't expect to come here and enjoy ours because it's very serious and we don't want you here.' The politicians were blinded. 'They are part of the Commonwealth; they fought for us in two world wars,' they said. Of course they did, but I still wouldn't have given them full rights. I would have allowed in people who'd shown educational ability, the people who want to become doctors, civil servants and so on, given them three or five years of training and then sent them back. It's hindsight, I know, but even in those early days, we at the Rotary Club were saying, 'These people have got to stop coming in', and people turned their backs on it. The people who were coming over here were straight from the canefields.

We've always said, 'Anybody who's a member of our colonies is free to come into this country.' Undoubtedly there's a lot who come in just to draw the dole. I personally think we'd be much better off if nobody could draw national assistance until they'd been in a job for six months. They come here and, within a month, they're living off the state, whether they're black, yellow, or any other colour. I think that's wrong. I've got two Indian friends. One's a doctor and the other's a business associate, and they're always amazed at the number of Indians and West Indians floating around. Where do they all come from? Whereas they came in with nothing, they're now starting to climb the business ladder and very shortly, if we don't watch it, they'll be getting ahead of us.

When my sister emigrated to Canada, thirteen years ago, there were a lot of strict requirements which had to be met before she went; the fact that she had a British passport meant nothing at all. She had to have a strict medical examination and her husband had to give an assurance that they weren't going to need any form of assistance from the Canadian government. In other words: 'Yes, you can come in, but you've got to contribute something to the economy in the process', which I thought was a rather good idea. I think what rankles with the taxpayer is that a lot of them have come in over the years and we've had to support them. And they're astute enough to find out the best way of getting as much money as they possibly can, to the detriment of some of the English businesses. I don't say this lightly, because I've spoken to one or two of our employees who have left and who'd seen things going on whereby they can get money out of the country while we can't. I'm not going to do an Enoch Powell and say, 'Deport the lot of them!' That's quite impracticable. We're not the only country like this; Germany has got a lot of Turks creating an awful lot of trouble. I just hope to God they don't breed like rabbits till we're outnumbered. But I think they will.

As a lifelong taxpayer, Mr Wark considers he has contributed appreciably to the UK's economy and objects to what he feels is scrounging off the state. The main reason he feels that immigration control should have been more restrictive than it was is that mass migration has upset a kind of economic balance in which 'you can only get out of the system what you put in'. Unemployment, both seasonal and structural, is inevitable in any advanced economy, and he appreciates that; but those unfortunate enough to be out of work will have made some input in their tax and National Insurance contributions. This he can accept. What he can't agree to is the idea of migrants and their dependants entering the country, having made no significant contribution, and drawing out financial assistance. This wrecks the balance, in Mr Wark's opinion. He recognizes the moral dilemma involved in offering colonized countries citizenship rights and then reneging on them; but economic considerations override all others.

As its members will readily acknowledge, the middle-class is not beset by the same kind of problem as the workingclass and does not see race relations as problematic in the same way. The issues have been inflated so as to give the impression that a crisis is imminent. This only exacerbates the situation; what is required is more patience and a faith in the natural process of assimilation. Interference by governments may have been intended as a resolution but, in the middleclass perspective, it created new problems. Certainly, it did for this class of employers and entrepreneurs, whose freedom of choice was suddenly restricted and who were no longer at liberty to discriminate as they saw appropriate to their interests. The paradox is that more government interference would have been encouraged in the 1950s and 1960s when migration to the UK from the New Commonwealth peaked. Maybe the effects are not directly felt by employers and professionals, especially those nearing or in retirement, but there remains a strong sense of resentment. After all, they believe their contributions, made over perhaps a forty-year period, are being drained away by scroungers from overseas and their offspring, who have contributed little or nothing to the nation's economy.

The middleclass elderly share few of the worries that infect the workingclass. Their views are not motivated by insecurity over their houses or their personal safety. They are not destabilized by the prospect of their businesses or professions being taken over by ethnic minorities. They are, however, anxious about changes that threaten to upset the equilibrium they value so much. Too much cultural diversity can lead to the destruction of the homogeneous and standardized world in which they have prospered. Government intervention threatens to break the free spirit of *laissez-faire* which has been pivotal in their careers. A new growing generation of takers will paralyse the country's productive system. In their own lifetimes, they have seen the UK decline to the status of a secondary economic power; now ethnic minorities will help push it further downwards. Expressed thus, this last point tends to oversimplify the elderly middleclass perspective; for a great many residents of Edgabston in particular are careful to distinguish between different ethnic groups and to evaluate their contributions accordingly. We have already noted how the likes of Mr Armitt attribute to Asians some of the positive values traditionally associated with the Protestant ethic ('urge and drive', etc.) and credit them with making some attempt to integrate. Blacks, on the other hand, are depicted as fetchers and carriers. These are either bland assumptions or superficial observations; but other Edgbaston residents have thought more deeply about the reasons for such images.

There's a fine line between discrimination and preference

The manner in which the Jews have risen from the depths of material deprivation, displacement and centuries-long racism would be an object lesson for the ethnic minorities. Anti-Semitism, in all its monstrous forms, has devastated the Jewish community, socially and physically; yet, in many areas of the Western world, Jews have acquired the status of an élite group. They populate the boardrooms of commercial companies, fill influential positions in politics and occupy important roles in the professions. Their success in these areas has attributed, in part, to their past Diaspora. Scattered, fragmented and lacking both resources and cohesion, the Jews have faced the additional problem of racism and discrimination. The Diaspora is of paramount importance to the Jews, and they are continually reminded of their past deprivation; it contributes towards the community's integration and spirit of commonality – features which have helped build the Jews' success.

As might be expected, middleclass Jews feel a certain empathy with minority groups which are currently experiencing problems associated with racism: systematic exclusion from jobs, denial of access to property, physical and verbal abuse and so on. Many Jews have overcome these, yet are still aware of them, albeit from a safer distance than blacks and Asians. As a result, there is an understanding.

'I identify very much with the immigrants, especially the Indians, because I can almost see my grandfather when I see them with their turbans and beards,' Alex Zebrowski discloses. 'My father, as a boy, won scholarships to grammar school and then to university and a degree, but with my grandparents it was different – harder – and I see the same things now, the same problems. For instance, when our grandparents came across [from Poland] nobody helped them at all; they strove to get on.'

Mr Zebrowski is now 62 and was only a child at the start of the Depression. His grandfather, a Polish Jew, struggled in poverty virtually throughout his life, but provided his son with a reasonable education; the grammarschool place led to university and then to a ministry career. Mr Zebrowski himself is a dentist. His practice is in Edgbaston, where he also lives; it is, of course, an area to which many upwardly mobile Asians are drawn, and the parallels between the Jewish and the Asian experience are not lost on Mr Zebrowski.

I think you've got to compare the Jewish community with the Asiatic; they're striving also to get scholarships and improve themselves. The others, West Indians, could possibly be compared with the Irish in that they don't strive for academic work or to better themselves; they're both satisfied with labouring jobs, and that seems to be the sort of work they like to do. I think it may be something to do with the racialism amongst the various groups. I have a girl working for me who's Jamaican, and she has a child who's ready to go to school. So she asked me if she could go and look at a school. When she came back I asked her if she liked it and she said, 'No, there are too many Asians there.' So I said, 'I'm surprised that you say things like that.' She said, 'Well, they smell', and came out with all the usual things. It rather amazed me.

Then again, I've been up against this question all my life. When I was in the forces, I was posted to Egypt and we had to go the long way round via the Cape and we stopped at Freetown. The boat was taken into port by a coloured pilot, and he wanted to go ashore so he called the captain of a tug passing by and said, 'Can you give me a lift?' The captain said, 'Why should I give a coloured bastard a lift? Not on your life!' All the personnel standing with me were horrified that this man could call the coloured chap that. And then we went to Egypt, and after being there a year or so, all these chaps were exactly the same. In the hangars – I worked with aircraft; I was a fitter – we worked with Egyptians. One day I was standing there talking to this Egyptian and I had my arm around him. When I went back to the barracks they said, 'You ought to be ashamed of yourself putting your hands on a wog like that. *We* don't do that sort of thing.' Of course, we hadn't got the coloured population in this country at that time, so it was their first meeting with them.

I'm not sure things have changed to a great extent. I've always worked with coloured colleagues, like the coloured nurse in the surgery. The other girls get on all right with them, but at times they let things out. For instance, we had an Indian girl working and I noticed, if she ever brought food in, sweets and so on, not curries or anything, the other girls would put it in their mouths later and spit it out again, saying, 'Ugh, foreign muck!' I've had coloured staff for years, not because anyone said I had to have a certain percentage, but because they come to me and they've been the best, so I picked them. As individuals, they're different, but not because of their colour. They're at a disadvantage in the job market. Some of us are Jewish-looking, others are not; so it's not quite so marked there. I would have thought we'd have noticed prejudice much more if we were coloured.

I think something strange is happening. I see some of our people, the more religious, in a sense, sheltering behind the coloureds. Now, when I was a boy, however religious a person was, he would go to school, and everything was done for him to be as English as possible. My father wore a dogcollar; he had a university education, so he spoke good English, and he got a good synagogue job because of this. We were taught to be very patriotic to the extreme and rather play down the religion. We lived in the East End of London in the 1930s, the heart of Mosley's area. In those days you would have been too scared to wear your skullcap outside the house. Nowadays you see the more religious types with the heads covered. They feel comfort; they feel that wearing their little skullcap and one or two other things is nothing compared to a Sikh with his turban. They see immigrants and feel, in a way, they can shelter behind them. Rather interesting. I don't feel it's religious pride alone; it's mythology, keeping their difference.

Guided by his past personal experience, Mr Zebrowski believed at one stage that the tension of the late 1930s would dissolve, as would what was then called 'the colour problem'. 'I thought there is something in the English that's inborn: tolerance and understanding' – but not now: 'I don't see it. I don't believe it'll get worse, as some say; I believe their fears are ill-founded. I think the main thing that has to be done is to stop using being deprived as an excuse.' The lessons of the Jewish past are that adversity can be overcome and that perseverance is the quintessential characteristic:

People make being deprived the excuse. But it isn't the reason for not getting on. They encourage coloured to use it as an excuse. They feel they are more deprived and so expect them to commit more crime and hide behind the excuse. What annoys me is when a crime is committed and people say, 'Oh, it's living conditions.' With my grandparents in the 1930s, things were very bad indeed, but that was never an excuse for crime. Being out of work and living in poor conditions doesn't justify crime for anybody.

Mr Zebrowski speculates that people's awareness of skin colour will disappear in the future, but not the immediate future: 'Within two or three generations, I should think.'

Bernard Reuben agrees: 'I think the situation will change. I think employers will employ on merit. To my mind, there's no difference between a completely uneducated coloured boy and a noncoloured boy. I don't know how employers of labour view it now, but I think people will just as soon employ a coloured boy as anybody else in the future. I don't think it'll be a big issue in a few years' time.' Mr Reuben is also Jewish, and his conception of race relations concurs with Mr Zebrowski's in several, but not all, respects. He agrees that the current situation bears a resemblance to the Jewish experience, with the added ingredient of colour. The significance of this, he contends, will disappear: 'People are getting used to the idea of seeing coloured people now. Coloured seeking employment used to be unusual and a little bit unacceptable. They were strange, but now they're commonplace.'

Mr Reuben, who is company director of a fashion house is 65 and lives in Solihull, having been based in the West Midlands his whole life. His ideas are slightly more benign than Mr Zebrowski's possibly because of his lack of exposure to the cruder forms of racism; he is convinced that racism is simply a matter of unfamiliarity. 'If I was to say to you that an employer used to look at a coloured person and say, "My staff will feel uncomfortable working with him because he's strange, he's got different habits", I wouldn't call that racial. I think employers felt more that it was their staff that would object to working with the man than they objected to employing him.' In other words, the suggestion is that staff rather than employers have been chiefly responsible for excluding blacks and Asians from jobs.

'There's a fine line between discrimination and preference. You've got a man who's going to employ a person and he's got a coloured boy and a white boy and chooses the white boy. How can you prove discrimination? I don't think it's possible really: if the man says the white boy is the right choice for him, that's it.'

And if there is a firm that continually 'prefers' whites over blacks, or if property sellers refuse to sell to Asians?

This is a different aspect. I think that a body of people, say, a family, is entitled to ask into its home who it wants to. A golf club is a similar situation. Frankly, I can't see why a body of golfers, if they want to keep their club that way, shouldn't be allowed to. I can't see what a coloured would want to join the club for, if it didn't want him. I'm a Jew and I wouldn't want to go to a club that opposed Jewish membership. It happens, of course, so I can't see why coloured people don't adopt the same policy as Jews and have their own golf club, in the same way as an ethnic body puts up its own mosque, or whatever.

In Mr Reuben's perspective, there is nothing particularly problematic about perpetual discrimination. Taking note of the Jewish example, he advocates the setting up of ethnic businesses, exclusive social clubs, segregated property areas and so on. If ethnic minority individuals are excluded, they are inevitably going to generalize this experience and feel collectively excluded: 'It's for exactly this reason that the Jewish golf club was formed by a number of quite wealthy Jewish people who realized they didn't want to be members of clubs where they felt uncomfortable, even if they managed to get membership.' Mr Reuben, it should be stressed, comes from a relatively comfortable family background, his father passing the family business to his control more than twenty years ago. He has no personal recollection of being a victim of anti-Semitism, nor does he feel that racism has affected his career.

'The intensity of feeling against the Jews has probably died in the last thirty years, and I think this will happen to coloured people as well, given time,' he states.

It would seem that this view is based on the presumption that blacks and Asians will not remain socially isolated and materially poor. For Mr Reuben's argument is that ethnic minorities, repelled by certain areas of society, will generate stronger feelings of affinity, pool resources and build their own ethnically exclusive institutions.

Many might argue that Mr Reuben underestimates both the nature and effects of racial discrimination, but he anticipates the objection:

I don't really take the hard line that many people of my race would do. I'm quite happy to let people do what they want to do, to be free. I take moderate views about these things. If I meet you, I either like you or I don't. It doesn't mean to say I hate you. I don't want to mix with you socially; you're unacceptable to me. 'Anti-Jewishness' and anti-Semitism are two different things: 'anti-Jewishness' is not wanting to associate with Jewish people; anti-Semitism is something else, a hatred. If people have been brought up and taught to dislike Jewish people, that will stay with them for most of their lives, and they won't associate with Jews. They don't necessarily hate them as a race. It's a very fine distinction.

Too fine for some, who would want to argue that the effects are pretty much the same despite the slightly different thoughts and motivations behind them. Mr Reuben, however, feels that what is popularly mistaken for racism is, in fact, an 'anti-coloured' tendency based solely on unfamiliarity, an unfamiliarity he has experienced personally.

'I would have been about 6 or 7 when I first saw a coloured person,' he recalls. 'It was something unusual to me, and I suppose I didn't enjoy the experience because it was something I wasn't used to. But now I feel a lot of sympathy for them, even though I can't do much to influence things now.'

The last comment prefaces Mr Reuben's more general conclusions, which tie in perfectly with those of the other members of the elderly middleclass: 'I think it will change, gradually, in a natural way. It can't be forced upon people, which is why I talked about the membership of clubs. I don't think it's the right way: to make people accept people they don't want. I think attitudes will change as they have done towards Jews in a natural way over the course of time.'

The elderly middleclass perspective on race is wrapped up in a broader *Weltanschauung*, or world view. It is a view such people have acquired and internalized through their working careers and one to which they hold fast in their mature years. Their success has been based on certain principles and values that have proved sound and effective. They see little reason not to apply them to every possible area of life, including race relations. Centrally, they invest faith in the value of free competition and open markets as a way of encouraging excellence and flushing out the weak and inadequate. Any legal intrusion into 'natural' areas of social life is deemed undesirable and, ultimately, detrimental. Race relations legislation is a case in point: it introduces a forced compliance often against the wills and judgements of employers who have striven to make a commercial success of their business.

'What you put into the system, you take out' is a shorthand way of expressing another value: balance is maintained in the system while contributors continue to be the main beneficiaries of state assistance. The balance has been upset, however, by the entry of outside non-contributors, and the endproduct is a system overload. Not all migrant groups stand accused of overloading the system: entrepreneurial and professional Asians appear to have contributed their fair share. They, more than any other nonwhites, seem to embody the capitalist ethos: an acquisitive nature, a zest for hard work and an ambition many see as unsurpassed, even by whites. By contrast the other main ethnic group, West Indians, is generally disparaged, its relationship to British society being seen by many as parasitic.

The elderly middleclass has flourished in a society of patterned regularity and conformity to rules. It values strong norms and censures deviation. Asians, it is hoped, will in time assimilate to white standards; as their careers in white society progress they will 'whiten' themselves in attitude and posture. There is little tolerance of diversity and unorthodoxy, or for those not prepared to toe the line. Homogeneity is the desired goal. The elderly middleclass is confident this will come — not soon perhaps, almost certainly not in its members' lifetimes; but in due, natural course there will be an assimilation that will make redundant all questions relating to race. This view may come as relief to many, but perhaps not to members of ethnic groups too advanced in years to appreciate the predicted decline in racism. They have lived through the troublesome early period in British race relations and have emerged not wholly unscathed by their experiences. We turn to them in Chapter 10.

Chapter Ten

Swallowing the Bitter Pill
– Ethnic Minorities

I don't put it down to being black

In spite of the confidence of the elderly middleclass, there are some members of society who are equally convinced that racism will not disappear in time. 'Look at it this way: prejudice was here from the very beginning and so shall it be in the end.' The words are those of Grace Powers, a Jamaican-born woman of 51, who migrated to England in 1954 when she was 19.

I don't think it's something that anybody will be able to do anything about until the end of the world. It's not something that's strange to us West Indian people, because we are prejudiced in our own way. Putting it down to colour isn't bad in itself. If people are just talking about you, saying, 'I don't like you because you're white, or because you are black', then that's nothing at all to me. I remember when I was a child in Jamaica, there used to be some lighter-coloured people than myself and they used to have a thing about the colour bit, so that isn't strange. But it's when you get to victimization, then it's bad, if you're victimized *because* of your colour. If you can't get a job because of your colour, or you get the worst housing, that's bad. I don't put that down to prejudice, though: that's victimization.

Like Mr Reuben in Chapter 9, who distinguished 'anti-

Jewishness' from anti-Semitism, Mrs Powers believes that prejudice based on a dislike of a certain group of people is not particularly harmful. But when this is converted into a systematic exclusion from jobs or a denial of housing, she feels there are genuine victims. Mrs Powers, in her thirty-one years in the UK, has experienced both kinds. She followed her parents to Birmingham at the time of the mass West Indian efflux and, at the age of 27, married a West Indian carpenter, by whom she had two daughters. The marriage was annulled when she was 35, and she brought up the two children. They lived in a succession of council flats, ending up in Newtown in 1974. For the past six years she has lived alone. 'I wouldn't say it's any tougher living here than any other district. I haven't had so many problems with white people in Newtown as I've had with my own people.'

Mrs Powers's impression is that prejudice and victimization operate at two different levels. The levels equate roughly to what social scientists call personal and institutional racism. The first manifests in everyday encounters and involves a person or group singling out another person or group for unequal treatment. This, for Mrs Powers, is not particularly dangerous; she has been affected by it her whole life – even in Jamaica where fine gradients in skin colour may have social significance, and the lighter skin often carries more status and prestige. Mrs Powers claims she has also come face to face with this in the UK and she cites examples of being served last in a shopful of people, being refused admission to a workingmen's club, or, in the 1960s, being barred from using a laundrette.

Institutional racism usually involves organizations rather than people; individuals never have to accept responsibility for the racism, for it operates in an anonymous way. Mrs Powers refers to it as victimization, meaning that blacks as a category of people could be made to wait longer on housing lists or be prevented from getting a job on the grounds of their colour. This is not due to any individual's decision: it just happens that way. Take an example: in sections of industry, it could be that blacks are under-represented in the total workforce. Personnel department staff swear they are not racists; directors shrug their shoulders at the suggestion; trade union shop stewards find the idea absurd. No one, it seems, is denying blacks jobs. Yet they are still not getting the jobs. Why? The reasons for this may lie in the routine practices of the industry. Boards of directors and managers are probably all white, as are union representatives. Key positions are occupied by whites, who can make decisions that stick. The managing director of a particular organization might assert: 'This firm is not racist. I do not handle the recruitment, though.' Personnel boss: 'I'm not racist in my policies, but I do have to consider the people best suited to the jobs, and sometimes the unions are very fussy.' Union official: 'Neither I nor my union are racist at all, but some of my members, who've trained for years in this country to learn their craft, might object to having an immigrant, who hasn't achieved as much as them, working alongside them.'

And so it goes on. Nobody in the organization accepts the blame, but racism still exists, and blacks don't get jobs. Anonymous, institutional racism can be present in schools, hospitals, the housing market and virtually any sphere where there is the opportunity for what Mrs Powers calls 'victimization'. If change is to come, it will be initiated by 'the people at the top', she says. Her argument is that prejudice flourishes where there is racist victimization; and prejudice will not disappear.

Ordinary workingclass people haven't got much power, so they can't do much to improve the situation between black and white. People are like children; you get teachers, and people just follow what they hear.

I can't prove that it's happened to me, but I tend to think this is what's happening through my own experience. English people are no fools because they can do things to you that leave you, at the end of the day, feeling guilty, instead of *them* feeling guilty. Supposing they don't give you a job because you're black; it's only your feeling that it's because you're black. But if you go for a job and they say they haven't got a job for you, they don't say it's because you're black, they're much more polite than that. You have to prove it in a different way. Let's look at this house: there's a lot of things need doing to it and I've been to the council and nothing gets done. Now, if I like, I can put this down to the fact that I'm black, but where's that going to get me? Does that mean they'll come and do the repairs if I go down to the council and tell them that? They'll just look at me and say, "There's a million people in your position." And if it comes to proving it, they'll bring out a list of white people in the same condition. I don't prove a thing. I don't think it helps, because nothing's going to change people's feelings.

When Mrs Powers moved to the UK, she harboured a vague idea about a return to Jamaica at some unspecified time in the future, hopefully enriched by a prosperous stay in Britain. Such ambitions were common amongst early immigrants but so few were realized that the whole notion became known as 'the myth of return'. Even after marrying, she and her husband still talked about going back. Only after the birth of her second daughter did she resign herself to living permanently in the UK.

I wouldn't say my quality of life has improved in all the years I've been here. At the moment, I'm not working; I'm looking for a job. And I've got this [two-bedroomed council] house which isn't my own, but I'm not blaming anybody. I'm just one of many, therefore I can't blame society for my standard of life. I wouldn't put it down to being black; we've never had any real problems about being black.

She has heard disapproving comments in the streets, especially in the 1960s, and has been shunned by neighbours, although not in Newtown, but she dismisses such experiences.

It never bothered us [her family]. We got mixed into everything and we never got any *rejection* nowhere, from nobody. We don't stick with other black people; black people don't stick with other blacks just because they're black; it's just that around here you've got a lot of black people chunked together, thrown together, and a lot aren't working. I think the council thinks that we're supposed to understand each other better. But I don't think that's right. Say I wanted to borrow a pound from a friend down the road, well, she wouldn't have any money to lend me, so it doesn't make it any better. A lot of junk gets thrown into Newtown. I just put it down to the fact that the council thinks that people who are unemployed should be able to cope with each other better, whether you're white or black.

Younger members of the black community might call Mrs Powers a defeatist rather than a realist, for, although she has obviously come to terms with the problem of racism, she prefers to adapt to it and not confront – less still oppose – it. Like many other ethnic minority elderly, who migrated to Britain in the 1950s and 1960s, she was surprised at first at the way skin colour held social significance, a significance she had encountered in a slightly different way in the West Indies. It was hardly a devastating revelation, however, and she was able to negotiate her way through the next two decades. What bitterness she feels is not so much against white people, but against institutions which she feels are loaded against the interests of blacks.

Despite her low profile posture, Mrs Powers is critical of certain elements of British society. Other migrants of over twenty years' standing are more content.

'No problem to me at all,' Joan Ellis says, answering a question about the effects of racism and discrimination. 'When we first arrived, the English were stupid; they thought we were monkeys. But over the past twenty years attitudes are less ignorant. There are some who're still stupid, but they never bother us. I think they're getting more civilized now.'

Her 60-year-old husband, George, agrees, whilst acknowledging: 'It goes on behind your back. People in England don't discriminate against you to your face, but you know it's there. I don't know why they want to. I'm just happy with everybody.' The couple have been married for twenty years and have one son living in Birmingham and two daughters who were born in the UK but moved to Jamaica. The myth of return held sway with them.

'We always intended to return,' reflects Mr Ellis. 'But now we're well and truly settled. I honestly don't see what all the trouble's about half the time. Some of the people who complain have never seen the West Indies. They don't know; they haven't travelled; they've seen nothing, and they talk about "problems". They don't understand.'

Mr Ellis's contentment is not derived from the prosperity he has found in England. Anything but: he has worked as a factory piece-worker, a bottle washer and a swimming baths attendant; he was forced to stop work due to ill health after his second heart attack. Both he and his 54-year-old wife live on pensions in Chelmsley Wood, an area in which they feel 'lonely' but 'too old for a move'.

They don't punish; they nourish

No issue divides West Indian generations as fiercely as the police. Second-generation blacks in the UK are generally unremitting in condemning the police as racist intimidators. Older folk, such as Mr and Mrs Ellis, are equally unremitting in their eulogizing. 'I've got nothing wrong to say of the police,' asserts Mr Ellis. 'You've got to have authority to back the law. I can't live without the law, so why shouldn't I follow it? And if I don't, then I deserve to be punished. But I've never been ill-abused by the police'.

Mrs Powers, like Mr and Mrs Ellis, holds the British police in high esteem. But, while Mr and Mrs Ellis are firm in their criticism of younger generations, Mrs Powers is sympathetic:

I don't think the youth are to be blamed for everything, as they are. It may look as if they're more rebellious, but I'm not too sure if they even know what they're meant to be rebelling against, or what they're doing it for. At the end of the day, they're getting nowhere at all. They look as if they're a totally different generation to us, but I don't think they're more rebellious. They just need something to believe in.

Some commentators would contend that the growth of the rastafarian movement amongst black youths is a response to this need for 'something to believe in'. Indeed, my own study of the subject, *Rastaman* (1983), suggests that the movement is much more than this, in so far as it provides a mode of political expression for youths who felt the social system of Babylon inimical to their own interests.

Mrs Powers does not wish to dignify the movement in this way: 'The rastas today don't know a damn thing about rastafarianism. Maybe they're looking for some answers. But most of the people who came across in the fifties and sixties had it rough and it was the same for them and they didn't turn out to be rastas.'

Mr and Mrs Ellis are more forceful: they deny that there is a basic similarity between age groups.'They're completely different from us,' says Mrs Ellis indignantly. 'They seem to follow a doctrine: "Your ways are not my ways, so my thoughts are higher than yours." They're in a completely different world.' Mr Ellis believes that the much-discussed tension between black youth and the police is 'the youth's fault'. He is fulsome in his comments on this point: 'If I am on the streets any time of day or night, police don't stop me and ask me this and that. If police do so to younger blacks, it must be because of the way they act. They continually do things out of the law. They just demand things.'

Mr Ellis reasons that the stance adopted by black youth is due, in large part, to an absence of parental discipline:

The reason why a lot of kids are like they are is that the government takes away the father's authority over the child. If you handle the child like you should, the government is on your back. What my father and mother did to me and what we did to our children never did them no harm; it did them good. Say you have a child, and the boy becomes 16 and he's out till twelve, one, two o'clock in the morning. He comes in, and you say, 'Well, then? I been telling you that you shouldn't be out so late at night because you'll end up getting involved in things that don't concern you.' You give him a smack, and he goes straight to the police. The police come to you and tell you that, if you hit him again, they're going to lock you up. What can you do?

When youths go and do things wrong, they let him have probation. After a person has done wrong, he must be punished. But they don't punish; they nourish! Say I want to collect some money and I wait for you one night and lick the life out of you and take away your money. They catch me and what do they do? The whole country has to feed me. The only thing I don't have is freedom to run about. But if I start moaning, they give me time off. They're encouraging me to do wrong.

Mrs Ellis concurs, adding that schools are also contributors to the lack of discipline; they also teach 'sex education and a pack of nonsense'.

The Ellis account of alleged black lawlessness allows blame to settle not so much on the West Indian family, but on a state that has usurped too much responsibility from parents. Left to handle things in their own somewhat authoritarian way, West Indian parents would have instilled some orthodoxy into their children and, through compulsion, made them conform rather than resist in the manner of Leon and others in Chapter 7. Mrs Powers, on the other hand, is incredulous at the received wisdom about black youth's involvement in street crime. She believes the media have been myth-making; in her eyes, black youth are not the habitual criminals many take them to be. This view is consistent with her general apprehension of a continuity rather than a break between the generations and contrasts markedly with the Ellis perception. Without attempting to exonerate young blacks, Mrs Powers argued for a more rational assessment of their position. She also contests the popular view in Newtown that black youths prey on white victims only. In fact, she herself feels as much a target for muggers as anybody else:

When a mugger goes out to mug, I don't think he cares who the hell you are. The Asians are doing it, the whites are doing it and the blacks are doing it.

In Newtown, most of the crime is committed by black youths, but that's because they outnumber the whites here and in Handsworth. They don't care who their victims are. People reckon they don't pick on other blacks, but black people aren't as outgoing as whites. For instance, two old white ladies could be living in our flats and, if they get lonely and want to go for a walk, they don't stop and think; they just up and go for a walk when and where they like. And they become victims. You find most West Indian people, especially women, are more stop-at-home and, when they have to go out, they're accompanied by men friends or three or four other women. If somebody is going to mug somebody, he wouldn't mug a group; he'd go for one or maybe two. They don't go out of their way to mug white victims; they look for easy targets.

Mrs Powers is at what might be seen as the liberal extreme of the older West Indian community. Her calls for more tolerance and analysis are not widely echoed, and older West Indians are for the most part as uncritical in their acceptance of the present order of things as they are critical of the younger blacks who seem to be bringing the whole community into disrepute. Although they tend to resist comparisons, some West Indians acknowledge that the Asian communities have maintained an admirably tight grip on their younger generations and seem not to experience disciplinary problems in the same way as blacks. Yet older Asians are wary of changes in their own community; they more than West Indians have undergone cultural changes, the effects of which they have somehow had to contain. West Indians at least had the advantage of sharing some features with white society: language, religion, dress, a familiarity with the British education system. Most Asians had none of these in common.

I've heard the smell of our food frightens people

It is doubtful if any section of the population has been so thoroughly disoriented as older members of the Asian community. Migrating to the UK implicated them in huge changes. They entered an environment in which personal and social values were obscure. Customs, laws and mores were confusing, and tastes, preferences and habits be-wildering. Moving from the Third World into the First has been a momentous change for them. Apart from the physical environment, they had to contend with the technological environment which dominated people's lives, particularly in the cities, to which the original migrants gravitated in search of work. As if such changes were not in themselves enough, Asians, perhaps more than West Indians, had to endure the brunt of racist attacks. 'Pakibashing', as the ritual became known, was rife in the early 1970s and surfaced once more at the start of the 1980s. Racist hostility is even today most frequently vented on Asians, who have acquired a reputation for passivity, thus making themselves soft targets.

Twenty-five years after arriving in the UK, many Asians can still speak very little English. So dramatically different was the new world that many retreated from it, building ethnic enclaves in which traditional beliefs, values and habits could be perpetuated, in spite of the outside influences of modern industrial society. There is a great variation in the background and religion of Asians in the UK, a consequence of which different groups have adapted in different ways. Yet there is an underlying similarity in the methods used by Asians in maintaining ethnic boundaries and preserving cultural identities. Ethnicity is transmitted from one generation to the next by using Asian dialects, by teaching traditional religion and by instilling the values associated with the homeland rather than the 'new' society. In terms of perpetuating early ethnic subcultures, Asians have been successful. For how much longer? This is another question: younger groups steeped in a totally different culture will be absorbed much more readily than their elders and may fail to recognize the relevance of their traditional cultures. In itself this may further marginalize elderly Asians, as they see their children or grandchildren abandoning the beliefs and values that have been so integral to Asian ethnicity. The respect traditionally reserved for seniority is under threat, as is elders' wisdom. They can no longer demand respect as of right; instead they may receive ridicule for clinging to elements of the past which seem to have no purpose in modern society.

Rajkamauri Bhatti has grudgingly accepted that Asian youth are defining a new role for themselves in which they must separate from the traditional community. She understands why they move away from their home areas in search of jobs and promotion and why they will marry out of their religion. She regrets it, but sees it as inevitable. At the age of 52 and after seventeen years in the UK (always in Birmingham), she has become used to a new form of community, and this is reflected in her comments.

'I was 35 when I came here,' she says (with the assistance of her daughter):

My husband was 53. We met in Kenya. My greatgrandfather settled in Kenya in 1895 and for generations my family have been British subjects. Now we are here and my two children will be truly British. We are gypsies really. When we came to England, my husband and I had to split up for a short while and stay with friends and relatives. We had enough money to maintain ourselves for one year and put a deposit down on a house in Lozells. I had learnt English at school in Kenya, so we didn't have too much trouble. My husband found a job as a car mechanic and then began his own business, but he is too old now. But we were able to buy a better house here [in Edgbaston].

With many other Asians who migrated to the UK from Kenya in 1968, Mrs Bhatti became by default part of a national scare. Spurred on by parliamentary and press campaigns for restrictions on incoming migrants, the then Home Secretary, James Callaghan, passed a Commonwealth Immigrants Act (1968) that gained the dubious distinction of being, as the *New Statesman* put it, 'The first incontestably racialist law to be placed on the statute book.' The Act ensured that only those British passport holders with 'substantial connections' with the UK had an automatic right of entry. 'Substantial connections' were defined as having at least a grandfather born in Britain, a condition which facilitated the entry of many white British passport holders living in Australia, New Zealand, Canada and what was then Rhodesia (Zimbabwe), but which effectively blocked the entry of further Asians from Kenya holding equivalent passport credentials. The Bill passed through all its stages in a record three days, and within a month of the passing of the Act, Enoch Powell MP made his infamous 'rivers of blood' speech in Birmingham. The recession of the 1960s, although quite modest compared to 1980s standards, helped to sharpen the edges of the race issue. Conservative Party leader Edward Heath's decision to remove Powell from the shadow cabinet provoked a staggering workingclass response: thousands stopped work and demonstrated in support of Powell and his depictions of immigrants as threats to the nation. Petitions signed by trade union members were presented at Westminster; rallies were staged, and MPs opposing Powell were barracked.

It was against this background of widespread resentment and animosity towards the black and especially the Asian population that Mrs Bhatti and her family arrived in Britain. If they were to infer a message from the Labour Party's legislation it would have been: our existing anti-discrimination laws should assure you that we are doing all we can to preserve your rights as equal citizens of the UK but, as our new immigration law makes clear, we don't want any more of your kind here! Yet, while Mrs Bhatti remembers a general and expected sense of dislocation, she cannot concentrate her mind on specific instances of racism:

I suppose if I had been looking for it, it would have been there, but I couldn't exactly say people were so unfriendly. Really, we got a lot of help when we first came to Britain, mainly from elderly people. We probably stuck to each other as a family to start with, but we never went through the terrible times that some Asians go through. Mostly, English people either ignored us or helped us out.

This early experience formed a kind of matrix for Mrs Bhatti's later impressions, especially of life in the innercity:

Prejudice does happen and it will happen if we go out to the countryside and places out of the city. But people there are not only prejudiced towards Asians, they're prejudiced towards the Irish and Scottish as well. This is what I have understood, and we should not go to areas where we're not accepted. Now, we don't go out very much at all. We did feel as if people didn't want us when we went out looking for a house. I don't know where this attitude of prejudice comes from. I've heard that the smell of our food frightens people, or perhaps they think we're dirty. I have to admit that some Asians are dirty; it's because they come from different backgrounds of poverty. I'm not speaking badly about white people now, but I think they become very depressed and worried over nothing, whereas Asian people can afford to put up with problems. White people can't put up with even minor problems and they become very corrupted. For instance, now that unemployment is high, they are blaming the Asians for it.

They are forgetting the fact that Asians came into the country because they needed them for jobs; many Asians helped start industries. So they must realize that, if there is unemployment, it's not the fault of Asians. What the English are now doing is injecting the thoughts of prejudice into their children's heads. I think Asian people will fight back against these ideas. Naturally, if someone is attacking you, confronting you, you have to do something, retaliate. And Asian people have only just started to do that. They seem to put up with a lot naturally, but they must snap if pushed too hard.'

Mrs Bhatti's daughters were children when they first arrived in the UK; now they are grown and have children of their own. Maintaining her daughters' ethnic identity was no particular problem to her, but she anticipates problems with her grandchildren. This is why she would like to see the whole family stay in the area:

We have a mosque now, which we didn't when we first came. The schools have begun multicultural education and I think this is very important for the children: they must celebrate different festivals from their own and other children's cultures. They also have special concessions for Muslim girls to be allowed to wear trousers. I think that, if white children are confused about this, or even if our own children are confused, then it is the fundamental duty of parents to explain the differences between them to their children to help them understand the differences in people's cultures. We need to explain who we are and where we belong. If I go to a Western society and dress in Western-style clothes and pretend to be a Western person, will I be accepted as one? No, I wouldn't. I have distinct looks and distinct ways. But I also think people from Asia tend to be narrow minded; if they are in England, they must also learn some of the methods and ways of English people.

The English always write about prejudice and discrimination, but they don't realize that Asian people have often been through worse times than this. If youths spit at you or call you names or beat you, this is still small. Some people have lost their homes and have lived in poverty or have had to leave their family and live in different lands. Asians have been forced to do these things, so prejudice is a very small thing by comparison.

Mrs Bhatti's suggestion is that Asians, if only because of their history, have become toughened to the rigours of life. Having to contend with racialist discrimination, even if it manifests in physical violence, is not a huge problem. Asians, she goes on to argue, retaliate indirectly, progressing in education and building businesses, rather than meeting fire with fire. 'There's too much fuss made about prejudice,' she insists, perhaps surprisingly in view of the continued reportage of attacks on Asians. But she qualifies this: 'If the press ignored it, it might go away; making it public makes others want to join in.' The sensationalist coverage afforded 'pakibashing' in the 1970s goes some way to supporting this view.

She is aware that many Asians have had to swallow a bitter pill, but for her own part has always found life satisfactory. What fears she does have are not of the whites:

I've got good neighbours on both sides of me, so that's some comfort. But I'm always worried about who will move in. I'm especially worried about West Indians. I think there are certain West Indians and Asians also who create a bad name for everybody. We used to live next door to a West Indian family which was very bad. Some were rastafarians, and I think they burgled our house. After that, we had some English move in, and they were violent, so they were nearly as bad. They weren't violent to us, but to their own family; he used to drink a lot and break windows and things. But they aren't like all English. I have known many English friends and I haven't experienced any racial antagonism from them. They have been very nice to us over the years.

Mrs Bhatti is acutely aware that Asians have been singled out by many reactionary groups, particularly innercity youths who make assaults on Asians an almost ceremonial event. 'My husband was attacked on two occasions for no reason, but I don't think the people who did it were like all English; they were idiots.' Mrs Bhatti knows of the intensity of anti-Asian feeling in some sections of the community and of the fears of an Asian takeover, at which she scoffs:

What they don't see is ordinary people like myself. I have no fortune and the friends I have who do have shops or firms are not rich people just because they can own their own houses or drive their own cars. The secret of these Asians is that, first, they have to be business minded and, second, you must have a family. I have seen people start businesses with nothing at all. I have seen shops where I have had to add up all the groceries for myself and tell the shopkeeper how much it is because he didn't speak good English; but he kept trying and trying till he made the shop a success. You see it in an area like Lozells, where one shop is taken over by Asians and suddenly all the shops are run by Asians and there is hardly an English shop left. I use Asian shops for everything. I go to the city centre when I need something special. I think Asians seem to make good businesses in poor areas; the more you go into poorer housing areas, the richer the Asians are. I suppose it's because they know how to survive better.

It is interesting that not one of the ethnic group members featured in this chapter denies that racism exists or that it can have deeply injurious effects; yet they all feel the need to downplay its impact in their own lives. It is as if they accuse writers like myself of exaggerating racism and discrimination, pointing up its existence and the damage it can cause to people's lives, whilst, in reality the recipients, being no strangers to problems, manage to pull through their tribulations adequately. These are older members of the ethnic community and are perhaps less inclined to protest as vigorously as younger members. They have acquired in maturity the quality of stoicism – not a desirable quality as seen by more militant ethnics, but one which has enabled them to withstand some of the adverse treatment administered, especially in the late 1960s and early 1970s. Their postures are built on the perception that life is hard enough for a migrant without bringing additional problems to bear by making grief public. They had the benefit of a facility that enabled them to analyse present circumstances and compare them with past ones. Both past and present are unsatisfactory in their own ways. The general conclusion seems to be: it's not perfect here, but it's still a shade better than what we've been through before, so why shout about it? Memories are full of worse problems than these. Such a conclusion has kept the older ethnic minority generation in a low profile.

Part Four

Problem-Solvers of the Future

Chapter Eleven

Multicultural Challenges
– Schools

At the end of the day, they all live in England

The headmaster of Firs Junior School, Chelmsley, has an assumption. 'Everyone has a certain degree of racialism in their make-up. Somewhere deep down, there's a certain resistance in everyone, and how it shows itself depends on many things. One's education is often the counter to this. Basic racialism is a root feeling, and I can only hope that our educational development at a personal level is a sufficient cover to keep it under control.'

This idea is shared by many other headteachers, for example, the head of St Catherine's Roman Catholic School, in Edgbaston: 'In a sense everybody's prejudiced; it's in our blood, isn't it? I suppose it's because we ruled the bloody world, the English. So we are prejudiced, and I am conscious that we have to change.'

And at Solihull's Tudor Grange High School, the head-teacher's view coincides: 'Everybody is prejudiced. Xenophobia is there and, if you deny it, you're living in cloud cuckoo land. It's a very natural thing to fear strangers. The difficulty is to get over it.'

Few teachers in any part of the country would deny that racism affects their schools, indeed the entire educational system. Not all would agree with the previous views that everyone is racially prejudiced or that education is merely a 'cover', something to keep prejudices under control. Many would argue that education can and should forestall racism: presuming that racist ideas abound in society and reach the child via many different influences, formal education offers alternatives which can give the child sufficient intellectual equipment to repel the ideas or at least deny them credibility. Whether one believes racism is inevitable or contingent on other conditions, however, does not necessarily interfere with educational policies in regard to racism: the official line is that it will not be tolerated. For instance, the City of Birmingham's Education Committee, in its report to the Chief Education Officer (February 1984), identified three main objectives in regard to race and ethnic relations. They were:

(1) Preparing all pupils for life in a multicultural society, building upon the strengths of cultural diversity.
(2) Providing for the particular needs of children, having regard for their ethnic, cultural and historical background.
(3) Being aware of and countering racialism and the discriminatory practices to which it gives rise.

There is a virtual unanimity in all education authorities in England and Wales about the desirability of these aims and the urgency with which they should be achieved. Yet there is no corresponding consensus about the content or application of policies designed to achieve them. The four areas in focus – Newtown, Chelmsley, Edgbaston and Solihull – were chosen specifically to reflect national patterns and, in the sphere of education, they do: a mishmash of different and, sometimes, contradictory policies applied unevenly and without clear purpose.

It is impossible to exclude education from any discussion of race and ethnic relations. Some would emphasize its reactionary value as an ideological support for a capitalist system based on class inequalities. The educational system is seen as a mechanism through which capitalism disseminates beliefs and values about the legitimacy of the existing structure of society. By imbuing children and youths with a commitment to society, it minimizes the possibilities for serious criticism or opposition. Education, the argument runs, is part of the state's apparatus for perpetuating the system and maintaining a solid status quo. Cast under a different spotlight, education is seen as a positive and essential experience: first, by equipping the child to be an aware, sensitive and contributing member of society; second, by providing the opportunities and resources to enable the child to gain the qualifications that may lead to a well-paying, prestigious job; and, third, by learning from and about others the child may liberate him- or herself from the ignorance and prejudices of preceding generations.

Education authorities naturally favour the second perspective and attempt to arrange their schools' curricula and services so as to enhance children's awareness, maximize their opportunities to succeed and liberate themselves from nescience. The 1944 Education Act, the cornerstone of the UK's educational policy, provided universal secondary education for all children up till the age of 15 (now 16) free of charge and so established the basis for equality of opportunity for children regardless of class background and ethnic origin. This, at least, was the theory: in practice, class and ethnic backgrounds continue to exert decisive influences over the quality of education a child will receive and therefore over his or her ultimate destination in society.

Multicultural education (mce) is, in essence, a mode of teaching and curriculum design intended to reflect the pluralistic, or multifaceted, nature of society. So, where there is ethnic diversity, education should mirror this. As originally conceived, mce was thought to be relevant only in areas where more than 2 per cent of children on school rolls were of New Commonwealth or Pakistani background. Financial assistance was made available to authorities in these areas under Section 11 of the 1966 Local Government Act. This was amended in 1982 to include areas showing 'substantial numbers' of ethnic minority children in their schools. As a result, an area such as Barnsley, with a predominantly white school population, is ineligible for funds, whereas nearby Bradford, with a large ethnic population and many years' experience with mce, has had finance available and has expanded programmes so that they reach all white areas under the authority's control.

In Solihull the Director of Education, sees little use for mce, arguing: 'Although we are fully aware of the problems of multi-ethnic groups . . . we have very few children from ethnic minorities in our schools . . . and we have not as yet had to formulate a written policy, nor have we begun any initiatives.'

The implication is that mce is for the benefit of ethnic minority pupils, rather than their white counterparts. Throughout England and Wales there are local education authorities without any multicultural policy that have had very few ethnic pupils and fail to see the relevance of mce to their area because of this fact. Yet almost exactly the opposite awareness is shown in some other areas without ethnic minority populations. For example, Suffolk's policy statement acknowledges that, in a rural area such as it is,

the relevance of making a positive approach to multicultural education may not be immediately apparent . . . However, multi-cultural education implies far more than such limited contact with ethnic minority groups; it involves the whole of the education service in preparing its members to take their place in the society in which they are living. All children . . . need to be given an understanding of how society changes and of the constituent groups within that society.

Sunderland's Director of Education goes further in

arguing that mce is 'even more necessary' in areas of low ethnic density.

The Solihull stance is in direct contradiction to this. According to the headteacher of St Peter's Roman Catholic Secondary School (2.85 per cent ethnic enrolment), it 'reflects the view of the majority of people in the borough'. But the view is not above criticism: 'I think there's a certain smugness in Solihull; too much affluence is a weakness. School curricula do need to change, but if we tackled it by calling it "multiethnic" or "multicultural", we'd attract quite a bit of hostility. To tackle it directly would cause problems.'

The reasons for his believing this are spelled out by the head of Tudor Grange School (1 per cent ethnic enrolment):

In this area, parents are very, very success conscious. They want their children to emerge at the end of their schooling with nine or ten O-levels, and if you attempt to introduce anything that appears to them to be a waste of time, they're against it. We've tried two periods a week of General Studies with a moral-ethical element – racism comes into it – for fifth-years. Now, if we introduced even that on a bigger scale there would be considerable parental opposition.

Some heads agree with the basic conservative principle. 'I've no misgivings on the idea that people should understand each other despite their backgrounds,' states Solihull's Malvern Hall Secondary School's headteacher. 'I've just got reservations on balance. At the end of the day, they all live in England and they ought to know their own culture, the traditional one.'

And, back at Tudor Grange:

I do think that *if* you were in an area that is dominated by an ethnic population, you would have to make certain adaptations in the curriculum to suit that area. I can't see sense in teaching children from other cultures solely a British-oriented curriculum.

But I would be absolutely against switching from the British-oriented one entirely; because, if there is to be any bias in the educational system, it should be towards the British traditional subject areas.

Such sentiments however, cause some embarrassment amongst other headteachers of the area. 'I don't go all the way with the official Solihull viewpoint. Just because you don't have ethnic minorities doesn't mean to say you shouldn't give some thought to the position in the country as a whole,' suggests the St Peter's Roman Catholic School headteacher. 'We try to encourage wider perspectives, and I think we've got to prepare pupils for the society in the country at large, making children aware of the problems.' Similarly, at Alderbrook School (1 per cent ethnic enrolment), in Solihull, the headteacher believes that 'Even though we have a very low percentage of nonwhite and nonBritish children in this school, the pupils will be in situations where their attitudes and understanding will be influential and important. I think that it [mce] should be part of the compulsory core of the curriculum in all schools.' Neither school has initiated any planned mce programme as yet, however.

It could be argued that, no matter what *ex cathedra* statements pour out of the education authority's office, the individual schools in every area will operate with a fair degree of independence and tailor their curricula and pedagogies to suit their own requirements as they see them. Birmingham has a monitoring unit to try to ensure consistency in its schools' implementation of mce, but Chelmsley schools have no equivalent. 'It isn't so much a policy in Chelmsley as a lack of one,' observes the head of Simon Digby School. 'I would imagine that, if we as a school wanted to introduce multicultural education and set about doing it, there wouldn't be any objection. So I can't really blame our negligence on the authority.' She goes on:

The thing is, we've been looking at our curriculum and we've got to be concerned about special needs, about language across the curriculum, about the equality of the sexes in education. The fact that we've not got round to it is not because we don't believe in it; it's just the problem of having to do the day-to-day bit and then introduce new ideas into the curriculum. It's just time. The fact that we're able to indulge in this negligence is because there are no major issues forcing us to face up to it. Nothing positive is done to go against multicultural education. What we haven't done is look at the issue as a whole and make sure it is done.

No primary or secondary school in Chelmsley has a planned mce programme. Presumably, it will take the aforementioned 'major issue' to prompt some initiative. This is, of course, a euphemism for a high ethnic minority enrolment, and in this sense the issue has been confronting Newtown schools for between ten and fifteen years. Mce underwent a kind of evolution, as depicted by an Anglesey Junior School teacher:

The first stage we went through was the area of Black and Brown Studies. We felt we must do something to reflect the cultures of the children who were in the school. But that developed into a realization that, with a lot of things we were doing, it was *how* we were doing them, as well as *what* we were doing, that was important: teacher attitudes particularly, and the expectations that we had of children. There have been a number of people in the school who thought that, because they came from the workingclass or ethnic groups, these children didn't have much ability. They were overlooking the point that these children are exceptionally talented; a number of them are operating in four languages, which quite a few of us could never do. The talents are different, but they are there nevertheless, and we should be making the most of them.

Teachers in Birmingham's workingclass innercity areas work in schools housing appreciable ethnic populations. In Newtown at least three schools have 95 per cent ethnic minority enrolments. So a sensitivity to the issues is expected. 'Good teaching practice' is what they aim at above all else. English as a Second Language is taught in all Newtown schools; inservice training is a continuous facility; curriculum topics are constantly revised in attempts to eliminate bias; parent–teacher contacts are fostered; but, as one head puts it: 'There's no substitute for good teaching practice … and this is learned through classroom experience.'

Schools are, in some ways, microcosms, miniature representations of the areas in which they are situated. 'The school itself reflects the area that it draws from,' observes the head of Chadvale Infants' School in Edgbaston:

It's almost like a village situation here; it nestles in a wood, with a brook going down the side. On the one side of the school, the housing starts at £80,000 and goes up; on the other the prices stick at £50,000. Our ratio of children is about 99 per cent Anglo-Saxon, and most of the children here come from a very well-equipped – for want of a better word – background. Most schools I've taught in before get a large number of children in such economic circumstances that they get free school dinners. Here there are four or five children out of 217.

I suppose initially most teachers here would have said, 'There's no need for us to look at multicultural approaches to subjects, because our children are not multicultural.' But even if schools don't necessarily have a cross-section, they don't live in a cushioned world. Kids here are privileged and ought to be made aware of what goes on in the rest of society. They walk down the street and see people with knotted handkerchiefs on their heads, with turbans, or a black face wearing rastafarian colours. They have to come to terms with this.

Such liberal outlooks are not typical of Edgbaston schools, most of which adopt a 'colour blind' approach, refusing to keep records of pupils' ethnic backgrounds and avoiding wherever possible the intrusion of ethnic issues in the curriculum. Coming under Birmingham's education authority, all Edgbaston state schools have a commitment to mce, technically at least — although, being the area it is, Edgbaston tends to remain aloof. Lee Mason School's head summed up the feeling, with his 'inbuilt suspicion' of radical changes. 'But,' he continues, 'if I had the Brixton riots on my doorstep, I might think differently' (41 per cent ethnic minority enrolment at his school).

There exists a deep conservatism in Edgbaston, a resistance to changes, especially those imposed by governments, which are tantamount to unwanted interference. Echoing the *laissez-faire* ideals of many of the area's residents, the headmistress of Edgbaston High School for Girls, which has about 9.4 per cent ethnic minority intake, opines:

I think most of the nonBritish parents who inquire about the possibility of their daughters coming here are looking for what they consider to be a British education, which is, incidentally, far more traditional than what even *I* would consider to be a British education. They're very ambitious, wanting their children to get on . . . But, obviously, as an independent school, we're not typical.

Research conducted by Parminder Bhachu supports this claim. She found that ethnic minority parents were interested only in securing their children qualifications and cared little for multicultural initiatives (1984).

Needless to say, Newtown and Chelmsley have no independent schools. Edgbaston and Solihull have six each, and, like every other public school in England and Wales, they operate no programme or policy of multicultural education. Across the board, independent schools demonstrate a complacency in their attitude to ethnic issues. The complete absence of anything resembling multicultural education is justified either by invoking the free market model, *à la* Edgbaston High, or by the Solihull-type use of the exclusion clause — initiatives are not required because the number of ethnic minority pupils is small.

'If one can imagine a school with above 75 per cent nonBritish pupils, I might be saying something different,' acknowledges Edgbaston High's head. 'But I still wonder whether the parents of that 75 per cent wouldn't be wanting a traditional British education. So I think I'd still be providing what they want.'

The point about independent schools is that they are exactly that: independent. Even in areas where local education authorities strenuously encourage multicultural policies, independent schools remain untouched. Inertia is a virtue in their eyes, and they hold on to Anglo traditions in the face of fairly widespread changes in education. Convenient as it is to ignore them, it is sobering to remember, as the head of Edgbaston's local authority Lee Mason Secondary School points out: 'Multicultural education is just as important in Solihull as it is in Aston. Especially in Solihull because they're the people who'll pull the power strings.'

Children currently being educated in independent schools are not the milkmen, assembly workers or unemployed of tomorrow. These are the people who will occupy key positions in society, in government, industry and the Civil Service – precisely the positions that give incumbents the potential power to change the shape of race relations. It is unlikely that the children of Newtown and Chelmsley will exert decisive influence on future society, much more likely that Solihull and Edgbaston children will. So it is perhaps disconcerting to realize that our future controllers are being educated in public schools offering little or no conception of the realities of a multicultural society. (See my article with Carl Bagley, 'Colour blind' (1985) for an expansion of this argument.)

In Heathfield Primary School on the outskirts of Newtown, there are 20 white children out of 298 on the school roll (6.71 per cent); the numerical majority is Asian. As part of a project, pupils were asked to depict a sporting scene of their choice, and their efforts would collectively form a frieze in the main hall. A group of black 10-year-olds chose to paint a cricket scene. Cricket is dominated by the West Indies national side, so it was a surprise to the school's headteacher to find the pupils had given the cricketers on their mural white faces. 'We've been using multicultural teaching here for years, and I thought we'd moved on from this business about black kids suffering from lack of self esteem and whatnot. But I had to scratch my head over this one.' He asked the artists their reasons: 'But none of them could answer why there were no blacks in the picture. They just shrugged their shoulders. And I thought then: there's still a lot of work to be done.'

The admission is laudable. Yet there remains the fact that, whilst of the four areas in this study Newtown has made most progress towards a genuinely multicultural education system, in a sense it needs mce the least. In recognizing that one of the central aims of mce is 'countering racialism and the discriminatory practices to which it gives rise' (see page 200), we have to confront the uncomfortable possibility that these are peculiarly white characteristics. One of the best conditions for the erosion of racism and racialism is sustained social contact and interpersonal relationships between ethnic groups that it produces. Newtown is conducive to this. The other areas are not nearly so conducive; so maybe it is in these predominantly white areas that multicultural programmes should be most advanced. After all, it is germane to multicultural philosophy that white children should benefit, perhaps more so than ethnics, from the expansion of awareness that mce is supposed to bring about. If multicultural education is about combating or forestalling racism, then its relevance is greatest in areas where there are few other resources with which to fight it. In other words, areas like Solihull, Chelmsley and, to a lesser extent, Edgbaston, precisely the areas where mce is least developed and where it is regarded as least relevant.

Only 14 per cent of the child's time

'Two years ago, we lifted up a child's desk top and there, written underneath, was, "We want jobs not wogs." And the child was asked, "What do you mean, wogs?" There were one or two West Indian children in the class. "Do you mean them?" the child was asked. "Oh no, I didn't mean them; they're my friends." ' The story comes from Firs Junior School in Chelmsley. The headteacher summoned the boy and told him: 'If your father thinks that way, that's up to your father. But there are other ways of thinking, and it's up to you at your age [13] to realize that there are alternatives and perhaps you should be thinking about what others have to say.'

In an area like Chelmsley, the potential for a conflict between ideas and values learned at home and those encouraged at school is great. As we have seen in previous chapters, racism filters down the generations, and, deprived of exposure to alternative images, children rely on those gleaned from parents and the media. More often than not, they unquestioningly accept outmoded stereotypes. Given the limited ethnic population of Chelmsley, the scope for modifying these stereotypes is small. The small numbers of blacks and Asians who are personally encountered are perceived as exceptions to the stereotypes: 'I didn't mean *them*.'

Another illustration of this type of excepting process comes from nearby Hodge Hill Comprehensive School for Girls, where the headteacher recalls a line of 13-year-olds awaiting a medical examination. The doctor appeared; he was Asian. 'Christ, I don't know what I'll do if they ask me to take my clothes off in front of a black man,' said one of the white girls, sounding alarmed. Overhearing her, the head-teacher interrupted. 'What about Meena and Rubeena and your other friends? They're the same colour.' About 55 per cent of the school's roll is of Asian background. The white girl didn't even hesitate: 'But they're different; they're my friends.' As the headteacher comments: 'They actually separate out the stereotyping from their daily experience.'

Hodge Hill is exceptional in its high Asian profile. It is situated on the extreme edge of Chelmsley and its catchment area has a large Asian concentration, unlike Chelmsley itself. The example, however, does point up the power of parents' views and ideas in influencing the outlook of children. Presuming that racism is not a totally natural phenomenon and something we inherit, we are drawn to the conclusion that it must be learned. Sure, the propensity to prejudice and discriminate against groups or categories of people is built into our physiological makeup, but the manner in which this propensity is converted into ideas and actions is influenced by social factors. Children draw ideas from parents: many parents have racist ideas; schools are committed against racism. So the child is sometimes at the centre of a conceptual tug-of-war. The problem is summed up by a Firs Infant School teacher: 'If we're teaching children in school about racism and the problems for black people, and they're going home and getting a completely different set of ideas from their parents, they won't know which way to turn.'

Researchers on both sides of the Atlantic have for long debated the relative influences on the child of the home and the school. Way back in the 1930s E. L. Horowitz completed a study of United States children and concluded that negative evaluations of blacks were not determined by contact with black people, but by contacts with influential people, mainly parents, who held negative evaluations (1936). Many studies since then have thrown up contradictory evidence, some laying the accent on the family as the dominant influence, others emphasizing the school and still others introducing other factors to account for why the school can assume prime importance in some contexts and not in others. In short, there is no clear association between parents' attitudes towards ethnic minorities and children's attitudes.

Paul Hartmann and Charles Husband produced interesting evidence, suggesting that some areas of high immigrant settlement in England had norms, or unwritten rules of thought and behaviour, of hostility towards blacks (1974). Each area's norms, they concluded, had a greater effect on the development of racism than did parents' attitudes. Parents' influence on children's attitudes and beliefs was not dismissed, although no direct relationship was found. Yet, even allowing for the impact of area norms and the absence of a *direct* transmission of attitudes, it would be foolish to underestimate the power of parents' beliefs on their children. It is difficult to imagine any child not in some way influenced by his or her parents' beliefs about and attitudes towards ethnic minorities. Even if parents make no conscious attempt to teach their children to adopt a particular outlook, it is still highly unlikely that children's thoughts will remain uninfluenced by them. As Alfred Davey points out: 'Children's attitudes towards minority groups will be fashioned through the kind of social education in human relationships provided by parental example, and the beliefs and sentiments implicit in their reactions to various cultural differences' (1983, p. 148).

A child's perspectives are forged in many different contexts, and many of the influences may clash. Inevitably, a child acquires negative evaluations of others as he or she picks up prejudices about 'us' and 'them': learning the patterns of association and disassociation, the linguistic labels that can be applied to people they include and those they exclude and the behaviour appropriate to each. The category of race reduces ambiguity and helps the child superficially to order and rank his or her environment. Since all schools are more or less committed to less divisive perspectives there is the possibility of conflict. For seven hours a day, five days a week, children may develop in an atmosphere untainted by stereotyped images, prejudicial outlooks and racist theories. But once outside the school gates, they may well return to a situation in which racist identifications and evaluations are norms which are reinforced daily.

Imagine a child's quandary when he returns home from school to tell his father, 'Dad, at school today we learned about how black peoples were taken from Africa, chained up and made to be the slaves of whites.' 'Too bloody right as well,' his father answers, confirming the factual reality of the lesson whilst undermining the moral message imparted at school. This can manifest in the child's posture at school and may eventually be drawn to the attention of the head, as has been the case at Castle Vale School:

Oddly enough, when I've approached white parents, they've always made out, 'Oh, he didn't get it from me: he must have picked it up from the playground or on the street.' They will never admit to it, never admit to being racially prejudiced. I can only think to one parent admitting to be racially intolerant. She was very racially prejudiced and she was rude to an Asian chap at a parents–teachers meeting.

Racist name-calling, graffiti and physical intimidation are much bigger and more regular problems in Chelmsley and Newtown than they are in the other two areas. Understandably, the school personnel are more adept at dealing with them. The head of Heathfield Primary School gives an example:

The worst thing you can do is announce it in assembly or anything public like that. I had a chap here in my office for calling somebody a 'black bastard'. I said 'What did you call so-and-so?' 'Nothing, sir.' 'You're lying.' 'A black bastard, sir.' 'I see. Why?' 'Dunno, sir.' So I said, 'Well, I'll tell you one thing now. In this school we've got children from all parts of the world, all colours, all religions. Now, have you heard this from home?' Because I think there's a certain populace around here like that. 'Yes, sir.' So

213

I said, 'I don't care where it comes from; what's more important is that I'm not having it in this school.' Full stop. Now, I dare say I haven't converted him.

So what happens if the child goes home unconverted and tells his father, who happens to hold his racist views very clearly and objects to some 'wet' liberal-type schoolteacher telling his son what to think and what not to think?

I say to the father his views are wrong in my opinion. They're his views, and if he wants to have them at home, that's his choice. I can do nothing about that. But what I'm positive about is that, if his children persist in using language like that and offending people, I'll throw his kid out. That's his choice. I know it's just shifting the problem on to somebody else, but what else can you do?

No headteacher in any of the areas could answer that question constructively. Technically, the headmaster would not be able to 'throw' the child out.

This is a familiar problem to all teachers in workingclass areas, less familiar but not unknown to those in middleclass areas. 'You may well be getting this indoctrination from the outside,' the headteacher of Edgbaston's Harborn Secondary School would tell the offender. 'You may well believe it. But that's not what we believe and we don't want it here, so change while you're in school.' Still, the admission: 'You're not going to change that boy's attitude; all you can do is contain it. If the school has failed to make its policy clear through the way it does assemblies, through its instruction in cultures, through the attitudes of its teachers, then, all right, it's failed. But you're not going to change his home.'

Some teachers tend to downplay the influence of the school, citing the family in formative years and the peer group in later years as more significant factors in the development of racism. According to the head of Edgbaston's Chadvale Infants' School:

The pressure of the peer group becomes the important influence once they come to the end of the first year of secondary school. I think the parents, unless they're very strong, lose influence at that stage, and teachers come a very bad third. So the work has to be done before that, at junior school, so that at least some of it will stick when their friends become the dominant factor. Even then, there are children who've left me who I thought would never be classed as racist in their attitude; but they come back using the terms, 'paki' and 'wog', when they've been third year secondary children [aged 13]. Now, that has been undone from when they left here, because the parents haven't changed, so it must be down to the peer group. And when they get in their teens, it often seems to be the right thing to do to be one of the pack and it's good to go paki-bashing or give West Indians a hard time.

Interestingly, teachers holding such views are, in the main, from middleclass areas. Teachers in workingclass areas prefer to assume more responsibility and see themselves as active agents in the child's all-round development throughout the whole school career.

'Only 14 per cent of a child's time may be spent at school, but the influence of the school is more than 14 per cent on the child,' the head of Chelmsley's Firs Junior School argues. 'We represent authority, something much bigger than 14 per cent. I think on an estate like this there is a fair degree of acceptance of the school's authority and a willingness to listen to the school. A willingness to conform, perhaps.'

Despite this confidence, the uncomfortable reality may be that children from workingclass areas are amongst the least likely groups to be influenced by teachers and the school ethos generally. The reasons for this are summed up by the head of Chelmsley's Simon Digby School, which is clearly not middleclass in composition:

The sort of children who are influenced by the school are those children who can respond to the sort of middleclass education ideal that we all provide; the child who can do O-levels, proceed to A-levels and then go into further education and then fit in the system. You're likely to influence them 'cause there's something in it for them. But the majority of children aren't going to fit into that. I think their home background is far more important to them. Its influence is far stronger than that of the school.

From a different vantage point, the headteacher of the independent Edgbaston High School reaches a broadly similar conclusion:

Schools should be on the side of the angels; we should be putting over the morally correct view. But since schools are part of society and not separate from it, you can't expect them to be totally dissimilar in the values they are reflecting. If the school gets too out of step with the values of society, I think it will put itself in a position of having very little influence at all. You can't be out of step. A school should take a rather different view perhaps from the majority of parents, but not so different that they feel they can't accept what's going on at all.

At Langley School (3 per cent ethnic minority enrolment) in Solihull, the headteacher argues that his school is only slightly, but quite deliberately, out of phase with parents: 'It's extremely important that we should modify and shape pupils' attitudes, not just support those they encounter at home.' The suggestion in these comments is that children from middleclass homes are more likely to be susceptible to the influences of the school, because the educational system is geared to the standards of the middle class. There is a solid body of research to support this claim, and it seems that middleclass children do tend to profit more from formal education than their workingclass counterparts, whose home environment may not be conducive to learning for a variety of reasons (lack of space, of stimuli, of materials; pressure to take part-time jobs; and so on). The teachers, perhaps intuitively, agree that not only will the middleclass child reap more benefit from the school in terms of intellectual gratification and paper qualifications, but that he or she will be more receptive to school influences.

The upshot of this plausible account is that children in places like Newtown and Chelmsley are likely to exerience a fundamental incompatibility between home and school values and to be less amenable to educational influences, in particular to multiethnic-related influences. Yet it is in such workingclass areas that multiethnic initiatives are most likely to have been taken. In middleclass areas, where there is an ostrich policy in regard to multiethnic curriculum development and staff training, children would be more open to school influences. Home influence is greatest in areas of material deprivation and insecurity – good conditions for the maintenance of racism.

Our *children,* our *schools,* our *culture*

Many teachers and policy-makers erroneously believe that they can produce an education appropriate to a multicultural society by introducing bits and pieces of ethnic content into curricula. A more sophisticated appraisal is that the whole school system has to be reformed: not only do curricula have to come under review, but teaching staff attitudes, perceptions and expectations must be changed, as must their actual teaching practices. This is all very well in theory, but teachers are as much products of their social environment as any other members of society are. Enlightened by years of training and education, yes; but social products just the same and sometimes steeped in traditions that are not entirely consistent with new modes of teaching. This often makes them resistant to change, especially change of the proportions implied by multicultural education. The schools in which substantial revisions have occurred over the past ten or fifteen years are situated in areas that have undergone demographic changes. As ethnic minority groups increased their size relative to the white population, schools were virtually forced to consider existing curricula and staff attitudes. The languages issue alone was enough to prompt serious thought on the introduction of English as a Second Language, or ESL as it is often called (sometimes E2L).

In other areas, where there was little or no ethnic minority presence, schools adopted a 'what's it got to do with us?' approach and merely observed changes in other areas' schools with a detached interest. Staff at the schools were given little opportunity to acquaint themselves with ethnic minority children, and their ideas about them would have been derived from secondary sources. These ideas would have filtered through to the children they taught. A whole body of research funded by the National Federation for Educational Research (NFER) in the 1970s found that teachers harboured stereotyped images of black and Asian children and that they tended to teach in an ethnocentric manner, that is, evaluating issues by reference to their own values and presuming that white Anglo beliefs and values were at the centre of everything.

The head of Solihull's Tudor Grange School still entertains misgivings about drastic reforms: 'If we were suddenly to revolutionize and have a multicultural curriculum, we wouldn't get away with it, frankly – even if we desired it. But I don't desire multicultural education, because I don't think, in the long run, it's going to be that way round.' It might seem reasonable to expect that changes since the 1970s have contributed to a reduction in ethnocentrism in teachers, especially in the light of the Report of the Committee of Inquiry into the Education of Children from Ethnic Minority Groups, chaired by Lord Swann, which exposed several areas of neglect in the education system and argued that in the classroom 'ethnocentrism can in fact be seen as synonymous with racism' (Swann, 1985, p. 25). Yet, the Solihull school's head continues:

My attitude would be that this is the culture of the country as it stands; it is the predominant culture and the immigrants – and I don't just mean coloured people; I mean, Irish, Poles, Chinese, whatever – have got to adapt to the culture of the country, rather than vice versa. It doesn't mean it's all one way, but it's the sensible attitude and I think we've got it the wrong way round. In the long run, what we're doing is probably going to create problems, rather than solve them.

If we look at a country like Brazil, which has a great mixture of races, how much did the immigrants there adapt to the culture they found? It was a European influx into an Indian culture; and what they did was crush the Indian culture almost out of existence. The Indian culture in Brazil is not very strong; it's only in what you might call the real backwoods that it's survived. Mostly, it's been a European-imported culture. Now, the immigrants into this country have not been in a similar position to impose their culture and, if they try to, they'll build up a bigger prejudice against themselves. History shows that we're going the wrong way; there should be more assimilation.

In this context, the process referred to means that minority groups lose all the distinctive aspects of their group identities and become absorbed by and subsumed within the majority group; they become similar to whites. The perspective is not confined to middleclass area schools, as the head of Castle Vale Nursery School, Chelmsley, demonstrates:

A lot of teachers really, if they spoke the truth, feel that it's gone too far: that *our own* children's culture is being neglected at the expense of teaching children a culture which they've got no experience of; that merely because of their birth, they are to be taught different culture attitudes, most of which they'll never have any need of. And yet *our own* children and the culture of this country are being neglected. A lot of teachers I've spoken to feel the same way . . . we're only creating more prejudice.

The Swann Report disagreed and found this line of reasoning to imply 'a denial of the fundamental freedom of all individuals to differ on aspects of their lives where no single way can justifiably be presented as universally appropriate' (1985, p. 4). (*Note*: The interim report of the committee, published in 1981, bore the embarrassing title, 'West Indian Children in our Schools'.) It remains the dominant approach of schools in 'white areas' like Solihull and Edgbaston, partly because of the inflexible ethnocentricity of their schools' heads and also because such areas fail to recognize fully the implications of their policies, or lack of them.

I don't want to sound snobbish about this, but because we don't tend to have too big a problem, we don't tend to tackle it and so it's, as it were, under the surface with many of our youngsters. I've no doubt that when they go out with their gang to football matches and so on they'll use the same sort of racist language, 'Niggers go home' and so on, that they hear outside school.

Thus acknowledges the head of St Peter's Roman Catholic School at Solihull, with an insight uncharacteristic of fellow teachers of the area.

Teachers in middleclass areas, whilst not still clinging to the kind of stereotyped image reported by the NFER in the 1970s, are still not fully cognizant of the possible consequences of their present inaction. Multicultural education may not be the panacea many claim it is: the schools employing it will not suddenly begin to churn out model nonracist humans completely freed of the prejudices that have hampered the judgement of their parents. But mce. is at least an initiative devised to rid the educational process of the kind of archaic notions and ethnocentric approach that sustain racism. And, in a way, it is paradoxical that its progress has been slowest in areas where pupils, as an Edgbaston teacher puts it, 'haven't got ethnic minorities within the school to use as a resource for learning about others'.

Clearly, the influence of the school on a child's values, beliefs and perceptions varies according to class, area and age. The precise degree of influence relative to other factors like the family and the peer group is virtually impossible to establish. Education nevertheless has a central role to play in race relations. It cannot reach adults who are convinced of the rightness of their values and the superiority of their beliefs. But it can affect the judgement and perception of future generations. Children are growing up in a multicultural society, even if those in areas such as Solihull may not be immediately aware of it. Schools that refuse to acknowledge this fact and hold fast to the sacrosanct traditional modes of teaching are not so much opting out of changes in the educational system as actively contributing to the perpetuation of racism. They are not adequately preparing their pupils for a society that has undergone considerable changes in its ethnic composition over the past three decades and are instead relying on a vague policy which does little more than maintain a culture in which racism, as we have seen in previous chapters, is the norm.

Chapter Twelve

The Wheels of the Race Relations Industry – Practitioners

Racism finds a place in any type of society

Misbegotten and misdirected as many people believe it to be, there is nevertheless a professional body of people operating with the ostensibly simple *raison d'être*, to eliminate or minimize the effects of racism. The race relations industry, as it is sometimes cynically called, comprises individuals and organizations unswervingly guided by the commitment to achieve equality of opportunity for all, regardless of background, belief, colour, or sex. Some organizations, like the Community Relations Council (CRC), have a fairly wide net and do not concern themselves especially with matters of race and ethnicity. Others, such as the Commission for Racial Equality (CRE), target issues of inequality and injustice as they affect ethnic minority groups. There are many other organizations, national and local, which in some way include ethnic matters in their problematic. Their personnel include *inter alia* youth and community workers, ethnic advisers, social workers and specialist education officers.

However they like to embellish their brief, all these

222

organizations share one central problem: racism. The many different cases and issues that involve ethnic conflict invariably have as their cause racism of one kind or another. Racism spawns many types of conflict, some covert and seldom detected, such as those involving immigration regulations, others obvious and visible, like outright violent confrontation. The perspectives occupying this chapter will be those of the personnel of the race relations industry. How these people conceive of racism affects the manner in which they tackle it.

Karen Forster (introduced in Chapter 5), an officer of the CRE, does not delude herself about her work. She realizes that, for all her everyday encounters with club owners, employers and teachers, her real foe lying behind these is racism, and she is not hopeful about the chances of defeating it:

First and foremost, the adult generation are a lost generation anyway. You can try and modify them simply by exposure, which doesn't work, or by some knowledge of the people who they seem to fear so much. But I'm very pessimistic about what you can really achieve there. It's all so much linked into the role and status of blacks in the world, rather than the black minority that happen to live in the Midlands. The whole history of the situation is so deep-rooted, so long-standing, that I reckon there's not much point in what I would regard as wasting too much time on the adult generation. You're going to get a few converts, or a few modified views, but some of these people round here are racists through and through and they'll take their views with them to the grave. Racism doesn't just disappear because you put a logical argument.

She entered the CRE via schoolteaching and has in the past four years changed her view of the role of her organization. Her original ideas have been eclipsed by more pragmatic considerations. 'The Commission would be quite wrong to try to cope with racism in a white community,' she states baldly. 'It's got a *specific* job to do: the elimination of discrimination rather than of the attitudes behind it.' This she sees as the first of two main functions, the other being 'the promotion of equality of opportunity', about which she has definite thoughts:

Early on, there was an attempt to approach the second main job of the Commission in a sort of multicultural kind of way. My own view is that that was again misguided, and that attempts that the Commission has made in the past to widen its provision of what it sees as equal opportunity have tended to use up very limited resources, in terms of staff, ideas, policy and all the rest of it, to no avail. In particular, the work we've tried to do with the police, local authorities' training in racial awareness, that sort of thing – a lot of time has gone into that and not been rewarded. We haven't great numbers of staff anyway, but given the number of staff we've got, a number of resources have gone into work on racist attitudes particularly, held by the police, teachers, etc. right across the board.

You can be a racialist but still not discriminate, because you've got no power to discriminate: you're not a boss; you haven't got a house to sell; so you shout abuse at children and hold racist views. But you're not a discriminator. We concentrate on the dicriminator. You can be a discriminator even though you don't personally hold racist views; you do it out of sheer ignorance. Or it's always been done this way so you continue to do it this way, as a lot of institutions do, because you're responding to the racism of the people you're with, the people you employ or the people you house. You know how they'll react if you bring in blacks to this kind of job or this kind of area, therefore you're going to adapt your policy so that that doesn't happen. The link is a reaction to racism, rather than you actually holding racist views. Unfortunately, many people in positions that affect the lives of others respond to racist views of others in what they do. It hasn't really got us anywhere; it's very time-consuming, and done in isolation, which is the way it's always done when the Commission's responding to these people, it really is a misuse of very limited resources.

Given the framework in which the CRE has to operate, Ms

Forster, 28, prefers to see her organization move away from its educative role and towards what she calls 'the strategic response'. With the statutory powers at the Commission's disposal, it can detect patterns of discrimination within particular industries, issue nondiscrimination notices and bring about sometimes 'radical change in company policy'. In this sense, Ms Forster sees the CRE as a kind of 'law enforcement agency', pushing industries and educational institutions to increase or maintain ethnic intakes. There is, however, a limit to this type of approach, and Ms Forster is concerned that the CRE will be running twice as hard to stay in the same place if it does not take a much more positive stance:

You're going to get a backlash from whites, but we must face the consequences. The biggest shift in moving forward occurred because of the Brixton riots in 1981 and probably the same will be true of Birmingham in 1985. That's real life. All the logic and reasoning and sound reasons for *not* doing things are all very well and so well documented that people can almost recite them by heart. But it doesn't cause them to do much. They'll worry about how much support they'll get locally, how many votes they're going to lose, and they'll do very little, if anything at all. You only get some shift when people in power start to think, 'What are these blacks going to get up to?' But that's what real life is like. It's not about logic and poetry; we respond to prejudices, fears. And it's getting to the position where the black community wants to see some recognizable change, some opening up of opportunities. The people in authority ought to be addressing themselves to the consequences of not responding to that.

So far, Ms Forster, born in Birmingham of Jamaican parents, has been rather vague in her allusions to social change, or 'shifts' as she prefers to call them. Accepting her view that those over the age of 45 are what she terms collectively 'a lost generation', what might be done, short of encouraging more disturbances on the scale of the 1981 and 1985 riots?

First of all, I'm very pessimistic about dealing with racism. I can't see any evidence to latch on to which will lead me to believe otherwise. Even in the United States, where the racism appears on the surface to be more deep seated, and they've had segregation, busing and the rest of it, you've got a much stronger black community and much stronger legislation in terms of education and employment. They've made judgements we're a million years from ever making here.

She would favour more political power for her Commission, especially in the areas of education and work. School-teachers, she believes, hold stereotyped views of ethnic children, certainly of those of West Indian background. And, in the manner of the self-fulfilling prophecy, minority children live up (or down) to the teachers' poor expectations of them.

I would look closely at teacher training, looking at what the courses offer and dealing properly with racism for all prospective teachers. For existing teachers, I would push for compulsory courses, exposing them to racial awareness. If you get teachers who are clearly unsuitable for working in a multiracial environment, then discrimination or other forms of racial abuse should be a serious disciplinary offence within their own work environment. Changing the whole curriculum is a massive task, but all syllabuses and materials that contribute in a pernicious way to reinforcing, if not actually introducing to children, racism have to be rooted out. Attitudes, many of which start at home and through the media, develop, but the school obviously plays a part in perpetuating them – often without any direct wish to do so – simply by the materials it uses.

There is nothing remarkably original about these suggested reforms. Ms Forster reiterates many of the proposals suggested in the past. But, she contends, they have remained only proposals and education authorities have still to consider their wider implications.

Whereas, in the past, a lot of attention has been paid to raising the level of self identity, particularly among Caribbean children, they moved on slightly to looking at innercity schools where you've got a very mixed school population and concentrating on curriculum changes there. I reckon that's not really on; where the work needs to be done is in the all white or nearly all white areas. That kind of reappraisal of the education system is urgent there, perhaps more urgent than in the innercity areas. I'd also get more black heads and black teachers into schools to expose children to black persons in authority over a longterm right through the school. This has got something to offer in terms of attitude forming.

The school would be the main site for Ms Forster's campaign, although she isolates the media as the most influential source of racist ideas. 'My aim would be to get children, when they grow up, to question what the media throw at them.'

Such schemes may sound idealistic coming from one so closely and practically involved with race relations, but Ms Forster believes that nothing short of wholesale changes in education will prevent an escalation of the events witnessed in the first half of the 1980s. She anticipates a strong antipathetic reaction to her ideas, as she has had plenty of experience gauging racism:

Well, you're going to get white backlash, but I reckon you're going to have to fly in the face of it and go ahead. Because you're going to have to do it at some point. The price to pay in terms of the level of discrimination – the effects of racism on part of the population – cannot be paid. That is too high a price to pay just to avoid raising somebody's hackles. The caution and all the rest of it that tends to be the response to any disagreement is counter-productive, because you're not going to be able to avoid a backlash; there's no possible way. Anybody who believes they can has no understanding of what racism's all about.

Ms Forster's understanding of racism is that it is part of the human condition, just like the universal destructive urge. She refutes any political analysis, arguing that 'Racism isn't that easy to eradicate; in the socialist states that exist, there is racism. It doesn't follow that because you change the social structure and the way things are run, attitudes such as racism can't find a role in the new structure. Racism finds a place in any kind of society.'

Robin Harley, a community worker in the Newtown area, makes a similar point: 'There is a strong tribalism in all people. When you go, as a white person, to see people, you're *their* representative.' He gives an example:

I was based at a junior school involved in a multicultural project and I got on particularly well with this one lady teacher there. But then her school pulled out and we lost contact. Now, remember, she was really all for the multicultural package. I met her recently, and there'd been some kind of problem with one of her children and she was upset and angry. Now, while she was in that mood she came out with all sorts of racialist things: that the school was favouring black pupils, etc. This is the tribal defence mechanism people have. But she'd only come out with this when we were talking on an individual basis; it didn't spill over into her work at school where she always leaned over backwards to help blacks. Yes, the tribalism is there. I even find it in any work with the churches. And it isn't confined to white people either; it's a trend in man.

Mr Harley is 32 and has been working full time in Newtown for four years. Like Ms Forster and, indeed, the majority of those continually facing the practical problems of race relations, Mr Harley believes in 'dealing with racialism in a positive way': in other words, *attacking* it in the schools. 'I think we've got to continue to press for legal reforms, reforms in police procedure and so on. But the main target is school. I want to be a problem solver, but I don't want to be a problem solver on a narrow definition of reality. I lay a strong emphasis on the educational system. I've learned from experience that this is where we have to start.'

He has also come to the conclusion, like Ms Forster, that older people are beyond his reach:

I think you tend to find with older people that they haven't entirely realized that the empire has been dismantled. Not that they ever knew what the empire was, but they tend to have, at best, rather paternalistic attitudes. It's very much to do with leadership and status, and these would apply to any newcomers; but in the case of black people, it seems to take them a long time to stop being a newcomer. In America it has taken two hundred years.

What seems to happen is that there's a vicious circle. Afro-Caribbean people are doing far less than they could do because they feel that they won't make any headway and then they are underrated by others who feel they aren't making any headway. They tend to always blame the next person for that, not themselves. So I think it's important to get so-called minorities into leadership roles, at any level, rather than let them carry on as dependent-type people. It's happening, but it's a slow process and the biggest resistance to it is racism. Even those who have friendly relations with Afro-Caribbeans and Asians still want them put at the back of the queue. So the main thing is to get people to the front. I know this one chap, a Jamaican, who's offering removal services. Now, he'll suit somebody else who desperately needs a cheap removal. This is quite a good example of a person being dependent on another person from another community and they will, either willingly or unwillingly, have to accept that from a psychological point of view.

It is interesting that Ms Forster and Mr Harley, both experienced workers 'at the coal-face', believe that education must be changed so that it is administered by more aware, better-informed people in such a way as to reflect a broader spectrum of interests. They also agree that ethnic minority group members need to be boosted to positions of seniority, leadership and responsibility, not only to prove to whites that they are capable, but to demonstrate to themselves and their ethnic community the possibility of breaking away from old, dependent positions.

Both practitioners are ultimately pessimistic about the possibilities of affecting racism through political change, or moving to 'a new structure' as Ms Forster puts it. Their reasons for this arise from the perception that racism transcends political systems.

'It's futile to use capitalism as a bogeyman,' asserts Mr Harley:

You can't go back to the Garden of Eden and rewrite history. What we've done is make ourselves incredibly powerful; powerful enough to blow ourselves off the face of the earth, powerful enough to feed the whole of the world or starve most of it, to enslave people or free them. We have the resources and feeding and freeing people are often part of the same thing, because very often the reason why they're not getting fed is that there are local bosses or caste systems or things like that that are getting in the way. So I'm not giving capitalism a clean bill of health. But who would say that the USSR is not capitalist? I've read books that prove absolutely that all countries which have accumulated wealth up to now can be described as capitalist.

Mr Harley seems to be suggesting that the political system of capitalism – and by this he includes both the West and the Soviet bloc – generates only potential and has no controlling force over attitudes, opinions and postures. The potential to free or enslave, to grant equality of opportunity or restrict it, is there. But individual human qualities determine the choices. This is a common view amongst race relations practitioners. Perhaps it is the experience of working so closely on a day-to-day basis with the problems that beset innercities that leads them to believe that racism is not simply a product of any one type of political system. Equally they are all committed to defeating it, refusing to accept that it is an unalterable human characteristic. From where might it derive, then?

A 'hearts and minds' integration of cultures?

'Culture,' answers Paul Broughton, the director of a social work department in Newtown:

But I think the breakdown is beginning. Just by people inhabiting the same classrooms and getting to know each other as people. Certainly that's what's happening here; we did racial awareness training so that the staff were introduced to it. It didn't do any good until we had coloured and Asian members of staff and then people related to them as people, and began to perceive that there was a difference between a Sikh and a Hindu, a Bangladeshi and a Pakistani and even a Pushtu and an Afghan. It very much depended upon the way in which you get the personal contact.

In this perspective, one which is shared by a great many social and community workers, racism wanes in direct proportion to familiarity. Mr Broughton believed it to be 'just a question of time', although tightly bonded families inhibit the process.

Friendships develop, but families are pretty exclusive anyway. One of the things I've often wondered about in racialism – and it came out in the awareness training – was to what extent were whites simply unaware that they were just relating to other families and to what extent were blacks aware of that? Families are pretty exclusive things – especially workingclass families – and I think there's been a lot of mythology about a 'community', and there's not been enough attention about the way families interact. You blame the obvious outsider. I was looking through some settlement records earlier on, and there was tremendous conflict with the Irish settlers who came here in the 1900s, with the same prejudice against them; they were ignorant; they came from hovels; they were Bog Irish; they were Catholic: very reminiscent of the present kind of racism. There's also the argument that it took forty to fifty years from the beginning of those immigrant ways for them to achieve equal status with the community. And they had to fight for it. Now we are only about thirty years into it. There are aspects of the problem that are the same.

It *is* true that the blacks are different, and somehow there's been a failure to get workingclass solidarity between blacks and whites. That's an appalling failure of the labour movement. The union movement's really alienated the Asians, so we haven't used that traditional method by which we got the Irish and other ethnic minorities into the main group. I don't think it's going to happen in the same way for both; there is more likelihood of gradual integration of the West Indians and the white community. I think there's much less chance of that with Asians because of the cultural difference, which is much greater. On the other hand, on the level of the work ethic and capitalist society, the chance of integration with the Indian subcontinent population is much greater. There's a definite admiration for Indian hard working, family solidarity in business, support for each other. It's astonishing how they work. I was in hospital next to an Indian, who took my name and address. The next year he set up an old trade printer's down the road, came in, undercut all the white printers' quotes that we'd got, produced excellent prototypes to show us and won the business.

With his similarly committed colleagues, Mr Broughton, 43, considers it essential that minority group members elevate themselves to business ownership and senior positions in commerce and industry – so essential, in fact, that he favours a programme of positive discrimination to realize this ambition. He harbours an optimism absent among many of his more junior colleagues. This may be a function of his seniority: if he is not convinced of the ultimate value of his work in this area, then his juniors certainly will not be. Or it could simply be that Mr Broughton's broader experience has made him more of a pragmatist: 'Is it so necessary always to look for a "hearts and minds" integration of cultures as opposed to a *modus vivendi* based upon as equal an opportunity as possible for all cultures, a pluralist approach?' As the problem is, in Mr Broughton's view, culturally based, so must its resolution be. Schools again: 'I believe in an educational system which establishes schools in a different way: as centres for basic education and *cultural* education as well.' So it is rather perplexing that Mr Broughton states: 'There is a case for Muslim schools' despite the fact that 'there is a better one for a universal education on basics and a diversified education system on other things'.

The assumption shared by virtually all practitioners is that racism is not so much an invariant quality of human nature as a quality of human culture. In other words, it expresses not a biological characteristic but a product of human intellect, something which is created, learned and passed down through generations. Some might argue that certain political arrangements are conducive to its creation and transmission. Not practitioners: in their perspective, racism operates independently of political systems. It follows that if racism is learned, it can be unlearned. Hence the emphasis on starting at the bottom, in schools.

Some, however, like Jeremy Calder, a community education officer, have reservations:

I think that all the goodwill in the world through the education system, be it through teachers, youth leaders, etc., is fine. But the fact is that a lot of the ideologies that are put into people's minds whilst they are children are very quickly dissipated by the time they get home because of prejudice, lack of understanding, lack of knowledge. There's a strong case to suggest that parents have already become prejudiced to such an extent that the good work is hammered out of their children in the home situation. The only thing to do is just keep plugging away: right, we are a multiracial society and multiracial societies take years to evolve. Look at Brazil.

Like Mr Broughton he wants a universal education with 'an element of multiculturalism as a core subject', but

I wouldn't teach Christianity. I wouldn't teach that God is beautiful, whether or not the 1944 Education Act says that C. of E. or whatever should be taught. I would ban sectarian schools. How can you argue the logic of not allowing Islamic schools when you allow Roman Catholic, Jewish and Church of England schools? What principle are you operating under? I would have an integrated school system whereby multifaith and multicultural identity were essential requirements of the curriculum. I would go further by making sure that options, in terms of subject matter,

233

included Afro-Caribbean, Asian studies, etc. I think we're going to go through a revolution in education.

Attitudes change, and people will forget they ever resented others

How one assesses the nature and scale of racism affects one's interpretations of its consequences, or more precisely, how to control those consequences. Many race relations practitioners, whilst acknowledging that changes of large proportions need to be made in education, would see their job as reaching beyond a *modus vivendi*. Community worker Alan Trower, for example, feels that what passes for racism is frequently no more than 'a conflict of lifestyles':

Let's take what might seem an extreme example of the 60- or 70-year-old who's suddenly got a new neighbour who's a 20-year-old single parent black girl. She's going to do things different to a 60-year-old because she comes from a different generation and a different culture, and these are unknown to the elderly person. But the younger person, mother or not, is not going to see loud music at midnight as being a problem because that's the way her culture has brought her up to believe it should be.

Geoff Waring, 30, a social worker, makes a similar point:

In practical terms, there are some things that are very wrong, such as the ridiculous situation of the tower blocks, where conflict is created by absolutely absurd mixes. Single parents with very young families plonked into tower blocks amongst aged whites. There's a recipe for conflict. It so happens that one is black and the other is white. But *we* respond to it in a way which makes it appear as colour prejudice.

In this interpretation, whites certainly prejudge ethnic minorities if only because of the availability of stereotyped images. But these are very much *idées reçues*, generally accepted notions that have not been studied critically.

'The typical situation is the white woman who says, "All blacks are terrible", and comes out with stereotypes,' argues Mr Waring. 'Then she gets some neighbours and, after a period, she begins to say, "Actually, black people aren't so bad; my neighbour is OK." Her attitude begins to change because of her experiences. If your behaviour and experience are one thing and your beliefs something else, there's going to be conflict, and you'll modify your ideas. And people will forget the fact that they ever resented others.'

Mr Trower isn't convinced that ideas and beliefs are necessarily so pliable and cites an actual case to illustrate his point:

A black single parent moved into a block of flats recently. At the end of her corridor, the door was broken and had a habit of slamming shut, the noise echoing through the floor when anybody used it. At first, the other residents on the floor considered the new neighbour OK. But, after a few weeks, the rest of the residents began to hear the door go bang at midnight and again at 4 a.m. At 6 a.m. they would hear her front door shut, followed by a clink and the corridor bang again. Because all the other residents had known each other for many years, they knew that the noises had to be coming from the black tenant. The noises were attributed by them as follows. The bang at twelve o'clock was her going out looking for a trick. The bang at four was her coming back with someone. The door shutting was the person leaving at six, and the clink was him putting the keys back through the letterbox after shutting her front door; you can't close them just by slamming them to. So by the process of 'bang-bang-slam-clink-bang' they constructed their idea of this woman as a prostitute and defined her as a problem. They called her 'the blackberry tart'. Over the past five years, the elderly have either died or moved out, and these people constituted a large percentage of the traditional workingclass residents who had lived on the estate before redevelopment. They've been replaced by young families or single parents who tend to be black. That's when problems arise.

Contrary to Mr Waring's forecast, Mr Trower has found that experiences can be fused with racist potential when stereotyped images exist. These prejudices form a mould into which experience can be 'poured', the mould in this case being the belief that all young black women are 'on the game'. The logic runs: the new neighbour is a black woman; therefore the new neighbour is 'on the game'. This might just as easily read: prostitutes are inferior beings; all black women are inferior beings; therefore all black women are prostitutes. This may violate the formal rules of logic, but it is a powerful syllogism in the minds of white residents.

Mr Trower's observations tell him that this type of reasoning does not have a racist foundation, but rather is based on a conflict of lifestyles: 'The problems start when you get a young person or family, especially from an ethnic background, living in amongst a group of elderly.' Perhaps so, but such conditions may not be sufficient, merely necessary, for the kind of conflict Mr Trower regularly encounters in his daily work. When combined with the racist assumptions that are shared by a great many white residents, they produce abrasive relationships that eventually serve to confirm old stereotypes, themselves based on racist ideas. Hence the self-perpetuating characteristic of racism.

In the above example, Mr Trower outlines how residents deduced from a general idea of blacks a specific interpretation of one woman. In another, he shows how a different process can result in a similar labelling: 'We have the classic example of the local licensee who was stabbed outside the Woodman pub. Even before it was reported, the gossip was there; they automatically thought it was a black person. If it turns out that it's a white person, they're very concerned: "Oh, it's a shame. Perhaps he's got a disturbed home" –

something like that, But if he's black, it's just the opposite: "All blacks are the same." '

Much conflict, particularly in the innercities, arises from the housing question. Again, Mr Trower believes that cultural difference stokes up the fires of resentment:

Comments have come along like, 'All the properties that become empty now are let to blacks.' Now, I don't think you can ever be in the position where Housing Departments are able to pick and choose who's going to be where. One of the reasons why it looks as if all the empty stock is offered to blacks is because whites are not on the move so much. The whites in Newtown tend to be elderly; it's only when they die off that the replacement of that person tends to be a black person. The housing itself tends to be a problem, because the whites tend to come to me and say, 'How can I get one of these properties? Every one that's available goes to a black person.' The council would say that each case is taken on its merit, but it's also a known fact that if a black person goes to the Housing Department and kicks up a lot of fuss, they're likely to get what they want. We – the whites – have been brought up to believe that you respect your elders. If you've got a complaint, don't go into it with both feet: be respectful and sit there, explain your problem and accept what the person says. So, I'm living in a two-bedroomed flat, and I've got two kids, a boy and a girl, and I go to Housing wanting a house. If I'm a white, it seems that I'm going to accept what housing has said: that I haven't got enough points. I go back to my four walls and I complain about it to my wife and we have a great argument about it. But it seems as if the attitude of the black is to say, 'I ain't moving until I get what I want!' And at the end of the day, they do tend to get what they're looking for, not because they're black, but because they're more vociferous.

It could be argued that Mr Trower shares the same stereotype as many of the community of people he serves. The image of 'pushy blacks' is a popular one amongst social and community workers. Analysing the frustration of whites, which often boils over into anger, Roger Keating, a Chelmsley social worker, begins with a question frequently asked of him by whites: 'The blacks can get more off the state than whites; why's that?' His answer is:

Because whites have a slowly disappearing pride. It's like drawing social security payments: the attitude of whites is that you don't do it – you work. Whereas the attitude of ethnics is, 'We'll get every penny we can.' I'm not saying that's wrong; it's their entitlement. But blacks are far more forward in going to get it than whites. It's the same with bills: blacks don't necessarily care if they pay their rates or electricity bills; they can shake it off.

In working so closely with a particular community, it is expected that practitioners absorb some of the popular ideas and beliefs, even if they are based more on folklore than on careful analysis. Still, Messrs Trower and Keating, like all the people whose views are represented in this chapter, have their fingers on the pulse. Their practical encounters are their data bases and they rely on common-sense and sound judgement. The Trower position is, bluntly stated, that cultural differences as manifested in lifestyles are the essential source of friction amongst ethnic groups. Racist stereotypes come into play after the tension has been created and, inevitably, add appreciably to the conflict, perhaps giving it a new dimension. Mr Trower and many of his professional colleagues feel disinclined to attribute racism with too much efficacy in generating conflict. The conflict, like a fire, itself is started by the friction of two elements, and the racism acts as fuel helping the flames roar. But, they all argue, as the cultures meld, differences will become less apparent; stereotypes will not be invoked and racism will disappear.

Yet, others, like Makhan Sohpal, an officer of Birmingham Education Department's multicultural support unit, are less confident about the implications of ethnic change. 'The host community is prepared to accept people who are assimilated,' he premisses his argument. 'It satisfies the host community, giving it the feeling that others' assimilation is making them superior; their country is superior to a foreign country.' In this view, the only type of melding that will yield a change in whites' orientation to blacks is one in which ethnic groups assimilate, becoming similar to whites and losing their distinctive characteristics in the process. This, Mr Sohpal feels, will not happen:

Asians, Sikhs in particular, are not prepared to assimilate, to change their ways, their own specific culture patterns. They seek to stay as a community, speaking in their mother tongue. If you take the West Indians, they are assimilated to a large extent in terms of their habits, sport, religion and things like that. But because of their colour, they are not totally accepted. The degree of assimilation determines the attitude of the host community. Whites are prepared to give employment to and accept an individual who is assimilated rather than an individual who wears a turban or rastafarian locks.

This is the contrasting longterm perspective to that of people like Mr Trower, who believes racism to be like a footprint in sand that time will eventually erase: 'It's happening already in the schools where the cultures are mixing and children of all backgrounds are getting along.' Racism for Mr Sohpal also impresses like footprints – but footprints set in concrete. The only way whites will accept ethnic groups is if those groups 'whiten' themselves and become anglicized. And this process itself has racist implications for Mr Sohpal, for he believes that it will confirm whites' judgements of their own superiority. It will provide evidence of white culture's power to change others to its own requirements. So, whereas for Mr Trower the residual racism of parents – which he readily concedes 'undoes a lot of the good work done at school' – will disappear as the schoolchildren of the 1980s mature into adults, Mr Sohpal depicts a much less fluid image of the future, with ethnic groups intransigently sticking to their own cultures and 'the host community,' as he calls it, refusing to accept them as legitimate and equal participants in society.

Practitioners whose daily work brings them into direct contact with race relations situations do not speak with a unanimous voice. Their opinions, arguments and analyses are textured by their backgrounds and experiences and often conflict with each others. Conceptions of racism differ and so, as a consequence, do the preferred methods of combating it. All are committed to educational reform as a basic condition for the future. But whereas some view education as the fulcrum of significant change, others see it as only a hopeful gesture to the future.

The people considered in this chapter are neither ivory tower academics theorizing about the causes of racism, nor power wielding policy makers who have the political juice to be able to make decisions about how to tackle its consequences. Their working day is organized around coping with practical problems, many of them thrown up by racism. Some see such problems as insoluble, but ones which they have to confront all the same. It is for precisely this reason that a chapter has been devoted to the practitioners' perspective; for it is a perspective hewn out of practical day-to-day experience, insight and knowledge that serves as a recipe, a prescription for effecting something – rather than a grand scheme. Their outlooks are motivated by a need for practical policies, not by wishful thinking. It is difficult for them to be optimistic about the prospects when confronted by a bewildering spread of problems they have in their caseloads. They tread the muddy path of British race issues and know only too well the magnitude of racism in modern society. Some feel that the forbidding climate in which they work is changing, although not fast enough to avert more episodes like Brixton in 1981 and Birmingham in 1985. Such episodes, tragic as they may be, at least force public recognition and prompt change, according to virtually all practitioners. Others feel that nothing is likely to change in the foreseeable future. If anything, further economic downturn could result in even more job competition and perhaps a corresponding intensification of racism. The concluding chapter will assess how well founded their pessimism is, by examining the views of politicians in the areas.

Chapter Thirteen

Conclusion
– Politicians and Policy

A snake and a bullock

At a recent race relations seminar, the discussion centred on the effectiveness of existing legal measures designed to minimize, or even eliminate, racial discrimination. After three Acts of Parliament, consolidated and extended in 1976, we are entitled to ponder the effects of legal reforms in this area. During the seminar, a professor of sociology with a career's experience in race relations drew an interesting parallel between sections of the white population and general practitioners. According to professional codes of ethics, GPs are forbidden from engaging in sexual relationships with their patients. Yet no one seriously expects every GP to find every patient totally unattractive and to have no sexual leanings. The speaker commented that this would be both unreasonable and unrealistic. The problems resulting from GP-patient liaisons are manifest, and those taking the Hippocratic oath are instructed to observe their principles. In other words, no attempt can be made to influence thoughts and emotions, but *behaviour* must be controlled in the interests of the profession. The parallel is by no means exact, but race relations legislation tries to regulate behaviour without intruding into the minds of people. It states that people must not discriminate on racialist grounds; but it cannot, in the first instance at least, prevent them from harbouring racist thoughts. With this approach, racialism – the practice – is controlled by setting boundaries around people and regulating their manifest behaviour. Legislation cannot penetrate people's minds, so racism remains untouched.

This is only one interpretation and a somewhat pessimistic one. As this book has shown, racism of some form exists in all classes, in all places and amongst all age groups. Its logic is persuasive because it is constantly fused with relevance. Some writers argue, like Michael Banton, that 'prejudice in the minds of discriminators ... is to be understood as stemming from the pressure individuals feel to conform to what they believe to be the social norms prevailing in the groups to which they belong or seek to belong' (1985, p. 130). It follows that, provided people's patterns of behaviour can be changed by the imposition of race relations laws, then group norms will gradually change also, and new pressures to conform will emerge. Banton sees laws against discrimination as having vital importance not merely in a superficial sense – in inducing types of behaviour – but in a deeper, more lasting sense of introducing nonracist norms which people will eventually accept. Banton places great store in the value of race relations law as both a controlling and an educational instrument of social policy.

I begin this conclusion by outlining the possibilities and limitations of law as a central element of social policy in reducing racialism, because report after report suggests that racialism, or racial discrimination, is as widespread as it ever was in the UK. The conclusion of the Policy Studies Institute report of 1985 was that in the seventeen years following the 1968 Race Relations Act virtually nothing changed: racialism was and does flourish in all areas of society (Brown and Gay, 1985). Yet, ironically, in the late 1980s, for perhaps the first time in twenty years, there has been a strong feeling shared by all sections of society that the national government totally lacks commitment to the cause of equality of opportunity. The generally accepted goal of integration ushered in with the liberalism of the mid-1960s seems to have been jettisoned by an odd combination of white backlash, black separatism and interethnic rivalry. Some think that the Thatcher administration's unwillingness to sustain an initiative in this area contributed to the turbulence in 1985.

Labour MP Denis Howell, whose constituency includes Newtown, believes that the government's policies, or lack of them, have, as he puts it, 'fed back into the community'. More specifically, he cites the operation of immigration policies: 'The application of immigration laws is totally racialist. For example, Americans arriving here on a Boeing 737 are allowed through immigration control with the most cursory questions in thirty seconds flat. Asians will be kept eight hours. They are grilled. Not only them, but their relatives waiting outside to receive them are grilled. You'd think they'd committed a mortal sin if there's any discrepancies.'

Mr Howell uses this illustration to stress his point that 'the spirit of the community' in Newtown and other innercity areas has been upset by government policies. 'I spend a lot of my time recreating a belief in the system,' he says. 'Because part of the ethnic community's faith has been destroyed.' One could expand Mr Howell's argument. For, as well as enacting restrictive immigration legislation that has racist consequences, the Conservative administration, from the late 1970s onwards, attempted to rein back local authority spending; it side-stepped some of the wider implications of Lord Scarman's (1982) minimalist package of proposals in the light of the 1981 riots; and it drip-fed youths – black, white and Asian – with Youth Training Schemes and analogous programmes to divert their atten-

tion away from the deeper problems thrown up by unemployment – and unemployment has affected ethnic
minorities appreciably more than it has whites. Mr Howell
has ample backing for his view that the government has
shown itself lacking in moral commitment.

Yet the Conservative response is like the assurances of a
ship's captain that calm waters lie ahead when the ship is in
the midst of a storm: 'Don't panic! Better times are coming.'
Conservatives hold seats in the three areas studied other
than Newtown and the MPs are convinced that the present
crisis is but a phase and that race relations problems will
dissolve. Like their constituents, they believe impatience
has prompted many problems. A classic nineteenth century
liberal approach would have yielded better results, the
argument runs; let things follow a 'natural course', in other
words. However, in order for events to be able to follow
such a course, some control over the environment must be
implemented. This, to Mr Howell, is a contradiction; but to
John Taylor, MP for Solihull, it is essential to the whole
philosophy: 'It's rather like a snake that eats a small bullock,'
he says, referring to the UK's admission of New Commonwealth migrants. 'It's going to take a hell of a lot of digesting
and it distorts the outline and the configuration of our
society. We let in too many, too quickly.'

Dame Jill Knight, MP for Edgbaston, served on the
parliamentary Select Committee on Race Relations and
Immigration between 1969 and 1972. In this capacity she
received complaints from parents of children who were at
schools with high ethnic minority rolls. 'They complained
bitterly that their children weren't having a fair chance and,
indeed, they weren't; that was true,' she remembers.

There was no way that this country could just take on more and
more people, because we could see the problems of unemployment coming up. One of the things that worried me was when the
host community might turn against black people. We hadn't got
the housing or the hospital beds. We hadn't got the facilities

to care for just anyone who wished to come here. Our ability to absorb is very much less than somewhere like Australia where they're very much more strict than we've ever been about immigration. They've got huge tracts of land and so much wealth and so much facility for expansion. We needed immigration controls.

The MP for Meriden, which includes Chelmsley Wood, is Iain Mills, who prefaces his remarks with the disclaimer: 'I'm not an Enoch Powell "rivers of blood" man.' He does, however, align himself with other Conservatives in being 'a strong supporter of increased controls on immigration – of all colours of people.' Like his two colleagues, he believes historical mistakes were made in not restricting immigration sooner (the first formal restriction of Commonwealth migrants came in 1962). 'Had we been much more stringent on primary immigration, we would have been more generous with the Boat People [from Vietnam] and so on. Certainly, the tolerance level is quite low on this.' His view is that the 'tolerance level' was exceeded, causing an upset of the population's ethnic balance. 'Native whites would have tolerated a certain number of migrants, but their wrath was roused when the number of incoming migrants was allowed to go beyond the levels of tolerance.'

While Conservative ministers rue the lack of a clear and defined policy of immigration control in the past, they are suspicious of existing, or even mooted, policies designed to improve race relations in the future. While Labour's Mr Howell insists on the absolute necessity of anti-discrimination legislation and implicitly endorses Banton's theory of norm creation, his Tory peers favour a much 'freer' approach, though as Mrs Knight points out: 'One person's freedom is another person's deprivation.' Her reservations about race relations legislation are as deep as those of the Edgbaston constituents she serves:

The law is a very blunt instrument and, frequently, if you use it indiscriminately with the best of intentions to try to end a certain situation, you will have new difficulties that you never dreamed of springing out of that. This is precisely what has happened in race relations. You can say, 'We won't have any discrimination at all', and pass a law which says that. But, in passing the law, we are creating a new sort of discrimination.

The bottom line is: 'I would rather we had no more race relations laws, because I think they are counter-productive.'

Her reason for believing this is based on the philosophy that legal compulsion can work in specific circumstances but race relations do not yield such circumstances. Informal norm creation is a more reliable longterm possibility and Mrs Knight provides a simple illustration: 'There's no law that a chap's got to cut his lawn on a Sunday afternoon, but because everyone else in the road cuts their lawns on a Sunday afternoon and keeps the road neat and tidy, he's more likely to conform.' The difference between this perspective and that offered by Banton and others is apparent: for Mrs Knight, the law cannot induce the norm-governed behaviour and is more likely to arouse a reaction to it. So a law forbidding racial discrimination is destined to founder as surely as a law compelling householders to cut their lawns on Sunday afternoons. Appalled at the effrontery of such an imposition, people deliberately violate the law. 'It's like poking away at a sore; it gets worse,' opines Mrs Knight. 'Youngsters don't know anything about racism.' The very process of growing up in a multicultural society would guarantee an empathy that would, in time, negate prejudice.

Mr Mills agrees with the general principle that, as he phrases, it 'the more you force it, the more you force the opposition to it.' Race relations legislation has 'made not one jot of difference'. Despite his view that 'the Race Relations Act is valuable because it demonstrates that society and Parliament wished there would be no discrimination', Mr Mills believes that 'We should have abolished it.'

In this view, all race relations legislation is window dressing, what Mr Mills calls 'a PR exercise'.

The view that governments should abstain from interfering with individuals' actions, especially in race relations, is shared by Mr Taylor. He bases his argument on historical observations of the British national character. 'This country has a long history of tolerance,' he begins. 'There's a centuries-old British tradition of taking in aliens, Huguenots, Jews, Poles, provided you don't cram it and overheat the system. Our track record of absorbing aliens and other folk from other cultures could probably claim number one position in the world.' The groups of different cultures would, according to Mr Taylor, 'express their gratitude, fit themselves into the new environment, observe the law and customs and keep a bit of their own culture. It is a kind of reciprocal action that the host nation is pleased to get; it looks after the others and gives them the chance to protect their own individuality.'

The postwar period saw a wave of immigration to the UK, but it was not only the sheer scale of the migration that marked it off from its predecessors. Mr Taylor detects 'a difference in the basic attitude'. 'They think they came in by right, and they were,' he observes, referring to the fact that, as passport-holding British subjects, New Commonwealth migrants were entitled to entry. He expands:

They think they owe nothing to the customs and culture of the host, don't have to make concessions and do not move towards, or converge with, the environment they've joined. In many senses, they stay where they are in what seems, to the indigenous population, a slightly defiant way. This is where tensions arise. The British, who are basically a tolerant, peaceful, rather private people, expect concessions to be made in favour of their culture. When they see none, and, in fact, reversals in favour of the in-brought culture, resentment comes.

This is a revealing analysis and one which captures elements of the white middleclass orientation to race relations. Racism, to stretch the analysis, is an outgrowth of a more fundamental resentment felt by whites sensing an 'outside' group's refusal to compromise sufficiently and the government's capitulation to them. The ethnic minorities' 'defiance' spurs hostility. There is no recognition that the alleged defiance is an attempt by groups confronted by racialism and exclusion to preserve their cultures. Where Mr Taylor, or rather his constituents, see ethnicity as a symbol of defiance, others might see it, in its early stages at least, more as a canopy under which group members may shelter.

The common strands in all three Conservative MPs' outlook on the past and, indeed, future are that racism has been nourished by state intervention into what are essentially private domains; also that an absence of legislation would have allowed relations between different ethnic groups to develop 'naturally', that is, without the artificiality of legal compulsion. Ethnic minorities would have aided their reception had they been prepared to 'give in' more readily; instead of clinging to traditional cultures, they could have tried to assimilate with more vigour. Their failure to do so has further exacerbated relations with native whites and therefore has sustained racist ideas about separatism, natural differences and so on.

The programme for the future is reasonably simple and does not involve too much in the way of policy initiatives. Its premiss, as expressed by Mr Mills, is that 'Life is basically unfair and nothing's ever going to change that. Guys have the most unfortunate times during their lives and I don't really see why black guys should be any more protected than everybody else is from the unfairness of life.' The Mills position is that legislation to prevent racialism was ill conceived and that 'moral pressures and as much education as possible' are needed. 'Have a go at people,' implores Mr Mills, endorsing a longterm campaign aimed at re-education, but without legal backing. He is opposed to race relations laws and the race relations industry they have spawned. 'A far better industry would be the persuasion industry; perhaps we should employ Saatchi and Saatchi [the Conservative Party's advertising agents],' he advises. 'It's going to be a hellishly long job. There's no other solution. Why should we expect it from people with such a wide range of religious and cultural difference, from roast beef to curry?'

Mr Mills feels there is a case for abolishing race relations laws. His colleagues, whilst sympathizing, see this as impracticable. 'Whichever route seems to give least difficulties, upsets, worries and bitternesses as you pursue it' is Mrs Knight's chosen path for the future. No more legislation, as this is disruptive, she claims. The introduction of multi-cultural education is also a source of grief for many, and she would stick resolutely to a traditional British education while encouraging children of different ethnic backgrounds to retain pride in their own cultures. Mrs Knight's prescription, in short, is to do nothing that will arouse concern among the white community and this includes even giving the impression that policies specifically favour ethnic minorities. This would intimidate whites, she feels and she gives an example: 'I was in a sub-post office and saw this black child take a book and put it under her dress. I went across, but the child ran away and I told the postmaster. He said, "It happens all the time, but I dare not make a complaint. Nobody will take action because the child is black".' For Mrs Knight, then, confidence has to be restored to whites, who feel they are being made to pay for history. 'To imagine that you can set right injustices committed long ago by injustices now is a very shaky moral argument indeed.' Many of the implications of race relations laws are injurious to whites and can serve only to foster more resentment, she says.

Predictably, the same principle applies with greater force to the concept of affirmative action, by which ethnic minorities which have been disadvantaged in the past are given preference in the present, particularly in the areas of employment and higher education. 'Immoral,' is Mrs Knight's verdict, 'it's a tit-for-tat argument: "You were horrid to us, so now we're going to be horrid to you".' Mrs Knight's conception of the morality underlying affirmative action elicits agreement not only from her Tory colleagues, but from Mr Howell, who believes it to be 'divisive'. While Mr Howell is not as strongly opposed to the morality of programmes aimed at elevating ethnic sections of the community, he sees potential damage in elevating them over other sections. John Taylor also senses the problem: 'If you do go and help some more than other sections of society, then there are penalties for the other side.'

Both Mr Howell and Mr Taylor agree that a more general 'positive action' programme is desirable in the future. 'I would like to discriminate in favour of areas and help everybody in that area, whatever their colour.' Mr Howell feels that 'positive action', by which he means not only pumping money into target areas, but also 'balancing them out', should have begun in the 1960s or 1970s. 'What I wanted in the early days was a policy of positive action to maintain integrated communities, so the residents would have respect for each other. But you can't have integrated communities if it's all-white or all-coloured.'

Formulated during his period as under secretary of state in the Department of Education, 1969–70, Mr Howell's plan was that 'ghettoization', as it has come to be called, should be avoided through a policy of dispersal. *Involuntary* dispersal? Mr Howell argues that he would not necessarily be against compulsion, but 'When you're on a council housing waiting list, you can't have a house where you want to anyway.' His idea was that populations of the cities should be dispersed as far as possible in such a way as to prevent concentrations of ethnic groups in certain areas, his own area of Newtown being an example. The city Housing

Department would be the mechanism through which this was achieved. The City of Birmingham did operate a set-ratio dispersal policy between February 1969 and October 1975, when it was decided that, although true to the spirit of the 1968 Race Relations Act in attempting to foster integration, it was technically in contravention of it in allocating a maximum of one in six properties to nonwhites within a given block of premises or streets.

Mr Howell's programme for 'balanced communities' would have affected the ethnic composition of schools. A dispersed population would have obviated the alleged 'problem' of schools with majority ethnic rolls, which caused such a furore in the 1960s, when the Department of Education and Science sanctioned a recommendation that the proportion of immigrant children should not exceed 30 per cent in any one school. Mr Howell still agrees with this in principle and fails to acknowledge some of the racist implications made about the inevitability of falling educational standards once the 30 per cent figure has been passed.

Mr Howell's policies for the future principally differ from those of his Tory colleagues in the conception of the state's role. 'Things *don't* run their natural course,' he states. 'The arguments about principles of freedom and so on are useless.'

With the exception of his support for the CRE, there are no calls from any of the four MPs for policies directed at the problem of race relations. It is as if racist beliefs and thoughts were almost inevitable, given the clash of cultures that migration precipitated, and that racialist behaviour was one outcome. Whereas Mr Howell feels the need to minimize racialist behaviour, his Conservative counterparts place their faith in human nature. In contrast to this sanguine vision, some Tories – David Waddington, the immigration minister at the time of the 1985 riots, included – seriously consider the possibility of a system of government contract compliance, whereby private firms holding contracts with government departments would be instructed to recruit and promote specified numbers of ethnic minority employees or be penalized by having their contracts cancelled. (The system has operated with reasonable success in the United States.) None of the four politicians in question supports such a scheme, however; Mr Howell is the most sympathetic but fears the white backlash problem.

The problem is that he thinks *I am a problem*

There are at least two critical evaluations of the perspectives presented by the MPs of the four areas. First, we may detect a palpable lack of imaginative proposals to combat what is a powerful and enduring source of cleavage in modern society. Second, linked to this, there is a serious misunderstanding of the scope, severity and potentiality of racism today. The testimonies in this book reveal that racism has a rationale beyond sheer prejudice; it has a powerful significance that is not confined to any particular class, age, or geographical group; and it is most certainly not a characteristic only of extremists. Racism is pervasive and, given its currency amongst the young, is likely to continue to rupture ethnic relations in the future. Add to this the chastening economic climate and the disillusionment it nourishes and social policy coupled with mere rectitude appears a very frail instrument indeed.

'Racial disadvantage' was the problem to be tackled when the first Race Relations Bill was being drafted. Nowadays, institutional racism has replaced it, bringing with it a grimmer, more formidable foe. Anonymous and abstract as it may seem, this particular form of racism is sustained by people – not by people who actively support it, but those who do not make moves to oppose it. One need look no further than the chapters above on the middleclass to comprehend why institutional racism is maintained from the top by directors and other key decision makers. The chapters on the workingclass show why institutional racism is not challenged from below. Existing race relations laws are in practice unable to reach much of this concealed form of discrimination. The CRE, with its present method of operation, is often trying to exorcise ghosts from places where inhabitants deny their existence. Government contract compliance schemes can, at least, ensure a minimization of institutional forms of racism amongst those holding government contracts, although there are potential boomerang problems associated with any policy engineered by whites to give ethnic minorities assistance.

The lesson to be taken from this book is that policies aimed at the elimination of racialism can combat only symptoms. Even those accepting Banton's argument that new norms emerge from changing behaviour patterns have to concede that racism has a self-perpetuating potential that militates against the success of social policies. Racism, the root cause, prospers amongst groups who see no inherent moral wrongness in their beliefs. They believe they are, in some sense, superior and gladly accept the evidence of their senses that this is so. What Banton is suggesting is that, in time, in an environment where racialism has been excised, that evidence will suggest something very different: a fundamental equality. This would become evident once Asians and blacks were able to progress in a society uncluttered by racialist barriers. They would presumably demonstrate their ability and application in areas of education and work and, in the process, expose the inaccuracies of the negative, stereotyped images held, as we have seen, by many whites. Once the negative images have been replaced by more positive and genuine versions, then some of the ideas of racism will be reformulated.

This is one scenario; another is that racism is less

amenable to reformulation and that it is largely unaffected by what minority groups actually do. So deeply rooted in the very structure of society is racism, that even the manifest virtues of targeted groups can be transmuted into vices by what sociologist Robert Merton has called 'moral alchemy' (1980). In this altogether more sinister vision, the same behaviour may be evaluated differently according to the person or groups exhibiting it. If, for instance, white small business men and women work around the clock to build up their firm, they are considered industrious, resolute and eager to realize their capacities to the full. If Asians work the same hours, this bears witness to their 'sweatshop mentality', their 'ruthless disregard for and undercutting of British standards', their 'unfair competitive practices'. What might be interpreted as the whites' frugality can be seen as the Asians' miserly penny-pinching; good business sense becomes sharp practice. Likewise, a classic racist conception is that blacks are naturally suited for manual work: but do they draw praise for climbing the ladder of opportunity and securing jobs where intellect counts more than brawn? Or do they draw censure for opting for a 'parasitic way of life' instead of embracing the honesty of a good day's toil? White children might be rewarded for their efforts at study, whereas Asians could be seen as too effortful – always with 'their noses stuck in books', instead of going to discos and enjoying life like 'normal' kids. In sum, the right activity by the wrong people becomes an object of contempt, not honour. Only by holding the virtues exclusively to themselves can whites retain their distinction, prestige and power. As we have seen repeatedly in past chapters, whites express hostility and denigrate ethnic minorities for their sloth, their unwillingness to work within the system and their general failure in society. But they also resent 'too much' ambition and success, when the same minorities achieve it. This is not a contrived twist in whites' thinking, a calculated and deliberate reappraisal of the facts. It is a genuinely felt revulsion and one which appears both logical and rational to the believer. The consequence is that when blacks are labelled as incorrigibly inferior because they apparently do not manifest many of the virtues whites hold dear, this confirms the natural 'rightness' of their being assigned an inferior status in society. And when Asians are seen as having too many of the qualities valued by whites, it becomes clear that they are posing some sort of threat and need to be contained, by racialist practices if necessary. Blacks get damned for not achieving, Asians for achieving too much.

Both scenarios contain assumptions about the nature of racism, the first suggesting a less obdurate quality than the second. Policy makers must base their judgements on the first vision, while staying mindful of the limitations of all policies implied by the second. Getting results in terms of better-educated blacks and more successful Asians will most certainly kick away some of the props on which racism rests. What it will not do is guarantee that new structures of racism will not emerge. As vines wrap themselves around trellis-work, so the logic twists around the new structures of racism. Racism is not always moved by reasonable argument, nor by empirical refutation: its power is in its self-maintaining facility.

This is not intended to suggest that racism is locked into people's heads and that those believing in their own racial superiority (and, conversely, in the racial inferiority of others) will carry those beliefs with them to their graves – as Karen Forster argued. What this book does argue, however, is that a great deal of policy has underestimated the depth and complexity of racism. Racism is not just something that arises in times of depression when jobs are scarce and when visible scapegoats are sought. The responses of many of those interviewed here testify to this. Nor does racism 'break down at the point of human contact', as Mr Howell contends: sheer physical closeness can lead to empathy, understanding and tolerance under some conditions (like those shared by youths in Newtown), but it can also create tension and resentment. Even the removal of discriminatory behaviour and the opening up of opportunities for all ethnic groups will not necessarily translate into a radical change in thinking over the longer term, such is the resilience of racism.

It is a mistake to presume that racism is born out of and sustained by a lack of formal education. As this book has shown, many subscribing to racist beliefs are seemingly educated, articulate and intelligent people who project their views dispassionately and without apparent prejudice. Their arguments and views are consistent and often fervently held. Once this is recognized, then society can begin to confront the issue. Education is an obvious beginning, but, as I have argued, multicultural education will have less impact in workingclass schools than it will in middleclass (and especially independent) schools, where the perspectives of tomorrow's decision-makers are being forged. Their decisions may in the future affect the operation of institutional racism. To be effective in the longer term, multicultural education must gain a reception in all areas, by state and independent schools of all levels. Otherwise it is meaningless.

Racism in society's institutions can be actively discouraged, possibly by arming an organization such as the CRE, maligned as it has been, with more power to investigate and penalize. Government contract compliance carries with it many risks, but handled sensitively it could cut off the sustenance now provided for those holding stereotypical views about certain groups' incapabilities. Mr Mills's idea about the utilization of the 'persuasion industry' should not be taken lightly. As part of its campaign for sexual equality, France's Women's Rights Ministry has run a series of tv commercials illustrating metaphorically the obstacles facing women. (One showed two athletes, a boy and a girl, on their startingblocks: as they look up, the camera swings first to the boy's track, a flat sprint, then to the girl's, set up for a hurdle race.) Women are seeking to portray their situation in their search for equality of opportunity. The pursuit of ethnic equality might well be assisted by similar initiatives directed at employers and Mr Mills's suggestion that his own party's advertising agents be consulted should not be accepted as facetiously as he intends it.

Two basic assumptions underlie these remarks. The first is that the solutions to race relations problems are best tackled by striking at the cause rather than at the symptoms, that is, at white racism rather than at ethnic disadvantage. In the words of a black Newtown resident, imagining a discourse involving a white racist: '*I* haven't got a problem myself; the problem is that *he thinks* I am a problem.' The second assumption is that racism is not an inborn psychological constant. Of course, the proclivity to separate out others perceptually and arrange ideas about them in terms of types or categories is provided by our natural equipment. But the pattern of human thought that uses race as the criterion for separation is largely a product of the modifiable structure of society. Change the appropriate institutional and administrative conditions, and human thought will change too.

This book demonstrates that there are powerful forces opposing such change. The craving for order and stability which gives rise to a conservative mentality is by no means the exclusive property of those who have a vested interest in the preservation of the social order. Change is perceived as an enemy by members of all age groups and all classes. The racism we have documented derives not from blind prejudice, nor from a rejection or hatred of ethnic minorities, but from a fundamental acceptance of existing social standards, norms and institutions. Anxiety centres not so much on blacks and Asians – indeed, a great many white racists would encourage substantial improvements in the ethnic minorities' education, living conditions and occupational positions – but on the consequences of their presence. In the eyes of whites, ethnic minorities still symbolize disruptive changes which threaten their standard of living, more general cultural standards, or a combination of both.

It becomes possible to see why some whites can endorse ethnic claims for more equality and still recognize in them a threat to their own status. Ethnic groups are seen as bearers of change, and change brings with it uncertainty. The racism they express is not always based on the concept of inferior race, more on a sense of change of social interests, values and standards which will surely not improve their own conditions and may have dire consequences for them. This is not an emotional feeling, but an intellectual appraisal, an attempt to identify possible disruptions and organize views accordingly. This racism is the protective manoeuvre of people unaware of, or deliberately ignoring, the extent to which their own circumstances are products of historical and contemporary currents – currents which have conspired to weaken previously colonized peoples and to ensconce whites in temporary positions of privilege. Such positions are not willingly relinquished.

Bibliography

Banton, M. (1985), *Promoting Racial Harmony* (London: Cambridge University Press).

Bhachu, P. (1984), 'Multicultural education: parental views', *New Community*, vol. XII, no. 1 (winter), pp. 9–21.

Birmingham, City of (1984), *Report of Education Committee* (Birmingham: City Council).

Brown, C. and Gay, P. (1985), *Racial Discrimination: Seventeen Years after the Act* (London: Policy Studies Institute).

Cashmore, E. (1982), *Black Sportsmen* (London: Routledge & Kegan Paul).

Cashmore, E. (1983), *Rastaman* (London: Allen & Unwin).

Cashmore, E. (1984), *No Future* (London: Heinemann Educational Books).

Cashmore, E. and Bagley, C. (1985), 'Colour blind', *Times Educational Supplement*, no. 3574 (28 December).

Cashmore, E. and Troyna, B. (1983), *Introduction to Race Relations* (London: Routledge & Kegan Paul).

Davey, A. (1983), *Learning to Be Prejudiced* (London: Edward Arnold).

Hartmann, P. and Husband, C. (1974), *Racism and the Mass Media* (London: Davis Poynter).

Horowitz, E. (1936), 'The development of attitudes toward the Negro', *Archives of Psychology*, no. 194.

Kirp, D. (1979), *Doing Good by Doing Little* (London: University of California Press).

Merton, R. (1980), 'The self-fulfilling prophecy', in L. Coser (ed.), *The Pleasures of Sociology* (New York: Mentor), pp. 29–47.

Miles, R. (1982), *Racism and Migrant Labour* (London: Routledge & Kegan Paul).

O'Donnell, M. (1985), *Age and Generation* (London: Tavistock).

Runnymede Trust (1983), *Black Business Enterprise in Britain* (London: Runnymede Trust).

Scarman, Lord (1982), *The Scarman Report* (Harmondsworth: Penguin).

Seabrook, J. (1983), 'The crime of poverty', *New Society*, vol. 64, no. 1065 (14 April), pp. 63–4.

Swann, M. (1985), *Education for All* (London: HMSO).

Young, M. (1965), *The Rise of Meritocracy, 1870–2033* (Harmondsworth: Penguin).

Index